The Big Summer Activity Book

Anne and Peter Thomas

Floris Books

Explanation of the symbols

Age
- ⬡ end of third, fourth year
- ⬢ five to six/ beginning of the seventh year
- ❀ seven to nine years
- ✄ ten years and older

Number of participants
- ✳ unlimited
- N number of participants is N
- N⁺ minimum number of participants is N; there is no maximum
- N± minimum number of participants is N; there is no maximum, preferably an even number of participants
- N± minimum number of participants is N; the is no maximum, preferably an uneven number of participants

Indoor or outdoor
- ⌂ indoor activity
- ♀ outdoor activity

Type of activity
- ♟ table game
- ✂ creative activity
- ♪ music game
- ◐ ball game
- ✦ game with a blindfold
- 🚌 suitable for in the car
- ⊞ game with dice

Materials
- ► rope

Cover and layout: Ernst Thomassen
Illustrations: Annie Meussen
Illustration material in weather chapter: Meteo Consult, Wageningen

Translated by George Hall
Additional texts by: Reinier van den Berg, Manon van Loenen

First published in Dutch in 2006 under the title *Vakantieboek* by Christofoor Publishers, Zeist.

First published in English in 2006 by Floris Books, Edinburgh
© Uitgeverij Christofoor, Zeist 2006
English version © 2006 Floris Books

British Library CIP Data available

ISBN-10 0-86315-545-6
ISBN-13 978-086315-545-1

Printed in Slovenia

Contents

Foreword and Outline

You're off with the family for your long-awaited vacation. You get into the car or plane and after a surprisingly short time the inevitable question comes: 'Are we there yet?'

What do you do?

And what can you do on a rainy day on the campsite, or when the children have had enough of going to the beach every day?

These questions have led to the many games and other activities that form the principal part of this book. This book presents countless ideas for activities when travelling, outdoor games, countryside activities and what to do when it rains.

To compile a book with such a wide remit we needed help from others, which came primarily from dozens of parents who drew our attention to all kinds of situations, provided tips and shared their experiences. We held a small-scale survey among parents at two primary schools and the checklists were also filled in by many parents.

The introductory chapters are based mainly on real-life circumstances and perceptions that we and other parents have experienced while on vacation. Some things may seem exaggerated; however, some parents have genuinely experienced such situations and their tips have helped other people. Many parents may find the checklists too detailed, but everyone can select the items that are the most relevant to their situation.

Choosing your destination is, of course, a personal matter and is not discussed in the framework of this book.

Reinier van den Berg and Manon van Loenen wrote the chapters on *The weather* and *Nature,* respectively.

In addition, we enjoyed much co-operation in the form of interviews with Dr Paul Wormer, who is a member of the beach lifeguard team in the Netherlands as well as a mountain guide in the Swiss village of Grindelwald.

Others also assisted in writing various chapters: Christian Maclean *(The stars),* Jonathan Rosenberg (*Orientation*), and Francisca Rosenberg (*Friendship armbands*).

Much practical information has been taken from magazines and brochures from the Ministry of Foreign Affairs, local Area Health Authorities, pharmacists, health insurance companies, etc.

Departure points

The premise of this book is doing things together. As a parent, you will have to take the initiative or act as the games master or mistress with many of the 300 or so games and other activities described in this book. In addition, a number of things will require preparation and supervision.

Going on vacation does not by definition mean that you have to go *travelling* with your family. It is quite easy to make a short break, even a weekend, into something special.

A vacation should be a time of relaxation, a time in which you will be receptive to what is happening around you.

On the use of this book

The chapters on the weather, stars, nature and orientation are suitable for primary school children. You can go through them step by step with your children. Children of about eight years old can read, so they can become little weathermen and women, for example.

The contents of this book are not new and can be found in dozens of places, including similar, previously published books. But who really wants to travel with a whole box full of books?

The special features of this book include the large amount of information provided, its compactness, and the *Index according to type of game and age.* In the descriptions of the activities, symbols indicate the age(s) for which the activity is suited, the number of children who can participate, etc.

Several indices have been included at the end of the book so that you can find an activity in a more specific way. The most important index is:

✿ *The index according to type of activity, age, and number of participants.* Here, the index makes use of the symbols that are also displayed under the headings of the games and activities. As a result, all the information necessary for travelling games, outdoor games, party games, games in the countryside, or do-it-yourself activities for a rainy afternoon is available at a glance.
The other indices are:

✿ An alphabetical index of games, do-it-yourself and other activities

The symbols are explained on p. 4 In any instructions presented — how to use a compass, for instance, and in the DIY activities — the different steps are numbered chronologically.

Anne and Peter Thomas

1. Introduction

Whose vacation?

Babies and young children don't actually need vacations. Give them some sand and water and they're happy wherever they are. It may be a better idea to park the little one with his or her grandparents or to ask friends to look after your child(ren) in your own home while you go off with the older kids.

Children of different ages require a variety of solutions. You will certainly have to take the youngest child's capabilities into account. All the activities discussed in this book are accompanied by age indications. The division into age groups is based upon Bernard Lievegoed's book *Phases of Childhood*.

First year of life

In its first year of life, a newborn baby has to learn a great deal in order to develop from a helpless bundle of biology into a brave little explorer, crawling around trying to communicate how he or she feels. You may ask yourself if it is sensible to undertake long journeys with your child at this particular time. After all, the child has no need of a break. There is a substantial chance that the baby's natural rhythm will be disturbed and that this disruption will influence other family members.

Toddlers and infants

At this age, children are happy when their daily rhythm is not too disrupted and they can enjoy themselves playing in the garden or outside. Children in this phase of life are often inexhaustible. They enjoy undertaking small trips or going on short walks. Even if children are already accustomed to attending a day nursery, they still remain individuals. In terms of development, there are great differences between children: one child may be engrossed in his or her own private world whereas another is open and eager to participate with other children. When on vacation abroad, it is fascinating to see how the language barrier often presents no problem to children. At this stage, one can observe a change in the way infants play. Activity is not random: the game assumes a purpose, it begins to become more result-oriented.

Five to seven years

This is an extremely sociable age. The children are very approachable, begin to develop an interest in a great many phenomena and start to ask *why* things are as they are. They are beginning to become independent thinkers and, under proper supervision, are already capable of taking part in many games. But one should be careful when playing competitive games in which they have to vie against one another. If you take care that you do not overtax children in this age group, it is possible to have a truly enjoyable vacation.

Seven to nine years

You can ask much more of children in this age category, and they are old enough to accept stricter rules. They are pleased to demonstrate their abilities, and experience things in relation to others. Their stamina can be put to the test. To a considerable extent, children in this age group will be able to use this book on their own and find activities that they like. They will be pleased to help prepare for the vacation.

Ten years old and upward

You are now dealing with critical and independent children who like to be actively engaged in activities with their best friend(s). They are brazen and bold on one hand, but they are also approaching (pre)puberty and can also be unexpectedly sensitive and vulnerable. They want to be treated as people who can think and decide in an adult manner. Consequently, it is a good idea to involve them in any preparations at an early stage.

Three important factors

Whatever kind of vacation you choose, you always have to deal with three important factors, which you will find in many brochures concerning health. These factors are:

* water
* hygiene
* routine

Water

Everyone can endure a long period without eating, but not without drinking. This is particularly applicable to children. Babies, in particular, but also toddlers and infants tend to become dehydrated quite rapidly. It is warmer on the backseat of the car than in the front; the air in a plane is extremely dry; in warmer countries, you don't notice the heat if there is a refreshing breeze. Children two years old and upward need six extra cups of liquid a day. This also applies to adults. Babies ought to receive two to three extra nursing bottles (80 ml, 3 fl oz) of (boiled) water between feeds.

Tips:
* Never go on a trip without sufficient drinks.
* Take water, teas or diluted juice with you on every hike. Give older children their own water flask.

* Take care that children do not dehydrate, and that they consume enough liquid if they have a fever, and especially if they are suffering from diarrhoea.
* In some countries, it may be necessary to boil the water, especially in the third world.
* In these countries teach the children that they cannot simply drink water from the tap.
* Take water purification tablets with you.
* If you buy bottled water, check to see that the cap is sealed.

Hygiene

Children are adventurous. They touch everything. As a result, their hands quickly become dirty. They will often put their fingers in their mouths or eat food (sandwiches etc.) with their hands. When travelling, they will often lean against the car. You should ensure that the children wash their hands regularly with soap, especially when travelling.

Tips:
* On your travels, take a towel and a wet flannel with you in a plastic bag or box.
* Take wet wipes or tissues with you.
* Take a bar of disinfectant soap for along the way.
* Go to the toilet with your children to ensure that hygiene is as good as possible.

Routine

In general, a child is accustomed to his own routine. He receives meals at fixed times, the whole day has a regular pattern, and he goes to bed more or less at the same time every evening. All these things give a child a feeling of safety and security, which helps the child feel well. As soon as you alter this pattern, a child can begin to protest without being capable of explaining why. Above all, try to divide the occasionally lengthy travelling times in such a way that the smallest members of the family can also be accommodated. Of course, you cannot always stick rigidly to the daily routine. In hot countries, you could try to combine the routine with the long afternoon break (siesta) that is determined by the warm climate.

Routine not only concerns the time at which something happens, it also concerns the quality of the experience. For example, if a small child is used to a certain type of food, he will protest or even throw up if he is given strange food. For this reason, you should try to ensure a gradual change on vacation if necessary. Parents often take a jar of jam or peanut butter and some crackers with them to tide the children over.

Adjust the daily routine for the youngest member of the family and try to stick to it as much as possible. It is good for children to acclimatize to the new location. Do not get out and about immediately; you should familiarize the children with the environment gradually. Young children should not be in the sun for too long, and you must put something on their heads (see also pp.11f). Do not take small children too high in the mountains (see pp.114f). For additional information, please see the website of the Ramblers Association, *www.ramblers.org.uk*.

2. Preparations

Travel tips

Don't force those who stay at home to become detectives. Wherever you are, ensure that you can be contacted by those at home. If necessary, you can agree on a specific time that your mobile phone will be switched on.

Besides your destination address, it is advisable to give those at home a copy of your vacation plans, travelling arrangements and car (and trailer/caravan) details.

Keep in regular contact with home.

Passport and other data

Before you go, check the validity of your children's and your own passport or identity card. If necessary, seek information about the requirements of your destination in terms of passports and/or visas (from the travel agent, embassy or consulate). Be sure to take insurance papers, the telephone number needed to block your account in cases of a lost credit card etc., an address book.

Lost passports

If you lose your passport, you should immediately go to the police to report the loss. If this cannot be done, ask the consulate or the embassy for an acknowledgement that the passport has been lost. The consulate or the embassy may be able to give you temporary documentation that is valid for the rest of the trip. Lost passports are registered at a national level. Even if you find it again, you will not be able to use it.

Make sure your house is safe

* Ensure that your house looks occupied.
* A large amount of post visible behind the front door or in a post box indicates that no one is present. Ask friends, family or neighbours to help, or contact the Post Office to keep your mail.
* Ask someone to check your house regularly and to water the plants.
* Check all locks before you go.

Fig 10.1 Teddy-bear harness

* Place valuable items in a safe place.
* If necessary, ask the police about burglar prevention.

Remember to:
* throw all perishables away
* empty the garbage bins
* check the contents of the freezer and empty it if necessary
* check the water, gas, electricity, central heating
* switch off electrical equipment

Suitcase labels

There are always people who want to know when you are not at home. To them, that is the ideal time to pay a visit. Ensure that your address on the suitcase labels is not clearly visible to everyone. Use labels that can be screened off.

Card with emergency numbers

If something unpleasant happens during the vacation, you may be under pressure and have difficulty in finding an emergency number. Make a card about the same size as a credit card, showing important telephone numbers: general emergency centre, health insurance, number to block your credit card or mobile phone subscription, etc. Ensure that you always have easy access to this card.

Tips for going on vacation

It can be a minor disaster if your child loses his or her favourite doll or cuddly toy and won't go to sleep. There are parents who take a reserve doll just to be sure. You can even buy a new doll or make one, but your little one might not see this as an adequate solution. The following section presents patterns for a doll carrier bag, a teddy-bear harness, and a wrist strap. In this way, the children will always have their toys with them while travelling so they won't be easily lost.

Teddy-bear harness

✣ strong tape
 2 press fasteners (press studs)

Sew a harness to fit the teddy bear or other doll. It snaps shut by means of two press fasteners. Sew a piece of the same tape on to the top of the harness so that your child can hang the toy around his or her neck (see Fig 10.1). Use light stitches so that the tape will break off rather than strangling the child if it gets caught.

Doll carrier bag

✣ *piece of cloth*
 tape
 cord
 12 cm (5 inches) zip

The pattern shown in Figure 12.1 is quite large so that the doll will fit in it easily. There is space at the bottom for doll's clothes if required. You can adjust the measurements to suit your own wishes. The measurements do not include seams.

1 Cut the bag from double-folded cloth. Turn the cloth inside out and sew the outsides so that a bag is formed. Hem the edge of the hood. Turn the bag the right way out and insert the zip in the front.
2 Sew the tape on to the back so that the cord can pass through it.
3 Cut a strip of the same cloth for the shoulder strap. Fold it double, fold the seams to the inside and sew it up. Sew the strap to the bag in the way shown.
4 Pull a cord through the tape at the back.

Wrist strap

✣ *cord*
 strap

Tie the cord around the neck of the toy. Make a loop at the other end so that the wrist strap can pass through it. Wrap the wristband around your child's wrist.

Fig 11.2 Wrist attachment

Child's sunhat with neck protection

✣ *piece of cloth*
 a piece of interfacing
 2 buttons
 a piece of elastic

Children up to the age of (approximately) 15 years have skin that is very sensitive to the ultraviolet rays of the sun. So, here is a pattern for a sunhat with neck protection (a legionnaire's hat). The measurements stated do not include the seams (see Fig 12.2).

1 This pattern is based on a head circumference of 52 cm (20 $\frac{1}{2}$, but you can adjust the measurements to fit your needs.
   The part for the head consists of four identical quarters (a). You have to cut the cloth for the peak (b) twice, and for the neck protection (c) once. Finish the edges of the cloth with a zigzag stitch to prevent fraying.
2 For head section, sew two quarters together at one of the sides and do the same with the other two. Then sew the two halves thus formed to one another.

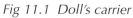

Fig 11.1 Doll's carrier

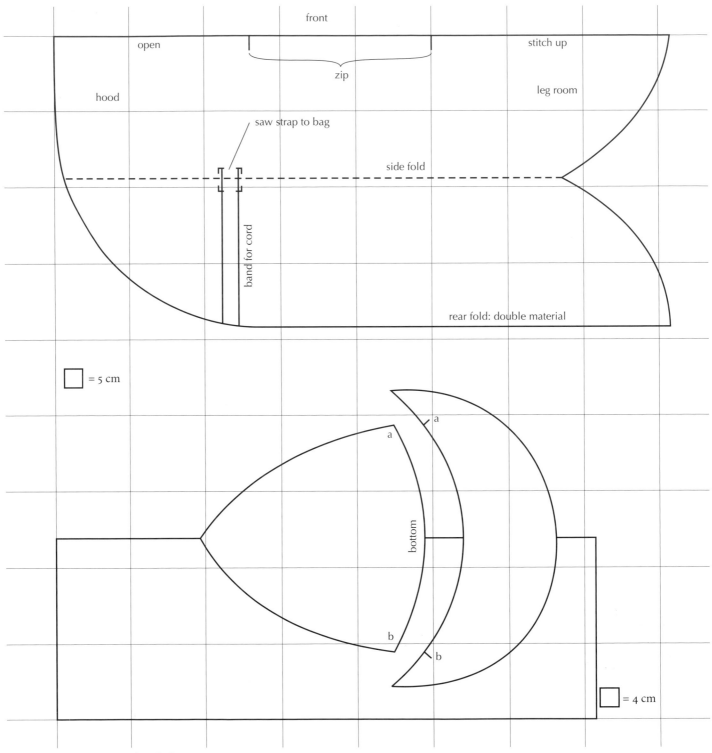

Fig 12.1 (top) Pattern for doll's carrier　　　　　　　　　　　　　　　*Fig 12.2 Pattern for a sunhat*

Lay the seams open and stitch the seams again at a distance of about 0.5 cm (¹/₄ in) from the existing seam.

3 You need two pieces for the *peak*. If you have very soft material you can reinforce one of them with interfacing. Lay the pieces inside out, one on top of the other. Sew up the round edge. Turn the material the right way out and stitch the seam again at a distance of about 0.5 cm (¹/₄ in) from the edge. Lay the outside of the peak against the one of the quarters. Fasten the middle of the peak to the middle of the headpiece with pins and sew the peak to the headpiece.

4 Seam the sides and bottom of the *neck protection* (c). Pin the middle of (c) to the middle of the rear quarter and sew them together.

Cut a strip of cloth about 3.5 cm (1¹/₂ in) long and to the width of (c), fold the edges up about 0.5 cm (¹/₄ in), and sew it to the side and back of (a) like a tunnel. Sew a button to the hat at both ends of this tunnel. Pull a piece of elastic (about 30 cm, 12 in) through the tunnel and attach it to the buttons.

Do not lose the little ones on the way

If you are going on vacation by train or plane, you will have to cope with busy stations and/or terminals. Before you know it, you have lost your youngest child. How can you prevent that?

❀ If your family situation allows it, agree beforehand which of the adults or the older children is going to supervise which of the little ones.

❀ If there are several small children, you can put a wrist strap or a harness on a potential stray.

❀ Papooses and/or backpacks for carrying young children are very handy. You can get carriers suitable for children up to 3 years depending on the weight of the child.

Give each child their own rucksack

Children often think they are tough if they carry their own backpack and their own flask. Give one to each child that can walk, appropriate for his or her age. A 5-year-old child should not carry more than 3 kg (6 lb); 5 kg (11 lb) is the limit for children up to 10 years old.

The size of the rucksack may determine how many toys can be taken on vacation. There are backpacks that children can draw on or write on with washable felt-tip pens.

Car seat tray

This car seat tray is a (brief)case (see Figure 14.2), of which one side can be zipped open and folded down like a table. It is supported by two tapes fixed to the front seat of the car. The compartments in the case allow

Fig 14.1

space for toys and food and drinks for the journey.

Car seat bag

✤ *piece of thick cloth*

It is easy to make a car seat bag yourself.

1 Take a robust piece of cloth as large as the backrest of the front car seat.
2 Make a large seam at the top into which you can insert a wooden

Fig 14.2

slat, so that the cloth will not sag down.
3 Sew a strong piece of tape to all four corners of the cloth in order to tie the cloth to the car seat.
4 Depending on the child's wishes (what does he or she want to take in the car?), sew a number of pockets on to the cloth.

Food in tropical countries

* If possible, switch to local food gradually.
* Take a packet of muesli with you, as is good for the digestion.
* Do not eat fruit that you have not peeled yourself.
* In open-air markets, choose stalls that are busy, as the food will be freshly prepared, and less likely to have been sitting around.
* If necessary, heat the food thoroughly to kill any bacteria.
* Take sufficient baby food with you if you are unsure that you can buy it at your destination.

Parents' questions:
Which destination?

The question *Where shall we go for our vacation?* is difficult to answer, especially if you have a family with children of different ages. Where should you choose if you have children aged five, eight and twelve years old, for example? You have the choice of:

* adapting the vacation to the youngest member of the family
* dividing the family in two, with one adult getting out and about with the older children and the other with the youngest. It sometimes a good idea to take one of the children's friends with you. (Be sure to make satisfactory agreements about contributions to

the costs, insurance and what to do in cases of illness.)

The characterization of the different age groups in the *Introduction* may help you with determining your destination and the activities undertaken.

The health of young children plays a major role when on vacation, but older children are also vulnerable. In many countries, a sick child need not be a real problem, but you do not wish to have to deal with any unpleasant surprises. The medical services abroad often work differently from our own. Accordingly, it is sensible to check the following points in advance:

* Are you capable of making yourself understood in the country you are visiting?
* Are there doctors in the vicinity of your destination, and which language(s) do they speak?
* Is there a hospital in the neighbourhood?
* Can you buy the 'right' baby food?
* Is there sufficient shade?
* How good is the water?
* If you are sleeping in rented accommodation or a hotel, ask in advance if the child's bed is actually big enough.

Can you involve the children in the preparations?

Many parents have asked us this question. It is not possible to give a simple answer and, of course, it depends on the ages of your children.

You can tell toddlers in advance about what is going to happen:

* 'We are going to be in the car for a long time and we will sleep in a hotel on the way.'
* 'We will go by train to a big building. Sometimes it takes a

long time before we can get on the aeroplane. You have to stay in your seat in the plane. When we get off ...' etc.

✿ 'Then we come to a country when the sun shines really brightly. You have to put a hat on when you're outside.'

You can provide lots of information to children of primary school age about your destination: what your accommodation will be like, all the things you can do, what you have to watch out for. The children will often come up with suggestions such as: 'Oh, then I should take this or that with me,' or 'That's what I want to do.' You can discuss with the children which toys they can take with them.

If your children can read, you can involve them in a different way with the preparations. They can go to the library and look for books and brochures on your destination. Get them to search for information on the Internet or help with planning the route.

Which toys and games should you take with you?

We received very varied responses to our survey question *What should you take with you for the journey?* They ranged from: 'take as little as possible, only a book of songs and games that one of the adults can make use of,' to 'let the children choose for themselves what they want to play with on the journey.' A CD with songs, perhaps with a walkman, is almost always a good travelling companion.

Some children would prefer to take their whole room with them on vacation. Is this convenient?

There are two things to consider here: on the one hand, you want your children to feel secure and to disrupt their routine as little as possible. Certain items, such as a cuddly toy, are often invaluable in this respect. On the other hand, it is good for children, especially older ones, to experience something new and refreshing on vacation, something that is completely different from what they experience at home. Familiar toys and games may be an obstacle to this fresh approach. Children should feel the urge to explore their surroundings on vacation. For this reason, it is advisable to take as few games and toys as possible with you.

Tips:
* One mother told us that she began compiling a folder, box or bag for each of her children long before the start of the trip. The contents depended on the specific interests of the child in question. For the horse-lover, she gathered all kinds of things about horses; and patches, threads and buttons for the DIY enthusiasts. She produced this material on a rainy day and the children were busy for hours.
* A play bag containing all kind of articles can also be useful if a child is bored.
* Making a *treasure chest* with your children before you go on vacation often gives a lot of pleasure. It is a decorated box that you can use to store all the treasures you find on vacation — a beautiful shell, a piece of rock crystal, etc.

Should we give the children a task for the journey?

You can involve the kids in the journey by giving them a specific task, depending on their age. A child of seven or eight years old could be the *luggage specialist,* for example. It would be his or her task to count the pieces of luggage when loading and unloading the car, at the airport or station, etc.

An older child could be the *platform specialist* at the station, and the oldest children could ensure that the tickets are in order for the check-in desk (under the watchful eyes of the parents).

Planning and travelling

* Draw up separate packing lists for along the way and for later.
* Keep in mind that you cannot drive very fast with children, and that you should stop regularly (at least once every two hours) for a comfort stop and to stretch your legs. Children should not sit still for too long.
* Drive as steadily as possible and do not swerve round bends; children suffer easily from motion sickness.
* If necessary, draw up a list of the numbers of the motorways, roads and junctions you are going to take, and stick it on the dashboard.
* Give small children an identification disc.
* Take small presents for along the way, like a pencil, a notepad, folders, etc. On long journeys, a small present now and again can work wonders.
* Do not leave children in the car on their own.
* Do not allow children under twelve years of age to sit in the front of the car.
* One of the adults should sit in the back with the children now and again.
* Take sweets that the children can suck on when the plane is taking off or landing.

Something to drink is also recommended. In the car, chewing gum or an apple may also help against motion sickness.
* Make an agreement about which of the adults or older children is going to look after which of the smaller ones.
* Ensure that there is enough fresh air in the car.
* Make sure there is enough shade in the car, particularly in the back.
* Allow the children enough scope for movement during the stops *en route* (see 'Games to stretch your muscels,' p. 128).
* A waste bin in the car avoids a lot of loose refuse on the floor.

3. Checklists

Documents

* passport(s) or identification card(s)
* visa, if necessary
* tickets
* a set of extra passport photos
* international vaccination certificate, if necessary
* health insurance
* animal passport, if necessary
* blood group card
* copy of travel insurance (are the children and any accompanying friends insured?)
* driving license
* car documents
* emergency numbers of the insurance
* spare keys (car, caravan, bikes)
* it can be useful to keep a photocopy of all your documents and keep these in a separate item of baggage

Finance

* money belt for under your shirt / bag for money and documents
* bank and/or credit card

Contact telephone numbers and addresses

* family and friends
* doctor
* pharmacy (in connection with medication)
* bank
* number to block bank/credit cards
* addresses and telephone numbers of embassies and consulates
* Mobile telephone and charger

Personal items

* diary / address book
* medication (for the entire vacation)
* (good) sunglasses
* spare set of spectacles or lenses

Household items

* small pack of washing powder
* thermos flask
* cool box with cool packs
* plate, cup, cutlery

Useful articles

* universal plug
* alarm clock
* (rechargeable) torch
* candles / matches
* plastic bags
* sewing kit
* toilet paper
* elastic bands
* safety pins
* washing line and clothes pegs
* neck cushion(s)
* garbage bags

For along the way

(in separate bag)
* knife (not in hand luggage, if flying)
* (plastic) spoons
* kitchen roll
* flannel
* towel
* piece of soap
* toilet paper
* cool box / cool packs
* thermos flask

For a car journey

* thermos flask
* cups
* sugar
* evaporated milk / milk powder
* spoons
* drinks for the kids
* sandwiches
* fruit
* savoury snacks
* sweets / lozenges
* paper tissues
* rubbish bin
* rubbish bag
* jerrycan or a couple of bottles of water (for children with motion sickness)
* flannel
* storage sleeves on the back of the front seats
* books
* small presents (as a surprise during the journey)
* coloured pencils, felt-tips
* paper / colouring book
* toys
* music for the children (tapes, CDs / walkman)

For hiking

* walking stick
* (small) backpack
* papoose / backpack for carrying child
* water bottle / thermos flask
* binoculars
* pocket knife with openers
* rope
* shooting stick
* sunhat
* sunglasses
* compass
* hiking map
* raincoats

Clothes

Take enough clothes and make sure you have a change of clothes if everything gets wet.

* climbing boots / hiking shoes
* shoe wax for waterproofing boots
* extra laces
* hat / neck protection

For babies and young children

* cuddly toys / rattles
* travel cot
* buggy
* papoose / backpack for carrying child
* cleaning towel / tissues
* blanket to lie down on
* nappies (diapers) and nappy bag
* waterproof sheet
* feeding bottle(s)
* baby food in jars (it is not always possible to buy what you want)
* bibs
* piece of cloth to darken the room / car
* T-shirts with long sleeves
* shorts
* sunhat with side flaps
* identity disc

Recreation

* reading materials
* (writing) paper / envelopes
* writing articles
* vacation diary
* sketch book / coloured pencils
* water paint paper, paint, brushes
* music instruments and sheet music
* adhesive tape / glue
* (video) camera (films)
* mini-tripod
* binoculars
* travel guides
* language guides
* book of flora and fauna
* map of the stars
* hiking map
* magnifying glass (text on maps is often very small)

Toys

* cuddly toy / toy cars
* books
* ball(s)
* skipping rope
* bucket / spade/ moulds
* sketch book and coloured pencils
* water colours, brushes
* wax crayons
* moulding clay
* folding paper
* walkman

Games etc.

* party games (see p. 200)
* dice
* skipping rope
* ball(s)
* boules

Tools / DIY material

Make a list of tools you might need depending on the activities you undertake.

* Allen keys / wrench for bikes
* magnifying glass
* reel of rope
* sticky tape
* scissors
* sewing kit

Travelling pharmacy

See page 25

First aid kit

* scissors for elastoplast dressing strip
* tweezers
* tweezers for removing ticks
* safety pins
* thermometer
* wound plasters
* sterile gauze
* sticking plaster
* emergency bandage
* (elastic) bandage
* swallowtail plaster for deep cuts
* antiseptic cream
* cotton wool
* triangular bandage
* insect repellent

When camping

* tent and accessories
* repair set
* extra guy ropes / tent pegs
* tent hammer
* small shovel
* groundsheet
* tent blanket
* sleeping bags
* mattresses / mats
* mosquito net
* torch (flashlight)
* water bag
* bucket
* camping furniture
* pots / kettle / frying pan
* plate / mug / cutlery
* chopping board
* butterdish
* gas cooker
* plastic basin / washing-up brush / sponge
* tea towel(s)
* dustpan and brush
* salt / herbs
* washing line

For the journey

* general route description / list of road numbers on the dashboard

Before leaving

* leave information behind: address(es), travel plans, data on car and trailer
* throw out perishables
* empty garbage bags / bins
* empty the fridge
* check water, gas, electricity, central heating
* check doors and windows
* place valuables in a safe place

4. In Cases of Illness

Over the last few years, increasing attention has been given to illnesses and problems that can occur when on vacation. We shall limit our summary to the most common of these. If you have to take medication, be sure to ask about the side effects. Not all medicines are suitable for pregnant women, for example, or for young children. There are often special medicines suitable for children. If you travel further afield or to another continent, it is advisable to obtain information in advance from your own pharmacy or from the local health department, especially about vaccinations.

Motion / travel sickness

Children are particularly prone to travel sickness — in the car, on a boat or plane. This usually results in nausea and vomiting.

Tips:
* Take plastic bags with you for any vomit.
* Take some sweets with you to suck on in the plane, or something to drink in a bottle. Sucking or drinking helps combat the earache that often accompanies taking off and landing.

Action

You cannot do much about travel sickness that suddenly appears. If you are travelling by car, you can stop, allow the sufferer some fresh air and wash his or her face with water.

Medication

* Ask at your local pharmacy. They will be able to help you. Remember, not all drugs are suitable for (young) children. Usually one has to take the pills about one hour before setting off. Ask about repeating the dose on the way.
* Nose drops or spray (Xylometazoline) for children with earache in the plane.

Diarrhoea

Diarrhoea is travel problem number one. It usually arises as a result of bacteria in polluted drinking water or contaminated food.

Children are particularly prone to diarrhoea due to the different eating habits abroad and the different climate. You have diarrhoea if you defaecate four times within twenty-four hours and the excrement is watery. Usually the problem clears up of its own accord after one or two days.

However, the body can lose much liquid, minerals and salts due to the diarrhoea, resulting in dehydration.

Tips, especially for tropical countries:
* Think about hygiene when preparing food.
* Do not eat unwashed fruit.
* Boil all vegetables.
* Drink (bottled) mineral water as much as possible, or boil the tap water.
* Be careful with soft drinks with ice in them, and do not eat scoop ice cream from street vendors.

Symptoms of dehydration

Infrequent urination (urine appears dark yellow), dry or sticky mouth and tongue. Lethargy. Not producing tears, sunken eyes. Markedly sunken fontanelle (the soft spot on the top of the head) in an infant.

Action

* With children under two years old, diarrhoea can quickly lead to complications. Consult a doctor. It is also advisable to consult a doctor if there is a fever as well as symptoms of dehydration, or if the diarrhoea lasts longer than two days. If the children are a little older, consult a doctor after three days.

* Seek a doctor's advice before giving anti-diarrhoea medication.
* Ensure that the person with diarrhoea regularly washes his or her hands with (hot) water and soap.
* Diarrhoea on its own won't do much harm. You have to drink a lot to replace the lost liquid: one to two litres (2 to 4 quars) a day. You can eat what your stomach accepts, but preferably not too many sweet items, spicy food or too much protein.
* Consult a doctor if the patient has diarrhoea, fever and cannot hold anything down in warm weather.

Medication

* Oral Rehydration Salts (ORS) help to replace liquid, salts and minerals lost because of diarrhoea. Dissolve one sachet in 200 ml (half pint) of (boiled) water. The mixture can be kept for a maximum of two hours outside the fridge and twenty-four hours in a fridge.

Dose: For children up to 20 kg (45 lb): 10 ml ORS solution per kg of body weight. Children over 20 kg and above: 200 ml (7 fl oz) each time.

Stomach and abdominal complaints

Stomach and abdominal complaints occur regularly in the summer, especially if you are in a foreign country. When camping, you do not always have a fridge at your disposal. As a result, bacteria in the food find it easier to multiply.

Action

If your stomach isn't working properly, if you are suffering from nausea and vomiting, it is better not to consume anything at all. After all, you will probably just throw it up again. When your insides have calmed down, you can begin with a few teaspoons of camomile tea. The body receives liquid and the camomile helps soothe the stomach.

After this, you can eat what you like. The complaints usually vanish within a couple of days. Children under two years old, however, run the risk of dehydration so it is advisable to consult a doctor.

Medication

* See the section on diarrhoea.
* Common Balm (*Melissa officinalis*): warms and relaxes the stomach when irritated. Take 3–5 drops with water every hour as required.
* *Bisacodyl:* in cases of constipation.

Sunburn

You can enjoy your sunshine as long as you do so sensibly. Sunlight activates the production of vitamin D in the skin and is good for some skin problems (eczema).

However, the sun radiates different kinds of ultra-violet rays, and UV-A and UV-B radiation can damage your health. Children under fifteen years old are generally sensitive to the harmful effects of UV radiation, but adults, too, must be careful. The lighter your skin, the greater your sensitivity. *Sunburn* is one of the directly visible harmful effects of UV radiation. Children who regularly suffer from sunburn can experience problems with their skin later on in life, so it is necessary to protect your skin against UV radiation.

Tips:
The following tips are important for children, but also apply to adults.

* Shade is better than full sunshine for the little ones. Always place a pram or buggy in the shade.
* Don't allow your children to be naked in the sun for too long.

Clothes, a sunhat, and sunglasses offer the best protection (see p. 11) for a pattern for a sunhat).

* Allow your skin to accustom gradually to the sun, and build up the amounts of exposure day by day.
* Use good-quality, high-factor sunlotion. Apply suncream at least thirty minutes before you go out in the sun. Repeat this every two hours. In the mountains, it is advisable to use an even higher factor. Do not forget your ears, chest or the back of your legs and arms, and the top of your feet if you are wearing sandals; protect your lips with lipsalve / a chapstick with UV filter.
* UV radiation is at its strongest between eleven and three. It is best to stick to the shade during these hours.

Action

If you stay in the sun too long, you can end up with livid, painful skin. In cases of sunburn, the skin is usually still intact and there are no blisters (first-degree burns).

Medication

There are many sunlotions with various protective factors. Ask at your pharmacy. An aftersun product can soothe a sensitive skin.

Burns

A child can easily incur a burn due to a small accident with fire or with hot tea or coffee. These are usually first-degree burns with red, painful skin that remains intact. Blisters are characteristic of second-degree burns, and the skin is seriously damaged with third-degree burns.

Action

* Contact a doctor immediately if there are second or third-degree burns.
* Cool the skin for at least 10 minutes, preferably in lukewarm, softly flowing water. Cold water can be very painful on burned skin.
* You can also dab the skin with compresses dipped in water with a little vinegar added to it (4 cups of water to 1 of vinegar) or lemon juice (2 cups of water to one of lemon juice). *Calendula lotion/ ointment* or *Weleda Combudoron Spray* can be directly sprayed on to the sore spot. If necessary, you can cover it with a compress.
* If there is light skin irritation, you can rub in *Weleda Combudoron gel* or *Weleda Citrus skin cream.* Use a cream that spreads easily. The gel version cools well.
* If the burns are more serious, do not rub anything into the skin. Cover it with a sterile compress or clean cloth.

Sunstroke

If you have been unprotected in the sun for too long, especially without a hat, you can become unwell due to sunstroke. Sunstroke is often caused by an accumulation of warmth in the body.

Tips:

* Make sure your head is covered and you are wearing sunglasses. Wear light and airy clothes. Do not allow children to walk naked in strong sunlight or in extreme heat for too long.
* Do not consume alcohol in any of the above-mentioned situations.

Symptoms

Someone who becomes unwell due to too much sunshine is very hot, lethargic, tired and sweaty. This is sometimes accompanied by a headache.

In cases of genuine sunstroke, the victim usually has a splitting headache, is somewhat befuddled and feels nauseous.

Action

* If you think that someone has become unwell due to the sun, encourage him or her to sit in the shade. Dab his or her head with a wet cloth and cool the wrists. This is a good way of cooling down.
* Do not allow a person in this condition to cool down under a cold shower or in the sea. All his or her skin pores are open in an attempt to lose warmth. If the skin comes in contact with cold water, the pores will close and the patient will become even warmer.
* Give the patient something to drink, but preferably not ice-cold water.

* If the patient has serious sun-stroke, he or she should not drink anything, as there is the risk of vomiting. Do not treat the skin and call in a doctor.
* Because a shortage of salt often plays a role, it is good to get the patient to drink a salt solution (1/2 teaspoon of salt in 1 litre of water) when he or she is feeling less nauseous. A little stock is also good.

Medication
* ORS (see Diarrhoea, p. 20)

Jellyfish stings

There may be jellyfish on the beach. Be careful when walking with bare feet, a sting from a jellyfish feels like a strong sting from a nettle. Red marks occur around the place of the sting.

Tips:
Do not rub or scratch even although it may itch. The jellyfish releases miniscule hollow arrows that stick in your skin. Rubbing breaks these arrows and makes the skin even itchier.

Action
Cool the skin by holding it underwater. The arrows are released. Azaron helps combat the itch and the pain. Vinegar can help neutralize the sting.

Tips:
It is advisable to ask locally about any marine life that may cause problems.

Ticks

Ticks are small brown-black insects that you find in many countries. They vary in size from 1 to 10 mm (up to 1/2 in) and live in wooded areas, bushes (especially bracken) and tall grass. Ticks are parasites, which attach themselves to your skin and drink your blood until they are full, which may take a couple of days. As a result, you may become infected with the bacteria that cause Lyme's disease (see below).

Tips:
* If children are foraging through high grass, bushes or the woods, make sure that they are wearing good shoes, a (T-)shirt with long sleeves and something on their heads.
* Check every day to see if ticks have nestled in their skin, and shake out the children's clothes above a white cloth or something similar. Ticks like to nestle in places where the skin is thinner, such as the groin, hollow of the knee, armpits, abdomen. With smaller children, they may be located on the neck or head.

Symptoms
After a few days, a large red patch appears at the location of the bite. Flu-like symptoms and fever, headache, and fatigue may be early symptoms of Lyme's disease (see below).

Action

* Remove the tick as quickly as possible with special tick pincers (see the first-aid list below). If you do so within twenty-four hours of the bite, the chance of infection is almost zero. Grab the tick as close to the skin as possible, and pull it out with a rotating movement.

  Try to avoid the body of the tick bursting, or leaving the front part in the skin. Do not use any fluid to get the tick out, it will only bite deeper into the skin.
* After you have removed the tick, clean the skin around the location of the bite with 70% alcohol or iodine tincture.
* Go to a doctor if you cannot get a part of the tick out of the skin.
* Make a note of the day that you found the tick on one of the family members. This could be important information for the doctor.

Lyme's disease

This illness develops in three stages. Occasionally, one of the stages will pass over without any symptoms.

Between three and twenty-one days after being bitten, a red, ring-shaped rash may form around the location of the bite and continue to expand. Symptoms: flu-like symptoms, fever, headache, fatigue. After a few weeks or months the victim may begin to suffer from problems with his or her joints, neurological complaints, facial paralysis, and heart problems. Months to years later, problems with the joints and walking and orientation disorders may arise.

Lyme's disease is not contagious.

Insect bites, bee and wasp stings

In principle, bees tend to avoid people. They only become aggressive if you stand in their flying route or approach their hive. Wasps, on the

other hand, are continually searching for sweet things (your sandwich, for example).

In warmer countries, there are many kinds of flies that like to bite in as dusk sets in.

Tips:
* Insects avoid tobacco smoke and also smoke from a candle. They do not like the smell of lemon. In the evening, insects are attracted to light. For this reason, you should not have any light on as long as insects can get in to your accommodation.

* In the evening, put on clothes that cover your body as much as possible.
* Protect your skin with an insect repellent. Do not put repellent on the hands or faces of children.
* Use a mosquito net at night if necessary.

Action

* Pull out the bee or wasp sting by scraping a credit card or something similar in one direction across the location of the sting. If you try to pull out the sting with your fingers or pincers, you may be squeezing the venom into the skin. But the most important thing to do is to get the sting out as quickly as possible.
* Cool the skin with a paste of baking soda for a bee sting and with diluted vinegar (1 vinegar: 4 water) for a wasp sting. Use a wet bandage on any swelling around the sting.
* Consult a doctor if the swelling becomes serious, or if the patient throws up, or if the patient has been stung in his or her mouth or throat.

Travelling pharmacy

(H) = homeopathic medication

As names of medications vary in different countries, ask a doctor or pharmacist for advice. Be aware that some medications can provoke allergic reactions or oversensitivity.

❋ *Motion/travel sickness / earache on the plane*

— medication against air, sea or car sickness
— nose spray for children with earache on the plane
— (H) *Weleda Rhinodoron* nose spray: begin using the spray one day before the journey and use it 3–4 times a day.

❋ *Diarrhoea*

— Oral Rehydration Salts (ORS)
— (H) *Weleda Carbo Betulae* tablets: for diarrhoea. Helps clean the intestines. Take two tablets with water every hour.

❋ *Stomach and abdominal complaints*

— Laxative against constipation
— (H) Balm *(Melissa officinalis)* for general unsettledness: feeling shaky, light flu, or stomach irritation (warmed and relaxes the stomach).
— (H) *Centaurea (Centaurium comp)*: laxative against constipation. Adults: up to 3 tablets three times a day; children: 1–2 tablets a day.

❋ *Sunburn*

— Suntan lotion
— (H) Weleda's Edelweiss Sun Products are available in factor 15 and 20

❋ *Burns*

— Calendula emulsion
— (H) *Weleda Combudoron* spray can be sprayed directly on the burn
— (H) With light skin irritation, you can rub in *Weleda Combudoron gel* or *Weleda Citrus skin cream.*

❋ *Sunstroke*

— Care plus Oral Rehydration Salts

❋ *Headache*

— painkiller
— (H) *Biodoron / Ferrum Quiartz* for people prone to headaches. 1–2 tablets three to six times a day, as required.

❋ *Insect bites, jellyfish stings, etc.*

— against insect bites or jellyfish stings. Rub into the skin.
— salve or after-bite powder
— (H) *Calendula* wound salve or spray: for insect bites, wounds, and sores
— (H) Weleda Citrus skin gel
— (H) *Combudoron* gel or spray: rub the gel thinly into the skin, or spray on to a wet compress.

First-aid kit

— scissors for bandages
— tweezers
— tick tweezers
— safety pins
— wound plasters
— sterile gauze
— sticking plaster
— emergency bandage
— (elastic) bandage
— swallow-tail plasters for cuts
— iodine tincture
— cotton wool
— triangular bandage
— insect repellent
— thermometer

5. The Weather

Introduction

It is fine to have good weather on your vacation. You can cope with one rainy day on the campsite but it won't do your spirits any good if it rains every day. If you are going where there is usually plenty of sunshine, the weather may change suddenly, more suddenly than we are used to at home. This applies both to the beach, where a sunny beach can rapidly become enveloped in mist, and to the mountains, where the weather can also alter dramatically.

This chapter provides much useful information on the weather:

* Why does a sunny summer's day suddenly give way to heavy rain and thunder?
* Why is it always much colder high up in the mountains and why is there snow there, even in mid-summer?

This chapter deals with these matters in more detail.

If your interest in the weather has been aroused, you can quite easily become a weatherman or woman. You will be able to recognize developments in the sky or changes in the wind, and this can be extremely useful. At least you will be able to seek shelter in good time if you see a shower coming!

It becomes more interesting if you begin to take measurements with a couple of simple instruments. For example, you can use a lemonade glass to determine how much rain has fallen. Nevertheless, you cannot completely do without the weather report in the newspaper or on television. If you understand the weather report, you will at least be well prepared for abrupt changes in the weather.

The sun: the weather engine

In our planetary system, the sun is the focus of everything. Well, this is not completely true — the moon orbits around the earth — but they both orbit the sun in tandem (see Fig 27.1).

The earth also turns on its own axis, like a spinning top, only much slower. The earth turns once every twenty-four hours. Figure 27.2 shows the movement of the earth with respect to the sun. Notice that the axis of the earth (the line connecting the two poles) is not vertical, but slants a little.

Sunlight

You can regard the sun as an enormous ball of fire that, fortunately, will take millions of years before it is burned out. The surface of the sun has a temperature of around 6 000°C.

This glowing ball transmits all kinds of radiation: visible radiation (we see the sun as a yellow or orange ball) and also invisible radiation.

It is light during the day thanks to the visible radiation. This sunlight also falls on the moon. The moon reflects some of this sunlight and that it why it gives a little light in the night. However, this visible light does not give us any warmth.

Fortunately, the sun also transmits invisible radiation. This so-called

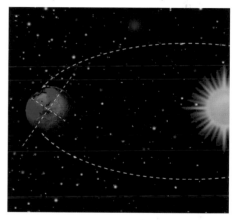

Fig 27.2 The position of the earth in relation to the sun (North Pole above, South Pole below)

Fig 27.1 The orbits of the earth and moon around the sun

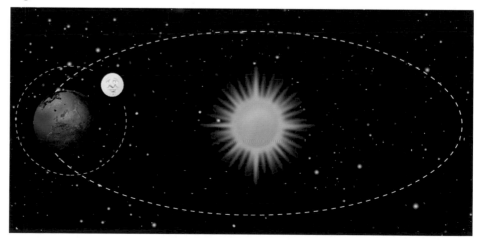

'shortwave' radiation is essential to us. We cannot see this radiation but it can heat up surfaces, such as our skin for example. The ground we are standing on, and the oceans, are warmed by the sun in this way.

The air is not warmed by this radiation, although we observe that it becomes warmer during the day. This is because the air passes over warmed ground or warmed seawater. You can perhaps compare it to the warm air that you feel rising above a central heating radiator. This air only becomes warmer when it has passed above or alongside the hot radiator. In this way, the sun warms the earth and the atmosphere (the air that surrounds the earth).

Seasons

However, the earth is not warmed up equally everywhere. This is not only because the earth turns on its axis and thus does not receive sunshine in the night, but also because the axis of the earth is slanting. In summer the sun is higher in the sky and its radiation falls more directly onto the surface of the earth. In winter, when the sun is lower, the same amount of radiation is spread over a far greater surface 'diluting' the heat. Note that when it is summer in the northern hemisphere it is winter in the southern hemisphere. And December and January are sumer in the southern hemisphere when it is cold in the north.

Fig 28.1

Summer   Winter

Air currents

As we said, not all regions of the earth are warmed up to the same extent during the course of the day or during the course of a year. There are great differences in this warming process. Northern Europe is cold in January, it is a little warmer in Spain, and it is tropically hot in Africa.

Warm air is lighter than cold air. You can see that if you look at a pot on the cooker, you see the hot air and the steam rising. Above a fire, you see the warm smoke rising. The air above the warm areas on the earth rises in the same way. Of course, if that was the only thing that happened, the people in the tropics would soon be gasping for air, all the oxygen we need to breathe would have disappeared.

Fortunately, there are also other processes taking place. When hot air rises, colder air rushes in from higher latitudes to replace the air that is rising. Of course, if great volumes of air sweep down from the north to fill up the shortage in the warmer areas,

the north would also have too little air. Luckily, this is not the case. The warm air that has risen spreads out at a great altitude. Some of this moves to the north. At great altitude, the air becomes cooler, becomes heavier, and slowly descends. In this way, the north gets its air back.

These air currents spread the excess warm air and excess cold air across large parts of the globe. Figure 28.2 shows the air circulation (explained by extra-large arrows just to be clear. In reality, this process takes place at an altitude of no more than 10 km, 35 000 ft, above the earth).

High and low-pressure areas

Despite the influx of air from other areas, there is just a little shortage of air in regions where air rises. In such cases, we speak of a low-pressure area or of a depression. Where air slowly descends from a great altitude, there is a surplus of air. There we find a high-pressure area.

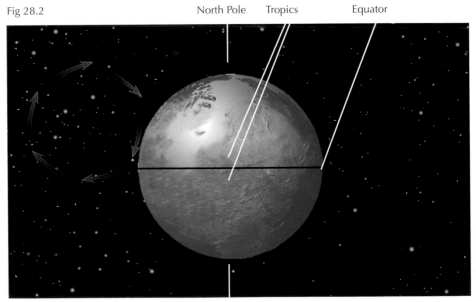

Fig 28.2   North Pole   Tropics   Equator

South Pole

This explanation is a little bit simpler than is actually the case. If the earth did not turn on its axis, the warmth would be much less efficiently distributed. High and low pressure areas wouldn't even exist! Probably, there would be hardly any weather at all.

The distribution of high and low pressure areas is closely related to the weather as we experience it. So you could say that there must be high and low-pressure areas to distribute the warmth across the earth 'more evenly.' These differences in high and low pressure give us the weather (rain, sunshine, wind) as we know it.

Without high and low pressure there would be no wind. Without the wind, the large amounts of warm air in the Tropics could not come to higher latitudes. And cold air could not flow to lower latitudes.

In and around low pressure areas, the weather is generally determined by clouds and precipitation: rain, hail or snow. In addition, it can be very windy or stormy in areas where the depression is deeper. We then speak of storm depressions. High pressure areas usually bring tranquil and good weather.

As you see, the sun is the true engine of the weather.

The ozone layer

A part of this UV radiation (UV-B) that penetrates to the earth is directly harmful to life on earth and to humans as well. This radiation can cause cancer. However, this harmful sort of UV radiation is stopped naturally by the ozone layer.

Ozone surrounds the earth, high above us in the stratosphere (above 10 km, 35 000 ft). But due to the air pollution (especially from CFC, the gas that used to be in spray-cans and refridgerators) the unstable ozone disintegrates, particularly in polar regions. This is the 'hole in the ozone layer.' As a result, an increasing amount of the harmful UV radiation is reaching the earth's surface. This means that lying in the sun is not the innocent pastime we imagined it to be. We have to protect ourselves against this UV radiation in other ways.

Temperature

Radiation from the sun eventually causes the air to warm up. The temperature usually rises during the day. At night, there is no sun. Not only the sun but also the earth sends out radiation. This is longwave radiation, which we can also feel. It is the same radiation that you feel near an open fire or near a hotplate, for example. Every object transmits heat, even your bike or a car. Mostly you don't feel it, because you yourself are about the same temperature. Since the object transmits heat, it cools down. Think about a hot cup of tea or coffee. Even if you place a lid on the mug, the liquid inside still becomes gradually cooler. The earth cools down at night in much the same way. Warm air flowing over ground that is cooling down also cools down. The air that flows just above the ground cools down most. That is why at night the air just above ground level is generally the coldest.

Sometimes the grass is white and frozen in the morning when the thermometer indicates that it is +3°C (37°F) one and a half metres (4 feet) above the ground. However, in the summer months, the nights are shorter and the temperature seldom falls as low as in winter.

The influence of the sea

Temperature is not only determined by the sun. Location is also important, especially in relation to the sea. The sea warms up more slowly than the land. With the prevailing south-west winds, relatively cool air is blown from the sea over the land. Once it is over land, it warms up more quickly. In summer, a wind on the beach can be quite fresh, under 20°C (68°F). But inland the temperature can quite easily rise to 22°C (72°F) or more.

After summer, the seawater cools down slowly. For this reason we see the reverse of this process in coastal areas from early autumn onward: if the wind comes from the sea, coastal areas can be warmer than inland ones.

If you are on the beach in June, and an offshore wind is blowing, it can become quite warm. This is because the wind is coming from inland, where the ground is warmer. The warmest days on the beach in the east occur when the wind is blowing from the west.

If the sea does not have a cooling effect on the temperature, the summer temperature can often rise to 25°C (77°F) and more. A day with a temperature of at least 30°C (86°F) is called a tropical day. These do not occur often in the UK. If so, they happen inland and not on the coast.

In Spain, the average temperature is around 30°C (86°F) in the summer. The map below displays the average temperatures in West European countries in the month of July. You will observe that the British Isles are rather cool in comparison to other Continental countries. The Scandinavian countries are roughly the same as the UK. This is because we are all surrounded by the sea.

We have not yet discussed the temperature in the mountains, which is completely different. We shall deal with that in more detail later.

Wind-chill factor

However, the temperature that your thermometer shows isn't everything. The wind and the amount of moisture in the air also determine how you experience the temperature, how the temperature feels. We refer to this as the chill factor, but it is impossible to measure this with any real accuracy.

If there is a strong breeze, a temperature of 30°C (86°F) does not feel too hot, but if there is no wind at all every step seems to cost energy and you are sweating profusely after a little while.

The amount of moisture in the air (the humidity) also plays a role here. If it is hot, you will sweat. Your skin becomes moist. If there is a dry wind, the sweat on your skin evaporates immediately, the moisture disappears. This evaporation process draws warmth from your body, so that your skin feels cooler. In moist air, the drops of sweat do not evaporate so easily so you do not experience the pleasant cooling effect. You soon feel sweaty and sticky.

In tropical countries, there is often a lack of wind and the humidity is high. You experience the weather as being rather clammy. In most southern European countries, the air is often quite dry, even with tropical temperatures, so that the weather feels very pleasant.

In cold weather in the winter or in the mountains, the chill factor again plays a major role. If there is no wind, a temperature of 10°C (50°F) can be quite acceptable, but a strong wind soon changes our perception of things. We can be chilled to the bone.

Temperature and altitude

We mostly speak of the temperature just above ground level. This is logical, of course, that is our living environment and that is the temperature we feel. As we get higher, the temperature gradually decreases. There is a direct correlation between altitude and temperature. The temperature decreases by 6°C with every 1 000 metres you climb (3°F per 1 000 ft) (see Fig 47.1).

You can see this if you go by plane. Many planes have a screen displaying flight data, such as the route flown, the altitude, and the temperature. If you fly high above France, which always seems to be warmer than the UK, you can see that the temperature outside is -60°C (-75°F)!

The correlation between altitude and temperature becomes clear if you go into the mountains. Even if it is warm in the valley, there is always snow on the peaks, the so-called 'perpetual snow' and, of course, that is only possible if it is much colder there.

Fig 30.1 Average afternoon temperatures in July

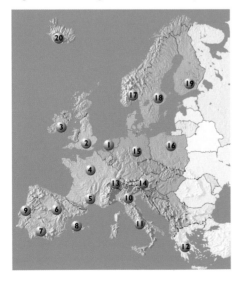

1	Amsterdam	21
2	London	22
3	Dublin	20
4	Paris	25
5	Marseilles	29
6	Madrid	31
7	Malaga	29
8	Palma de Mallorca	29
9	Lisbon	26
10	Venice	27
11	Rome	30
12	Athens	33
13	Zurich	25
14	Innsbruck	25
15	Berlin	24
16	Warsaw	24
17	Oslo	22
18	Stockholm	22
19	Helsinki	22
20	Reijkjavik	14

The clouds

Everyone has seen a cloud, and you sometimes see them too often! However, life on earth as we know it, in all its diversity, blaze of colour, and wealth of species, would not be possible without the clouds. Clouds are the suppliers of fresh water, our drinking water. Without clouds it would never rain and snow, and you could never go on a winter sports vacation.

Water, ice and water vapour

Water occurs in three forms — as liquid water as it comes out of the tap, in solid form as ice and in invisible gaseous form. Wherever you are, there is invisible water all around you: water vapour. Nevertheless, a large amount of water vapour is not necessarily a cloud — you cannot see water vapour but you can see a cloud. So what is a cloud?

A cloud is an amount of air that contains not only water vapour but also a lot of droplets (of liquid water) or ice crystals (solid water). These are things you can see. You can see that if it is misty — if you look closely you can see that it consists of countless droplets of water. So mist is therefore a cloud!

The question is: where does a cloud come from? To answer this, we have to look at a cloud's main ingredient: water, no matter in which form it occurs.

Condensation and evaporation

Water in one form can change into water in another. If water freezes it is a completely normal process. Water changes from liquid form to solid form. But water can also change into a gas. This is also an everyday process. You can see this when you are outside on a cold morning.

When you exhale, you can see your breath, and if you look at a pan of boiling potatoes, you see *clouds* of steam above the pan.

Air can only hold a certain amount of water vapour. If there is too much water vapour, the air cannot accommodate it and small visible droplets are formed. We call this *condensation*. The reverse process, when liquid water changes into water vapour, is called evaporation. If there has been a heavy shower of rain on a summer's day, the streets will be wet and full of puddles. If you come out an hour later, the street will probably have dried up completely, perhaps leaving a couple of puddles. The rest has evaporated. The water has not been destroyed or conjured away. It has become invisible and is floating all around us.

Temperature and humidity

In this process of evaporation and condensation, the temperature plays a decisive role. Warm air can hold more water vapour than cold air. Think about your breath on a cold morning. The air we breathe out is very moist. Within our bodies it is quite warm — 37°C (98°F) — and the air holds that moisture without us noticing it. But when we breathe out into the surrounding cold air, the air we breathe out cools down very quickly. The cooler air cannot hold all that moisture. So the water vapour turns into small droplets and we can suddenly see our breath. If the air surrounding our bodies is warm, in the summer for example, we do not see our breath, because the air we exhale scarcely cools down.

Water that is boiled turns into steam (water vapour). The warm and moist air above the pan rises upward. But this air comes into contact with cooler air, because the kitchen is only something like 20°C (68°F). So a process of condensation takes place and we see clouds of steam forming. Thus, the water in the pan changes into water vapour (due to evaporation) and then this water vapour changes into liquid water in the form of droplets (a process of condensation).

Air cooling down

Now we know how clouds are made: by the cooling down of moist air.

One of the simplest ways of cooling air down is to get it to rise to a greater altitude, where it is much colder, as we mentioned previously in this chapter. This rising air then cools down automatically and a cloud is formed.

This happens, for instance, when air is forced upwards when it comes into contact with a high range of mountains. Clouds are formed against the mountains.

Air also rises when the sun shines. The air above the ground becomes warmer and warm air is lighter than cold air. The warm air thus rises up, but becomes cooler again as it ascends. This generally produces a cloud (see Fig 33.1).

Birds and (hang)gliders make convenient use of these rising air currents by hitching a ride on them as they ascend. Since these air currents are relatively warm, we also refer to them as 'thermals.'

On the other hand, mist forms at ground level. The air does not rise at all but a dense cloud does manage to form. You must have seen something like it: mist that forms just above ground level after a nice (late) summer's day. Sometimes we refer to this as ground mist. How is it formed?

When the sun sets, the air cools down where it comes into contact with the ground, which cools down more quickly than the air. Cold air is heavier that warm air. The coldest air nestles at ground level. If it has been a warm day and there is moisture in the air, droplets of water will form in this cold air.

Air warming up

Clouds vanish as the air warms up. This happens when air descends. For example, air that has been forced up over the mountain descends again on the other side and the clouds disappear (see Fig 33.2). And mist dissolves when the sun gets up and the air becomes warmer.

Cloud layers and cumuli

We have seen how clouds can arise due to the air cooling down. Sometimes there is a whole layer of cloud (mist), on other occasions it is only an ascending air current. As a result, we see clouds with different appearances. We divide clouds into two general families:

* cloud layers (stratified clouds) and
* woolpacks (cumuli).

These families can be further subdivided into all sorts that are directly dependent on the altitude at which the cloud is formed. The table overleaf shows the division into families (layered clouds and woolpacks) and main types (low altitude, medium altitude, high altitude).

The list indicates that cumulonimbus occupies a special place. This cloud in the woolpack family is found at all levels. It is more or less the chief of all the clouds. It can take on immense dimensions and possesses the most marvellous forms and colours. Behind all this lurks an enormous destructive power.

The cumulonimbus

It is not without reason that cumulonimbus is the king of all clouds. Thunder only comes from this kind of cloud. Hail or a tornado always involves a cumulonimbus. This raincloud usually arises out of a normal woolpack, a cumulus. A woolpack gives few problems, the sun may disappear behind it for a time, that is all, but a cumulonimbus may make you soaking wet.

It is very handy if you can estimate whether or not an innocent cumulus is going to develop into a cumulonimbus. You have to take a good look at the sky.

Fig 33.1 Warm air rising below a cloud

Fig 33.2 Clouds forming at the top of a mountain dissolve as the air descents and warms up on the other side.

Fig 34.1

Fig 34.2

Fig 34.3

Fig 34.4

Fig 34.5

Fig 34.6

Fig 34.7

Fig 34.8

Fig 34.1 Low-hanging clouds, dark against a higher layer of cloud

Fig 34.2 Cumulus

Fig 34.3 The beautiful colours at sunset are typical of cirrus clouds

Fig 34.4 Cumulonimbus with its characteristic anvil shape

Fig 34.5 Stratocumulus

Fig 34.6 Altostratus

* If the normal woolpacks are quite small and they stay that way, you do not need to worry that the weather will suddenly change.
* But if the woolpacks continually grow in height and take on an ever-increasing size, there is really something going on.
* If you look closely at the top of a woolpack, you can often see how it is expanding upward.
* If this kind of woolpack more or less stays as it is and seems to be getting thicker and higher, the cloud may be developing into a raincloud, the cumulonimbus, but it is difficult to see this, you have to watch the sky carefully.
* As long as the top of the cauliflower-shaped cloud still has sharp contours, it still belongs to the woolpack group. As soon as the top of an expanding cloud becomes less clear-cut and seems to be acquiring more frayed edges, the cumulonimbus is beginning to appear. This growing cloud is already producing precipitation!
* As the cloud continues to grow, the top loses its bulging shape and becomes increasingly flat.

The surrounding air at these heights is very cold, below freezing. The bulging raincloud contains relatively warm air, heavy with moisture.

A fully-fledged cumulonimbus has the characteristic anvil or mushroom shape. At this stage, coupled with lightning and thunder, the moisture in the air freezes to ice particles which falling down grow into hailstones. They sometimes fall as hailstones, other times the hailstone melt into characteristic large thunderstorm drops.

Fig 34.7 Altocumulus, also referred to as 'fleecy clouds'

Fig 34.8 Cirrus

Altitude	Layered cloud	Woolpacks	
Low	Stratus (9)	Cumulus (10)	Cumulonimbus (12)
	Stratocumulus		
Medium	Altostratus (14)	Altocumulus (15)	Cumulonimbus
High	Cirrus (11, 16)	Cirrocumulus	Cumulonimbus

Pay attention to the clouds

Showers approaching

Besides examining the appearance of the raincloud, you should always look to see if the cloud is coming nearer or if it is passing by at a distance. Only if the cloud is definitely approaching can you expect a heavy shower within an hour. If the cloud gets closer you can no longer see its characteristic shape as it fills the sky with a large mass of dark cloud. A tightly packed porridge of clouds often appears under the cumulonimbus.

If you stand facing the cumulonimbus (see Fig 34.4) and the wind is coming from the left-hand side, the raincloud is more or less on its way toward you (see Fig 36.1). When the shower is nearby and it is becoming threateningly dark, the wind often becomes stronger, coming from the direction of the clouds. The wind usually feels noticeably colder. In general, in this situation, it will begin to rain within a few minutes. Thunder may already be audible.

Rain on the way

Stratified cloud can also tell you a lot about the weather that is on the way, such as a period of rain. Periods of rain are caused by a large area with stratified clouds that extend across a deep layer of the atmosphere.

In many cases, an approaching period of rain reveals itself by an increase in the amount of cloud in the higher layers of the atmosphere. We see extensive fields of cirrus clouds arriving, which have the tendency to become increasingly dense.

If this goes on for a few hours, the chance of rain increases greatly. It usually actually begins to rain when ribbons of cloud drift past at much lower altitudes.

You should also pay attention to the wind direction. First check which direction the cirrus clouds are coming from.

❀ If you stand facing the approaching cirrus clouds and the wind is noticeably coming from your left-hand side, this is an extra indication that rain is approaching (see Fig 36.3).

Fig 36.3 Rain on its way

Fig 36.4 Little chance of rain

Fig 36.1

Fig 36.2 The shower is close by

Fig 36.5 It will probably remain dry

* If the wind is coming from the direction you are facing, the chance of rain is small (Fig 36.4).
* If the wind is coming from your right-hand side, it will probably remain dry (Fig 36.5).

From the moment that the cirrus areas become more and more tightly packed (and the wind comes from the left-hand side), you almost always have enough time to seek shelter. It often takes around four hours before it actually begins to rain.

Precipitation

What is precipitation and how are rain, snow and hail formed?

They all make you wet, unless it is freezing of course. If you walk or cycle fast through mist, you also become wet. These mist droplets float in the air, they do not fall on to the ground. Mist is not precipitation, although things can become quite damp due to the mist. Think about dripping wet trees on a misty morning. Mist is low cloud.

Rain and drizzle

Most precipitation falls in the form of rain.

Rain only arises in the clouds. This takes place in two ways:

* The most simple way is that the miniscule droplets of water bump into one another, stick together, grow larger and finally, due to their weight, fall to the ground.
* Most rain, however, is created in a different way.

We have already seen that the atmosphere is much colder at high altitudes. Rainclouds are often located at an altitude of 3000 m (10000 ft) or more. The temperature is almost always below zero at such altitudes. If it is cold enough, snow crystals will form in the cloud. This happens at temperatures lower than -15°C (+5°F). These snow crystals gradually grow larger and eventually fall towards the ground, but as they fall, they pass through increasingly warm layers of air. They melt and fall upon the earth as raindrops. Even

if it rains in mid-summer, the raindrops will probably be melted snowflakes. This is a remarkable thought. However, if you are high up in the mountains you will see that this is not so remarkable. It regularly snows there, even in summer.

No large raindrops are formed in low-hanging cloud. The small droplets fall after a few collisions with one another. They reach the earth as tiny drops. They float a little because they are so light. This is a *drizzle*. You can become quite wet from drizzle though there is really not much precipitation. You probably won't see any puddles forming on the streets.

In the winter, rain or drizzle sometimes falls on the frozen earth, or the raindrops reach the ground although the temperature is a little below zero. This is perfectly possible if the temperature at 500 m (1600 ft) above ground level is above zero. In both cases, the drops will freeze when they hit the ground, becoming 'black ice' and it can be highly dangerous to traffic, because the roads turn into skating rinks. Sometimes the

-45°C
(-49°F)

-30°C
(-22°F)

-15°C
(+5°F)

-20°C
(-4°F)

0°C
(32°F)

Fig 38.1

Fig 38.2 a, b, c, snow crystals (enlarged approx. 15 ×)

layer of ice is even thick enough the allow skating on the pavement.

If the raindrops freeze before they reach the ground, they resemble small glass marbles. This is not hail but 'sleet' or 'frozen rain.' Frozen rain is transparent whereas hail is not, as we shall see below.

Snow

Snow only occurs in clouds that are sufficiently cold. The temperature in the cloud must be at least -10°C and preferably below -15°C (14° or 5°F). Ice crystals are formed at these temperatures, and can develop into snow crystals. A snow crystal is star-shaped and always has six points. It is certainly worthwhile examining a snowflake the next time it snows, but it is only really possible to study a snowflake properly if the temperature is below zero. You will also observe that every snowflake is different (see Fig 38.2, a–c).

Snow crystals can assume many different shapes. Separate snow-flakes often get stuck together in the clouds to form larger snowflakes. As the snowflake falls, it passes through air with a higher temper-ature. At temperatures of around zero, the snowflake becomes moist, and they stick a little. As a result, the snowflakes can sometimes become extremely large. Snowflakes of 5 cm (2 in) have been measured. Such large flakes do not melt very quickly and can reach the ground even though the temperature may be a few degrees above zero. This is often referred to as 'wet snow' or 'melting snow.'

Snow has more difficulty in melt-ing if the air is dry. In that case, even small snowflakes can reach the ground when the temperature is a couple of degree above zero.

Hail

Hail is a kind of precipitation that is only produced in the cumulonimbus cloud. If it hails, it only does so for a short time.

How is it possible that we occa-sionally have hailstones in the sum-mer? Even if it is boiling hot, you sometimes have a shower of hail-stones.

Hail arises in a raincloud at high altitude, where the temperature is perhaps -50° or -60°C (-60° or -75°F). Under the influence of certain air currents in this raincloud, a develop-ing hailstone can move around inside the cloud for quite some time. The hailstone does not fall to the earth immediately. As a result, due to col-lisions with small droplets of water, the hailstone can develop to reach the size of a marble, a golfball, a ten-nis ball, even a sizeable orange. The hailstone eventually falls to earth. A hailstone of this size reaches the ground in no more than five minutes and therefore has little time to melt. For that reason, there can be hail-stones even if the ground temperature is 30°C (86°F).

If you experience this kind of shower of hailstones in the sum-mer, it is worthwhile examining the hailstones as closely as possible. You will see, for instance, that most hail-stones are not neatly rounded. They resemble small meteorites with holes and protrusions. This is due to the collision with other hailstones in the raincloud.

Try to cut through a large hail-stone. With a bit of luck you will see that there are rings on the inside, bright white alternating with a glass-like colour. This tells you how often the hailstone has gone up and down within the raincloud.

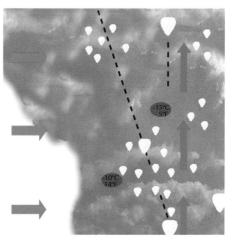

Fig 39.1   *Fig 39.2*

Hail is almost always preceded by a threatening, dark sky and you almost always hear a peal of thunder. If there is hail in the summer, it is best to go indoors or take shelter somewhere (but not under a tree!), because if a large hailstone falls at an enormous speed, it can hit you so hard that your life may be endangered.

Wind

The wind blows almost all the time, at least in the daytime. In the evening or at night, you may feel no wind at all. Wind is only air on the move. When it is windy, a lot of air is on the move at one time, and when there is a gentle breeze, this means that the air is only moving a little.

But why is the air almost always on the move? This involves high and low-pressure areas, which we dealt with earlier in this chapter. As mentioned, these differences in pressure are caused by variations in temperature.

In a low-pressure area, there is too little air, as it were. This shortage must be compensated, or filled in. Air from the surroundings flows to the low-pressure area, the wind gets up, and travels towards the centre of the low-pressure area, where there is the least air.

If there is a considerable shortage of air, a lot of air will be on the move. Meteorologists say that the depression is *very deep* or very active. The wind blows harder, a storm may even arise.

You see the same thing happening near a high-pressure area. There is too much air there and the air moves away from the high-pressure area. That, too, causes wind.

The rotation of the earth

The rotation of the earth on its axis also plays an important role in the generation of wind. The wind that is on the move toward the low-pressure areas does not take this rotation into account. As a result, the wind often does not go directly to the low-pressure area, it misses its goal. You can compare this to a situation where your friend is standing on a roundabout in the playground. If you throw a ball to your friend when he

Fig 40.1 and 40.2

or she is exactly opposite you, you see that he or she cannot catch it. The ball flies past, even though you did aim properly. The ball misses its goal because your friend moves on when the ball is on its way (see Fig 40.1 and 40.2).

That is also what happens when air is on its way to that low-pressure area.

The result is that the air does not travel directly to the low-pressure area but swirls around it. The wind blows around the low-pressure and the high-pressure areas.

Wind direction

In the northern hemisphere, the wind blows anti-clockwise around a low-pressure area, and in a clockwise direction around a high-pressure area.

South of the equator, in the southern hemisphere, the wind blows in exactly the opposite directions.

If you are looking north-east, and the wind is coming from the north-west, then you will know that the air pressure to your right is low and to your left it is high (see Fig 40.3).

You can examine the weather chart to see if this is true. Of course, it must be today's weather chart, not the one that refers to tomorrow or another day. Tomorrow's weather chart will probably be shown in the newspaper, so you can look to see from which direction the wind will blow tomorrow.

Fig 40.3

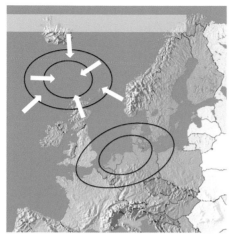

Fig 41.1

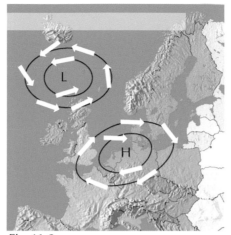

Fig 41.2

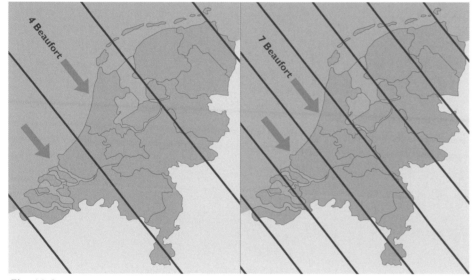

Fig 41.3

As we have seen, wind depends entirely on air pressure. The weather chart usually shows more than only high and low pressure areas. It also shows lines connecting places with the same air pressure. These lines are called *isobars*. The wind blows almost exactly along these lines in such a way that the air pressure to the left of the moving air is lower than that of the air to the right. In the south-

ern hemisphere the winds circle the opposite way around high and low pressure areas, so that the pressure to the right of the moving air is lower.

Wind force

As we have seen, the wind direction is determined by the division of high and low-pressure areas. But why is there sometimes a strong wind and at other times a breeze?

This has to do with amount of difference in the air pressure. If the air pressure in one place is much lower than in another, there will be a strong nearby wind. If there is not much difference, there will only be a breeze. You can see how much the air pressure between areas differs by looking at the distances between the isobars. If these lines are close together, there is a lot of difference within a small area, so the wind will be strong.

In the evening or at night, the wind usually becomes much weaker or even disappears altogether. This is not caused by changing air pressure. The strength of the wind is also determined by the temperature. If the lowest layer of air is colder than the air at a higher altitude (the reverse of what is normally the case), it is called a stable setting. The air (the wind) moving across the cold surface is then slowed down considerably. In the evening, the lower part of the atmosphere cools down most. As a result, the wind drops. After dawn, the lowest layer is soon warmed up, and that is why we often see the wind getting up an hour after dawn.

The strength of the wind is measured on the Beaufort Scale, which extends from 0 to 12 and is used in most weather reports.

The table in Fig 42.1 shows the scale and drescription.

When measuring the strength of the wind, the measurement refers to the wind force at a height of 10 m (30 ft) in more or less open ground. It will certainly not be stormy in the woods if there is gale force 9, and a tightly-packed city will be less windy than an open field. There is also less wind just above the ground. Even you lie flat on the ground, you will hardly notice the wind! On a high tower or spire, the wind is almost always stronger that at an altitude of 10 metres.

Beau-fort	Name	Wind speed		Description
		km/hour	m/h	
0	Calm	0–1	under 1	smoke rises vertically
1	Light air	1–5	1–3	smoke shows direction of wind
2	Light breeze	6–11	4–7	wind felt on fact; leaves rustle
3	Gentle breeze	12–19	8–12	leaves and small twigs in constant motion
4	Moderate breeze	20–28	13–18	raises dust and loose paper; small branches are moved
5	Fresh breeze	29–38	19–24	small trees in leaf begin to sway; crested wavelets
6	Strong breeze	39–49	25–31	large branches in motion; umbrellas used with difficulty
7	Near gale	50–61	32–38	whole trees in motion; inconvenience in walking against the wind
8	Gale	62–74	39–46	breaks twigs off trees; generally impedes progress
9	Strong gale	75–88	47–54	slight structural damage occurs; chimney pots and slates removed
10	Storm	89–102	55–63	trees uprooted; considerable structural damage occurs
11	Violent storm	103–117	64–72	widespread damage
12	Hurricane	over 117	73–136	devastation occurs

Fig 42.1 Beaufort scale

Thunderstorms

Places in the UK have thunder 15 to 20 times a year at the very most. Most thundery days occur in the summer months. Other places within Europe experience great differences in the amount of days with thunder.

Thunder only arises in an active raincloud, in the cumulonimbus. This kind of cloud is full of small droplets and ice crystals, which have an electric charge. This is because there is always an electrical field in the atmosphere around the earth. You cannot see or feel it, but it can be measured. The air currents in the clouds separate the small, light, positive particles from the negatively-charged particles. Then the top of the cloud can carry a positive charge, for example, while the bottom of the cloud can have a negative charge. The earth's surface also has an electrical charge.

Lightning

If the difference in electrical charge between the cloud and the earth — or between two clouds — is large enough, a kind of short circuit arises. A short, very strong current of electricity moves between the two. We see this as a bright bolt of lightning. A flash of lightning only lasts a fraction of a second, but there may be several flashes in succession, as if the current is being switched on and off. If the lightning is discharged in a dense mass of cloud, we do not see the bolt of lightning itself. We see a kind of extended, diffuse light. This is *sheet lightning*.

The temperature in the bolt of lightning is extremely high. The air can reach a temperature of 30 000°C, which is even hotter than the surface of the sun. The rapidly heated air expands quickly but cools down again immediately and shrinks. The many millions of air particles collide with one another in this process and this causes the accompanying sound: thunder.

Fig 42.2

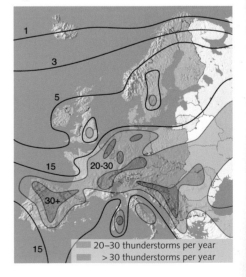

20–30 thunderstorms per year
> 30 thunderstorms per year

Thunder

Audible thunder always comes after the lightning. You can even calculate how far away the lightning was, because we know how quickly sound travels through air. It travels at a speed of around 1 200 kilometres (750 miles) an hour, thus faster than most jet planes. In 3 seconds, sound travels a distance of 1 kilometre (5 seconds per mile). So if you see a flash of lightning, you can start counting. If it takes 12 seconds before you hear the thunder, you will know that the lightning struck 4 km (2½ miles) away.

Watching lightning safely

It is better not to watch the lightning from close by if you are outdoors. It is advisable to stay indoors, at least 1 metre (3 feet) from the window. Close the windows. If you are outdoors, do not shelter under a tree in an open field. This is dangerous, as a tree may be struck by lightning.

You are completely safe in your car. In the car, you are in a metal shell and you are inaccessible to the destructive current of electricity.

After the thunderstorm, if you are certain that it has passed over, you can get out safely. The car has no electrical charge.

If thunder takes you by surprise in an open field or during a walk along the beach:

* Squat down on your haunches, with your legs reasonably close together. If you keep your feet together, less current will pass through your body than if you stand straddled. The greater the distance between your feet, the greater the chance that your feet will bridge a difference in electrical charge. Cows always stand with their legs wide apart, and they seldom if ever survive a bolt of lightning.

* Do not shelter near a metal fence or near your bicycle. Stay at a distance of at least 10 metres (30 feet) from metal objects.
* Stay away from the trees. High trees are easily struck by lightning.
* Do not go near a lamppost or an antenna.
* It is best not to shelter under an umbrella with a steel tip. You will just have to accept that you will get wet.

It is much better, of course, to keep a watchful eye on the weather in advance, certainly on days that the weather report forecasts showers and thunder.

Photographing lightning

You can take a photograph of lightning relatively easily. It must be dark and there must be a thundery shower that shows a flash of lightning at least every minute. You must have a camera that allows you to use a time-exposure. This is often indicated by a button showing the letter 'B' (on old cameras). Set up the camera and turn the button to time-exposure. Press the exposure lever and hold it down until you have seen a splendid flash of lightning in the camera's field of view. Then release the lever. If you do this a few times, you will be sure to capture at least one exciting photo. It is best to use a tripod, because otherwise it is very difficult to hold the camera absolutely still for so long. Try to keep the bright light of lampposts etc. out of the camera's field of vision. Always remember to photograph lightning from a safe distance, through a window if necessary.

Exceptional phenomena

We shall now look at a few well-known but nevertheless exceptional weather phenomena. Some of these occur only rarely, whereas others can be seen dozens of times a year.

Whirlwind and tornado

A whirlwind only arises in the cloud mass of a well-developed raincloud. It resembles an elephant's trunk or a hose that stretches from the clouds to just above the surface of the ground. Within this trunk or column, air is sucked upwards in a spiral, and has the same effect as a vacuum cleaner. As the whirlwind moves across the

earth's surface, extremely high wind speeds cause enormous destruction. Trees are blown down or uprooted and houses can also be badly damaged.

In the UK and most other European countries, whirlwinds may only occur a couple of times a year, mostly in the summer, during or in the immediate vicinity of a thundery shower. A whirlwind usually only lasts for a short time, and passes in a couple of minutes.

People in America speak of tornados, and sometimes of twisters. Tornados occur there much more often than in Europe. At least 1 000 tornados are reported there every year. Some of them have inconceivable power. They can raze a house to the ground or even pick up a truck and drop it a few hundred metres away.

Waterspouts

A waterspout is a whirlwind's little brother that occurs above the sea or above expansive lakes. It arises in the bottom part of a bulging raincloud. The force of this kind of whirlwind is usually less intense than that of a whirlwind, but nonetheless, it is better not to have it race over you. A sailing boat or a surfer will easily be overturned.

A waterspout will occasionally move on to land, but then it soon loses its shape and power.

Dust devils

The dust devil is the baby brother of the whirlwind, and occurs without the assistance of a (rain)cloud. It must be sunny and warm. The sky is often completely blue. An air whirl can arise above the heated ground and this can assume the shape of a small column. If the whirl occurs above sandy ground, you sometimes see a small whirling column filled with sand. These are almost always quite innocent but they may surprise you. A parasol is easy prey for a dust devil.

Rainbows

The most beautiful rainbows occur when the sun is low in the sky. Of course, it must be raining at the same time.

A rainbow is caused by rain droplets breaking the sunlight. White light is broken into the different colours that we clearly recognize in the rainbow. You must have your back to the sun. If there is bright sunlight, you sometimes see a double rainbow: there is a weaker rainbow next to the clear one (Fig 46.1). The legend says that there is a pot of gold at the end of the rainbow. You can always look for it, but do you think you could ever reach the spot where the rainbow touches the ground?

You can create a rainbow yourself if you wish, in your own garden for example. If the sun is low in the sky at the end of the afternoon, grab the garden hose and spray water into the air. Stand with your back to the sun. You will see your own rainbow.

Rings around the sun

You might have seen a beautiful ring around the sun (see Figs 46.2, 46.3). Sometimes there is a colourful lump on the ring; sometimes you only see this swelling and not the ring at all.

These rings are called *haloes*. These light phenomena are caused by reflection and the breaking of light in ice crystals. These ice crystals are part of a very thin transparent cloud, cirrus. Occasionally you get bright, colourful spots, usually in pairs on either side of the sun. These are called mock suns or sundogs (or parhelia).

Because cirrus is sometimes a herald of rain, there is a saying 'the bigger the ring, the nearer the rain.' However, you will often see a halo and the weather will remain fine. It is

Fig 46.1

Fig 46.2   Fig 46.3

best to listen to the weather forecast. Occasionally you will see a halo around the moon. The cause of this is the same as the halo around the sun.

The weather in the mountains

The mountains have their own climate. First of all, it is almost always colder in the mountains than in the valley. If you go on a long mountain hike and are wearing only short trousers and a T-shirt, you could well become cold as you progress. The higher you go, the colder it gets. In general, you can assume that for every 1 000 metres you climb, the temperature will drop by at least 6°C (3°F per 1 000 ft). For example, if you are in a valley at an altitude of 500 metres (1 600 ft) and it is 17°C (63°F), it will be 14°C (57°F) at an altitude of 1 000 metres (3 300 ft) and only 2°C (36°F) at a height of 3 000 metres (9 800 ft). If the mountains are high enough, you will be able to walk in the snow. Even in the Tropics, there are mountains with permanent snow.

Fig 47.1 The temperature at various altitudes

If it is too hot for you in the valley, a walk in the mountains is a good way to cool down.

The weather in the mountains can change very rapidly, and the differences within a single mountain area can vary greatly. Clouds and showers arise on one side of a mountain ridge, out of nothing it seems, whereas there is no hint of bad weather on the other side. Showers and thunder sometimes hang around one spot for quite a long time.

Take good note of the weather forecast given by the regional radio or weather station, and by the television and newspapers. You can even draw up a forecast yourself for the weather expected in the mountains. Clouds and showers gather on the windward side of a mountain ridge. This is the side receiving the wind. Thus, if the weather chart shows that a northern wind is blowing over the Alps, it is better not to 'pitch your tent' on the northern side of the high mountain ridges. A journey of 50 km (31 miles) southwards sometimes makes a world of difference. On the lee side of the mountain (sheltered from the wind), any clouds usually dissolve quickly and the chance of rain is smaller.

The weather on the coast

The weather on the beach may also surprise you as the sea has a considerable influence on the wind and weather.

The wind is almost always stronger on the coast than it is inland. This can make a huge difference, especially when the wind is coming from the sea. If the temperature is less than 22°C (72°F), the weather will seem fresh even if the sun is shining. The temperature of the seawater has a major influence on the air temperature. Weather reports sometimes show this on their charts. So, if you are thinking about going to the beach, be sure to take the wind direction into account.

The lower temperatures on the coast often mean that there are fewer clouds there than above inland areas. Threatening woolpacks may occur a few kilometres inland, but if you know that the wind is coming from the sea, there is a good chance that it will be sunny on the coast.

The wind may get up to a few strange tricks on the beach. Due to the differences in temperature between inland areas and the sea, a cool sea breeze may suddenly arise during the day. In the morning, it may be warm on the beach with a weak land breeze (blowing toward the sea). Later in the morning or in the afternoon, a fresh sea breeze or even a cold wind can suddenly begin blowing in from the sea. The temperature on the beach can then drop by 5 or even 10 degrees (8°–15°F). In particular, this kind of sea wind arises in the first half of the summer. Sometimes mist accompanies this cold sea breeze. Then it's certainly time to pack your things together. The rest of the day will probably stay this way.

The wind also causes waves. But waves roll on to the beach even

4 500 m
14 700 ft
-7°C (19°F)

3 000 m
9 800 ft
2°C (36°F)

1 000 m
3 300 ft
14°C (57°F)

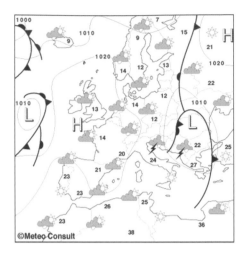

Fig 48.1

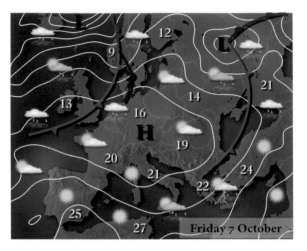

Fig 48.1

if there is no wind. Waves can be formed thousands of kilometres from the shore. Once they have been formed, they roll across the sea and eventually crash on to the beach, sometimes days later.

Splendid high waves are called *surf* or *breakers*.

The weather forecast

In newspapers

There are weather reports in almost all newspapers. Usually there is also a weather chart showing high and low-pressure areas, complete with isobars (so you will know which way the wind is blowing) and sometimes also weather fronts. A front is an extension of a low-pressure area, and forms the boundary between cold and warm air. If a front is pushing warm air aside as it goes, and is thus the front line of an area of cold air, we refer to this as a *cold front*. This is usually shown as a (blue) line with small triangles. Warm air is preceded by a *warm front,* which is shown by a

(red) line with semi-circles. Fronts are important, not only because of the differences in temperature on either side but also because it often rains along a front.

Most weather reports also show other small symbols that indicate what kind of weather it will be. The forecasted temperatures are also often shown, although some newspapers display a separate, coloured temperature chart.

In addition, the weather report may present a summary of the weather in other places (perhaps with a list).

If you are keeping a vacation diary, it may be a good idea to cut out the weather report and stick it on one of the pages.

On television

The weather man or woman on television uses the same kind of weather charts. They mostly show high and low-pressure areas and sometimes fronts and isobars. The satellite photos showing the distribution of clouds and sunshine are an attractive part of the TV weather reports. You can see at a glance what kind of weather

your family and friends at home are getting. You also often hear what the weather is going to be like for the rest of the week, which is handy if you are planning excursions.

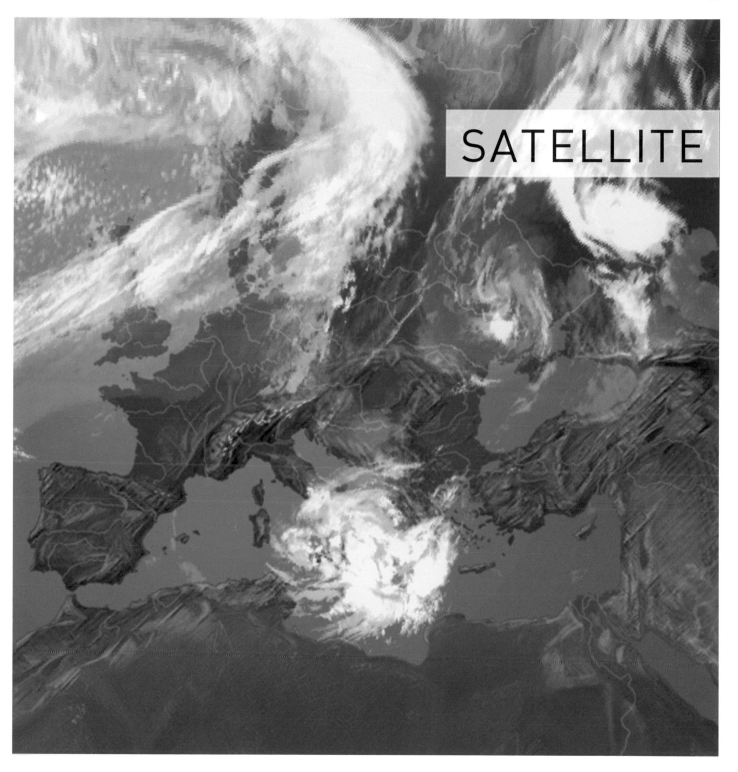

SATELLITE

6. The Stars

During vacations, you often go to bed later than normal. If you wait until it is completely dark on a summer's evening, when the sun has been down for some time you will see the sky gradually begin to light up with stars. If you really want to have a good look at the stars in the summer, you should actually stay up till midnight. Perhaps you will also see some fireflies then, too.

If there are no clouds and no nearby streetlights, you will observe an overwhelming number of glittering stars that form all kinds of figures and patterns, such as a triangle, a square, a curve or a cross.

The Milky Way

Besides all these groups of stars you will also see the MILKY WAY on a clear night. The Milky Way resembles a river, or a white stream that stretches from the north to the east and then towards the horizon in a south-easterly direction. With binoculars, you can see that the Milky Way actually consists of thousands and thousands of small stars. The broad starry river in the sky is special and rather beautiful. In the city, however, with light from the many streetlamps, you will not be able to see it.

The constellations

The groups of stars in the sky are referred to as constellations. Since ancient times they have all had names.

Many of the bright stars within these constellations also have their own names. The stars and constellations are usually called after figures from Greek mythology.

Some of the constellations are easily recognized by their shape. Others are more difficult, and with the complicated constellations it is quite a puzzle because the bright stars only indicate a part of the form.

If you want to recognize the constellations, the best way is to approach someone who already knows some of the constellations and who can explain them to you. After a couple of evenings, you will begin to recognize those constellations yourself. Then a star chart can be useful for finding other constellations. If you do not know anyone who can point out and name the stars in the sky, perhaps you can practise looking at the sky with the whole family.

It is advisable to begin on a night that it is not so clear as it is easier to find the most well-known constellations if you can only see the brightest stars. Be sure to find a place where you will have no interference from street lighting.

Before starting, you should find out where north, south, east and west are situated. In the spring, the sun rises in the east, at noon it is in the south, and it sets in the west. In the summer, sunrise has moved a little toward the north-east and sunset to the north-west. Of course, you can always use a compass.

Location

The place where you are also determines what you can see in the sky. In this chapter, we shall assume that you are in Central Europe or in the USA. There you can see all the stars associated with the northern hemisphere.

If you go further south, to Greece or Turkey, for example, you will see other stars.

If you go even further south, to the Canary Islands, for instance, or to Egypt, to Miami in Florida or to Taiwan, you will just be able to see the Pole Star low above the northern horizon. You will be able to see the Great Bear rise above the horizon and go down again, which is something we do not see further north.

At the equator (Ecuador, northern Brazil, Kenya, Singapore) the Pole Star is invisible in the haze of the horizon, but quite new constellations appear in the south. We can see stars (and at dawn, the sun) rising vertically in the east, and setting vertically in the west. Notice how fast it gets dark in the evening. The closer to the equator you get the steeper the sun sets. The steeper the angle, the quicker the sun sinks below the horizon, and so the shorter dusk is.

South of the equator (Southern Africa, Australia, New Zealand, South America) the movement is opposite to what has been described above. Sun, moon and stars still rise in the east and set in the west, but they move through the north instead of south, and so appear to move anticlockwise. This can be surprisingly disconcerting even when we know beforehand that this is what will happen!

Constellations in the northern summer sky

The Great Bear and the Plough (Big Dipper)

On a summer's night, look north. Do you see a group of seven bright stars? Together they have the shape of a kind of saucepan, or dipper. Four of the stars form a quad, resembling the pan itself. The other three form a slight curve attached to the pan, this is the handle. They form the constellation the GREAT BEAR. Now have a

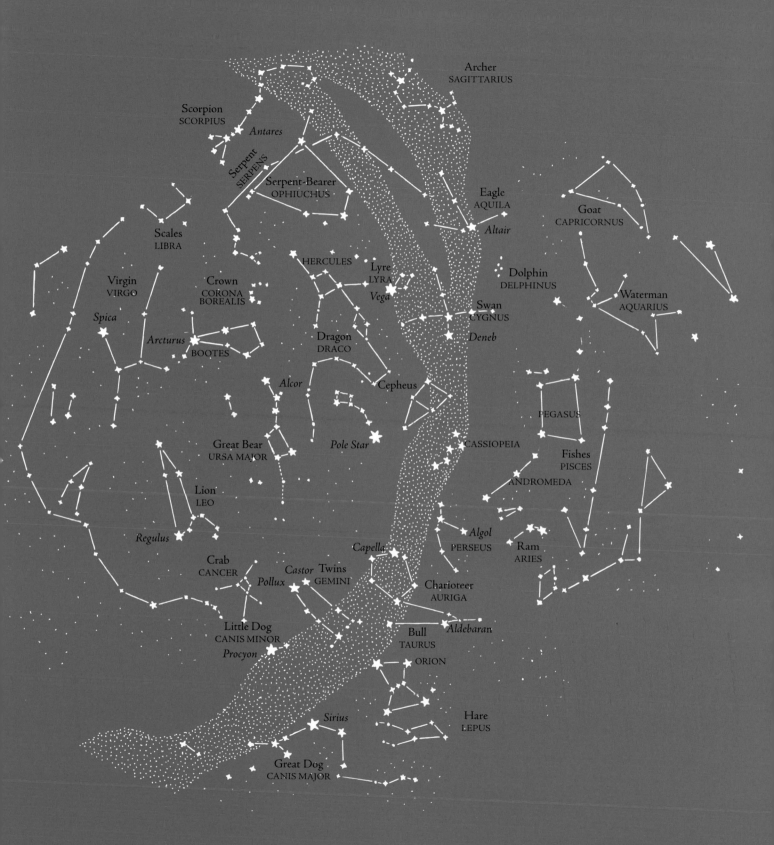

Archer
SAGITTARIUS

Scorpion
SCORPIUS

Antares

Serpent
SERPENS

Serpent-Bearer
OPHIUCHUS

Eagle
AQUILA

Altair

Goat
CAPRICORNUS

Scales
LIBRA

HERCULES

Lyre
LYRA

Vega

Dolphin
DELPHINUS

Waterman
AQUARIUS

Virgin
VIRGO

Crown
CORONA
BOREALIS

Swan
CYGNUS

Spica

Deneb

Arcturus

BOÖTES

Dragon
DRACO

PEGASUS

Alcor

Cepheus

Fishes
PISCES

Pole Star

CASSIOPEIA

Great Bear
URSA MAJOR

ANDROMEDA

Lion
LEO

Algol

PERSEUS

Ram
ARIES

Regulus

Capella

Crab
CANCER

Castor Twins

Charioteer
AURIGA

Pollux GEMINI

Little Dog
CANIS MINOR

Bull
TAURUS

Aldebaran

Procyon

ORION

Hare
LEPUS

Sirius

Great Dog
CANIS MAJOR

good look at the other, less bright stars that are grouped around the seven brighter ones. Can you recognize the shape of the bear? At the bottom you see the big paws, a large head at the front of the clear body and the tail. If you have sharp eyes, you will see a very small star next to the star in the middle of the handle. This star is called *Alcor,* and it sits like a horseman on the larger star below (see Fig 52.1). It was sometimes used to check eyesight.

The Pole Star

Now draw a line in your imagination between the two large stars in the Great Bear that are furthest away from the handle. Extend this line out of the top of the pan. At a distance of around five times the distance between the two large stars you will see a star that is conspicuous because there are no other stars in the direct surroundings. This is *Polaris,* the *Pole Star.* Once you have found it, you will always be able to

find it again because it is always at the same place in the northern sky at every moment of the day and night and at every time of the year.

Take another good look. In the summer you will be able to see six less bright stars that have the same shape as the Great Bear but are a smaller version of this. The Pole Star is the end of the handle (or tail). This group is called the LITTLE BEAR.

Dragon

The DRAGON wraps itself around the Little Bear like a snake. It is a chain of fainter stars. The tail of the Dragon stretches between both Bears, curves around the Little Bear and then turns sharply the other way, and ends right above your head in a diamond-shaped head.

Cassiopeia and Cepheus

Now follow the imaginary line from the Great Bear to the Pole Star and extend it further, doubling this entire distance. This is the constellation of

CASSIOPEIA which, depending on the time of year, looks like a W or M.

On a clear night, it is possible to see another constellation. Just above Cassiopeia you can see the less bright stars of CEPHEUS, which resembles a house upside down.

Constellations in the south-eastern summer sky

The Lyra

Until now, you have been looking at the northern sky. Now turn your sight to the south-east. Do you see the head of the Dragon right above your head? Just under that there is a very bright star. This is *Vega,* the brightest star in the constellation LYRA (or the Lyre). It is often the first star to become visible in the evening. Lyra is a very small constellation. Besides Vega, the other stars are hardly visible, but if you can find them, you will see a beautiful symmetrical form of a harp.

Fig 52.1 The Great Bear and the Little Bear

Fig 52.2 Constellations in the northern sky: the Great Bear, Little Bear, Dragon, Cassiopeia, and Cepheus

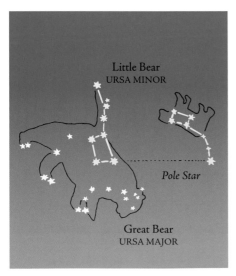

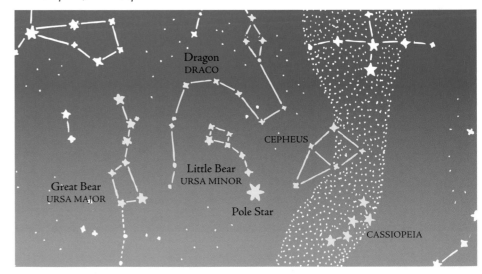

Swan, Eagle and Dolphin

If you now move your eyes down to the left, you will see the constellation CYGNUS (Latin for SWAN), which has a cross shape. It looks as if it is flying regally along the Milky Way, from north to south. The Swan has a long neck and two symmetrical wings that curve backwards a little. At the end of the short tail there is a bright star called *Deneb*. Move your eyes downwards to the right of the Swan, toward the southern horizon. There you will see the constellation AQUILA (Latin for EAGLE), which has a kind of T-shape. It is flying toward the Swan. The brightest star of the Eagle indicates its head. It is called *Altair*. The Eagle has no neck and the wings are smaller than those of the Swan. But the tail is very long.

Finally, quite near the Eagle, to the left of Altair (in the east of the sky) there is another small and faint constellation. This is DELPHINUS (Latin for DOLPHIN), which has the shape of a diamond with a tail.

If you look at the three constellations Swan, Eagle and Harp, you can see that each of them has one bright star. Together these three bright stars

Fig 53.1 Constellations in the south-eastern sky: the Harp, the Swan, the Eagle, and the Dolphin (summer triangle)

Fig 53.2 Constellations in the southern and western sky: Hercules, the Snake and the Serpent Bearer, and Bootes and the Northern Crown

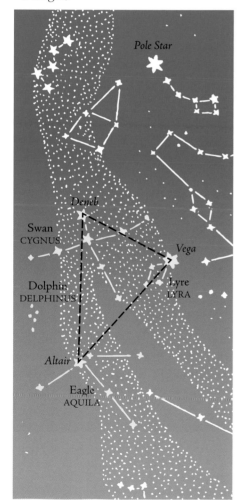

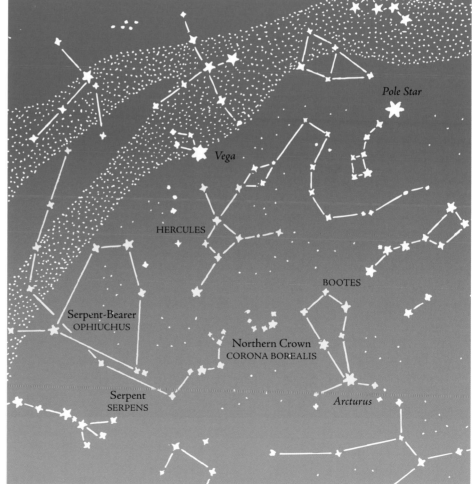

— Vega, Deneb, and Altair — form a triangle that is easily recognized in the summer sky: the *summer triangle.*

Constellations in the south-western summer sky

Hercules, the Serpent and the Serpent Bearer

Now go back to Vega in the Lyre. If you look to the right (westward), you will see the constellation HERCULES. The heart of the constellation is formed by a rectangle. Lines seem to extend from each corner of the rectangle; these are Hercules' limbs. One of them is close to the head of the Dragon.

There are two groups of stars which overlap one another just under the constellation Hercules. These are SERPENS (Latin for SERPENT) and OPHIUCUS (SERPENT-BEARER). The tail of the curved snake stretches out almost as far as the Eagle, the head is close to one of the limbs of Hercules.

Bootes and Corona Borealis

Westward again, past the constellation Hercules, ou will find two new constellations: CORONA BOREALIS (Latin for NORTHERN CROWN) and BOOTES (pronounced Bo-ohtes, the HERDSMAN). The Crown is formed by a circle of stars, not far from the head of the Serpent.

Bootes is just above (to the north of) the Crown. Bootes is also occasionally called the Ploughman or the Ox-driver. He has broad shoulders. You can hardly see his head because this star is so weak. *Arcturus,* a very bright star, is situated between his heels.

The zodiac in the summer sky

There are twelve constellations in the sky that are jointly called the *zodiac.* It is not easy to recognize them all, although you have probably heard their names: Aries, Taurus, Gemini, Cancer, Leo, Virgo, Libra, Scorpius, Sagittarius, Capricornus, Aquarius, and Pisces. These are Latin names for Ram, Bull, Twins, Crab, Lion, Virgin, Scales, Scorpion, Archer, Goat, Waterman and Fishes, respectively. These twelve constellations form a large ring around the sky.

While you see a part of the zodiac above the horizon in the evening, the rest remains invisible. As the year progresses, this ring gradually shifts around the sky. As a result, you see different constellations in the summer than you do in the winter. The spring sky is also different from the autumn sky.

We shall begin with the constellations that you see in the summer after the sun has set. These are Virgo, Libra and Scorpio. In the section on the winter sky, we shall explain the other constellations of the zodiac.

Virgo

It is easy to find the Great Bear. If you follow the curve of the pan handle, you will come to the bright star Arcturus in the constellation Bootes. If you keep on following this imaginary curve, you come to another bright star — *Spica,* the brightest star in the constellation VIRGO, the Virgin. *Spica* is the Latin name for the ear of corn she is holding in her left hand.

Virgo is a large constellation but it is not easily recognizable. It is not very clear — the stars are weak with the exception of Spica. In the summer, Virgo usually appears in a horizontal position in the south-west.

Libra, Scales

You will encounter LIBRA if you move left from Virgo (toward the south-east). It is a small constellation. Four stars represent the two balances and the bar of the scales. You can sometimes see a rather star in between the two stars of the bar.

Scorpius

In July, the constellation SCORPIO appears above the south-east horizon in the evening. It rises earlier in August, but if you are in Central Europe, you will not see it completely; its tail remains hidden behind the horizon. Only if you go south, to the Mediterranean Sea, for example, or the parts of the United States that do not border Canada, will you be able to see the whole of Scorpio. It is one of the most impressive constellations in the sky. The head has a reddish star called *Antares,* at the position of the neck. Then comes the splendid body extending to the curved tail with a sting at the end. You can also see two large pincers that embrace Libra.

Sagittarius, Archer

The constellation SAGITTARIUS is not easily recognizable, but you can often see the strong bow and arrow. If you draw a curve extending west from the Pole Star, along the Milky Way, you will see the bright star Deneb in the Swan. If you go further, you will see Altair, the head of the Eagle. Follow the curve and you will arrive at Sagittarius.

Fig 54.1 The constellations in the zodiac

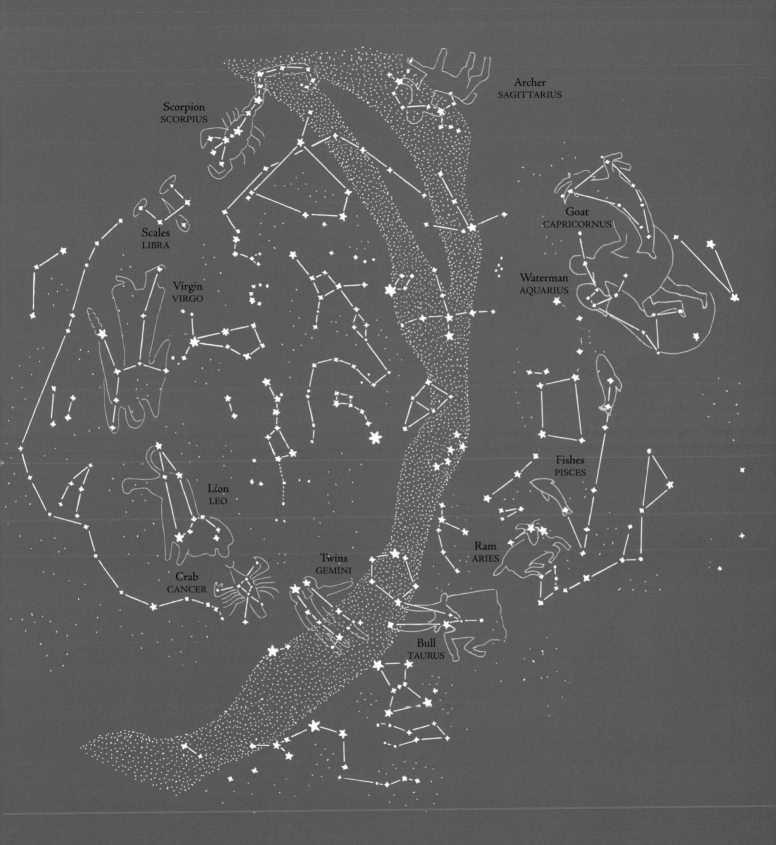

Scorpion
SCORPIUS

Archer
SAGITTARIUS

Scales
LIBRA

Goat
CAPRICORNUS

Virgin
VIRGO

Waterman
AQUARIUS

Fishes
PISCES

Lion
LEO

Crab
CANCER

Twins
GEMINI

Ram
ARIES

Bull
TAURUS

How do the stars move?

Seek out a certain constellation and have a good look at where it is at eight o'clock in the evening, for example. Look again the following evening at the same time, and once again a few days later. You will see that it is at the same place in the sky.

But you should try looking for it at 2 o'clock in the morning, for example. Can you still find it? Is it still at the same place? You will see that it has moved. It may have disappeared altogether. In order to find out how different constellations move in the sky, you have to look in various directions, because the stars move differently in the north, south, east and west.

Circumpolar stars

First examine the northern sky at different times of the night. Where is the W of Cassiopeia at eight o'clock in the evening? Diagonally under the Pole Star, to the right. And where is it at two o'clock in the morning? This constellation has moved and is

now above the Pole Star, a little to the right. The W has become an M. You may have taken a look at the Great Bear and the Little Bear, or the Dragon or Cepheus and discovered that they are all turning as well. The stars that are low on the horizon move from left to right, whereas those that are higher go from right to left. The Great Bear and the Little Bear, the Dragon, Cassiopeia, and Cepheus turn in a circle around the Pole Star once every twenty-four hours (anticlockwise). Of course, you can only see them when it is dark. These are called 'circumpolar stars' because they never set.

But there is another remarkable feature. Throughout the course of the year, these constellations shift position as they move around the Pole Star. If you go looking for the Great Bear in the autumn you will find it turned a quarter of a turn, *under* the Pole Star.

You can see these five constellations as well as the Pole Star every evening in temperate northern latitudes.

Fig 56.1 Cassiopeia turns around the Pole Star once every 24 hours

Movement of the other stars

If you were to stay up the whole night to look at the stars, you would see that most stars do not move across the sky like the circumpolar stars. They rise above the eastern horizon and move in a semi-circle toward the south, finally setting in the west. A star that is low in the southern sky in the early evening will set a couple of hours later in the south-western sky, and thus be visible for only a short time. Stars that are higher in the sky have to make a bigger curve and thus require more time before setting in the west. A star that rises above the eastern horizon just after sunset needs the entire night to climb to full height in the southern sky and will only set well past midnight or even early in the morning.

But this also means that as one constellation vanishes in the west another one rises in the east. So, if you were to stay up all night, or look at the sky at midnight, for example, you would see many more constellations. For instance, you would see that in the summer, the constellation Sagittarius appears behind Scorpio. In September, Sagittarius appears above the horizon a little earlier, shortly after sunset.

The winter sky

If you found it interesting to look at the sky in the evening, trying to recognize the various constellations, you may want to know something about the constellations that you are able to see when you are at home in the winter. You see other constellations in the winter than you do in the summer. Night falls earlier in the winter and the stars seem brighter in the cool winter air.

You will be able to see the circumpolar stars in the northern sky, because they are always there, but they now occupy a different position. The Great Bear has turned the other way around and is now in the east, to the right of the Pole Star. The Dragon is also situated there. To the west (left), you will see Cepheus and Cassiopeia, which now resembles an M rather than a W.

Perseus, Andromeda and Pegasus

In winter evenings, you will find PERSEUS directly above Cassiopeia, but this constellation is not easily recognized. Perseus has one exceptional star. It is sometimes bright, then faint and less visible. This is *Algol,* also sometimes called the 'Devil's Star,' because the ancient Greeks linked it to the terrible head of Medusa. Anyone who looked into the eyes of the monster Medusa was turned into stone. Assisted by the shield of the goddess Athena, Perseus was successful in hacking off Medusa's head.

The next constellation is ANDROMEDA. Draw a line from the Pole Star through Cassiopeia and you will come to the constellation Andromeda. It consists of four bright stars that lie in a gently curved line. Right next to that is the large constellation PEGASUS, the winged horse. A large square represents the body of the horse. The head and the front legs are furthest away from Andromeda.

Orion

If you look in a southerly direction, you will again find new constellations.

The largest and most impressive of these is the hunter, ORION. He has two big broad shoulders with a less bright star between these representing his head. In the middle, the three slightly slanting stars form the hunter's belt. At the bottom there are two strong feet. Orion's left foot (he is facing us, thus the one on our right) has a bright star called *Rigel* (which means 'foot' in Arabic). If it is a clear night, you will be able to see Orion's sword — the three small stars under his belt.

Canis Major and Canis Minor

The hunter, Orion, is accompanied by two dogs. Down to the left (the south-east) you will find the brightest star in the sky, *Sirius.* It is part of CANIS MAJOR (the GREAT DOG). In northern Europe, this constellation is always low in the sky and generally not completely visible. Only if you go further south can you see it in all its glory.

Above the bright Sirius, a little to the left (east), you will see two stars: a bright one, *Procyon,* and a dimmer one. Together they form CANIS MINOR (the LITTLE DOG).

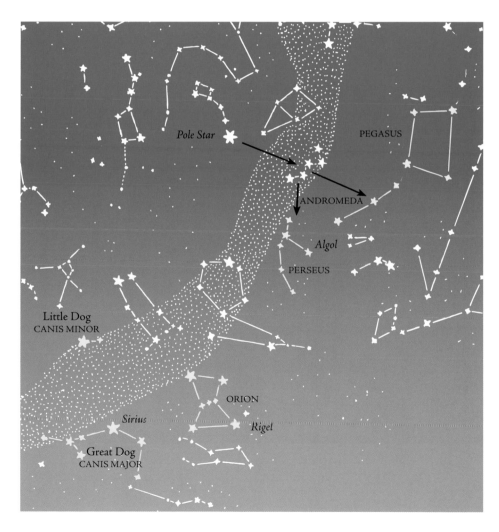

Fig 57.1 The northern sky in the winter: Perseus, Andromeda with Pegasus, and Orion with the Big Dog and the Little Dog

The Winter Cross

If you move your gaze from Orion towards the zenith, the imaginary point right above your head, you will meet a large pentagon: Auriga (the *Charioteer*) with the yellowish *Capella* as the brightest star. In conjunction with Orion, Auriga forms the vertical bar of an immense cross, of which the constellations *Taurus* and *Gemini* form the horizontal bar. Taurus is situated to the right, Gemini on the left.

The other constellations of the zodiac

We shall begin with the constellations that you can see above the horizon after sunset, in the autumn. Then, we shall describe the winter constellations, and end with the constellations that are visible in the spring.

Capricornus and Aquarius (Goat, Waterman)

The constellation of Capricornus (the Goat) resembles an elongated triangle with protruding horns and a tail. Go back to the Pole Star and draw a straight line through Deneb in the Swan (Cygnus) and another 1½ times this distance. You will come to the horns of the Goat (Capricorn). Capricorn is so close to the constellation Aquarius (the Waterman) that it seems to be part of it. It is not easy to recognize a man carrying a water jar. The jar itself consists of four stars.

Pisces (Fishes)

The large but faint constellation Pisces (Fishes) is visible on the western horizon. Pisces borders Aquarius and you can only see it in the autumn and early winter. It is low on the horizon and can only be seen if it is completely clear. In the winter, it will have vanished behind the horizon before the sun has set. In summer it is visible before dawn.

To find Pisces, first go to the Pole Star. Draw a straight line through Cassiopeia and you will come to the constellation Andromeda with the square representing Pegasus next to it. Extend the line further and you will arrive at the constellation Pisces. You can see two ovals: these are the two fish. They are connected to one another by two small cords of stars that join in a knot. The knot is the only star in Pisces that is reasonably bright.

Aries (Ram)

If you go eastward from Pisces, to the left, you will find the constellation Aries (the Ram). It is next to Perseus, on the right. It is not a large or conspicuous constellation. Two clearly visible stars represent the horns. A few faint stars represent the rest of the animal.

Taurus (Bull)

Taurus (the Bull) is one of the large and splendid constellations of the zodiac. The bright, reddish star, *Aldebaran*, is one of the eyes in the bull's head, which is formed by a symmetrical V of less visible stars. In the winter, the constellation has rotated a quarter of a turn: >. If you extend the arms of the V quite a distance, you arrive at two stars that indicate the tips of the horns. Under the head, you can vaguely see the forelegs. The bull's back is barely visible, it is formed by small very faint stars. One of the stars at the tip of the horns, that is closest to the Pole Star, is also a component of the constellation Auriga (the Charioteer), which is not part of the zodiac. At the shoulder of the bull, there is a small group of stars that resembles a miniature version of the Great Bear. This group is called the Pleiades, or the Seven Sisters. Mostly you can only see six stars, but on a clear night, you may see eight.

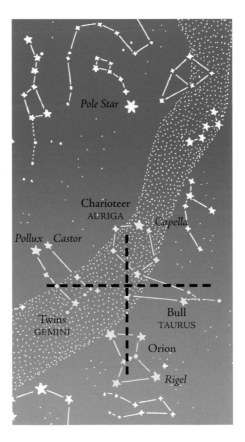

Fig 58.1 The Winter Cross

Gemini and Cancer (Twins, Crab)

The feet of GEMINI (the TWINS) begin just to the left of the horns of the Bull. At this time of year, you see Gemini lying almost flat in the sky. Two straight lines of stars indicate the bodies of the Twins. At the end of these, two bright stars, *Castor* and *Pollux,* represent the heads of the Twins.

To the left of Gemini there is another small constellation that is only faintly visible: CANCER (the CRAB). You can see the two pincers and the tail only if the sky is extremely clear. This also applies to *Praesepe,* a faint, cloud-like group of stars. Praesepe actually means 'manger.' If you use binoculars, you can see that two donkeys are eating from the manger: one star above and one below.

Leo (Lion)

If you look at the western sky on an early summer's evening, you will see the constellation LEO (the LION) rise low on the horizon, just behind Cancer. Leo is one of the most extensive constellations of the zodiac. Once you have seen and become familiar with this group of stars, you will find it easy to recognize the Lion. The front paw contains a bright star called *Regulus.* Above this is another bright star on the shoulder of the Lion, along with several other smaller ones that represent the head and the mane. Just as is the case with a real lion, the animal's back is somewhat smaller: a triangle of stars represents the hip, the back leg and the tail.

The moon

The phases of the moon

We are used to seeing the moon in its various forms. We call these the 'phases' of the moon. But do you know when the moon is waxing (getting bigger) or when it is waning (getting smaller)? Where will the moon be later in the evening or in a couple of days?

To be able to understand this, you have to follow the whole cycle of the moon in order to see its appearance gradually changing. It is best to begin when we first see the moon as a very thin sickle low above the western horizon, where the sun has just set. You will see that the bright part of the sickle is facing the sun (which has gone below the horizon).

If you look at the moon the following evening, you will see that it has grown, that the sickle has become fatter. It is now a bit further away from the sun and is higher in the sky. In the days that follow, you will see how the sickle continues to grow. This is the moon 'waxing.' It is increasingly high in the sky and goes down later and later.

You have now followed the moon for around five evenings. It now has a semi-circular shape. It looks like a half moon, but astronomers call it the 'first quarter' because it is 90° (a quarter circle) from the sun. It is now quite distant from the sun and sets around midnight. It rises around noon, so you can see it in the afternoon.

During the next week, the moon continues to grow until it is completely round. It is now 'full moon,' and the moon is situated exactly opposite the sun. It rises at sunset and sets as the sun rises, so you can see it all night. In summer, the full moon will be low in the sky at night. In contrast, the full moon is high in the sky during the long winter nights.

The moon enters its third week. Its fullness declines. This is the 'waning' moon. When it is half moon in the waning phase, astronomers call it the 'last quarter.' Have a good look: have you noticed that the rounded part is now on the other side? The moon now rises later and sets later. It is now only visible in the second half of the night and in the morning.

In the fourth week, the moon declines until it is only a thin sickle visible in the eastern sky in the early morning. Then the moon is invisible for days. Astronomers call this the new moon, even though there is nothing to be seen. About two days later it again appears in the evening sky. The cycle is complete. The moon takes around $29\frac{1}{2}$ days to go through the entire cycle.

To tell exactly when it is half moon, look carefully to see when the line between the lit and dark part of the moon is exactly straight. At the time of half moon the increase (or decrease) from one evening to the next is greatest, and you can see the shape of the line changing within a few hours. Check in a diary or newspaper to see how close you are — guessing to within three or four hours of the exact time is very good.

At full moon it is difficult to tell from looking at the shape of the moon whether it is a day or two before or after full moon. Observe the shadows on the surface of the moon. The surface consists of mountains and craters. When the moon is directly opposite the sun, that is at full moon, the sun shines directly onto the moon's surface, and there are hardly any shadows. Some time before and after exact full moon, the mountains and craters cast shadows.

If you see a thin sickle in the evening, how do you know if the moon is waxing or waning?

There is a small memory aid for this: if the sickle has the same curve as the letter 'b' (for 'beginning') it is waxing; if it has the same curve as the letter 'e' (for ending) it is waning.

In the southern hemisphere the crescent moon is the other way round — the waxing crescent looking like the waning one to the north, and similarly opposite or waning crescent.

The moon and the stars

Have a good look at the moon when it is in its first quarter. Do you see a group of stars (or a constellation) near the moon? Try to remember these so that you can recognize them the next day.

Look at the moon the following evening and try to find the constellation you saw the previous day. What has happened?

The moon has moved a good bit towards the left in relation to the constellation. If you look again the next night, you will see that the moon is even further away from that constella-

Fig 60.1 Phases of the moon

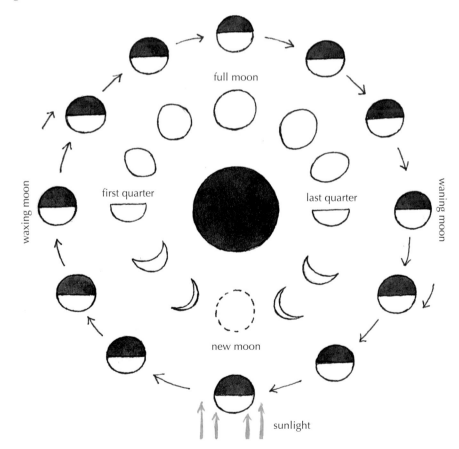

tion. In the southern hemisphere the moon moves to the right. As you see, the moon moves further along the sky every evening. It actually does this so quickly that you can even see the difference a couple of hours later.

If you look at the moon around 27 days after the first time you saw it in its first quarter, you will see that the moon is almost exactly at the same place in relation to the constellation that you saw and tried to remember. In order to establish this properly, you should not look at the moon too early, otherwise there is a chance that the constellation will not yet be visible at dusk. The 27 days mentioned is the time the moon takes to orbit the earth. This should be distinguished from the cycle of the moon's phases ($29^1/_2$ days) because, of course, as the moon orbits the earth, the earth orbits the sun. Thus the moon's position changes in relation to the sun.

The sun, the moon and the earth

If it is full moon on a clear night, you can easily see things around you in the moonlight, but how is this possible? It is known that the moon doesn't produce any light.

In the course of a whole year, the sun moves across the heavens through all the signs of the zodiac. Every month, it moves across one twelfth of the sky towards the next constellation.

In turn, the earth orbits the sun once a year, and the earth also turns on its own north-south axis once every twenty-four hours. As a result, a part of the earth is turned away from the sun every day. This part then experiences night. The part of the earth on which the sun is shining experiences daytime.

The moon also moves in a circle through the signs of the zodiac. On its journey, it receives light from the sun (see Fig 60.1). The part of the moon that is illuminated by the sun is visible to us here on earth. At the same time, the moon orbits the earth. Sometimes the moon is situated between the earth and the sun. Then the sunlight falls on the back of the moon, the side that we cannot see. The other side, the side facing us, is not illuminated, it is dark.

Eclipse of the sun (Solar eclipse)

One of the most impressive events in the sky is an eclipse of the sun. It actually happens quite regularly, but it happens at a different place every time, so the chance that it happens near you is quite small. Many people only experience it once in a lifetime. Sometimes, people go on a long journey just to see the eclipse.

An eclipse of the sun takes place because *the new moon moves exactly between the sun and the earth.* Fig 62.1 shows what happens in this situation. We see the moon as a black disc slowly gliding in front of the sun. As the moon moves in front of the sun, the shadow of the moon falls on the earth, moving from west to east.

At first it looks like a chunk has been taken out of the right-hand side of the sun (in the northern hemisphere). This 'chunk' grows until it covers the entire sun. Then the sun begins to become visible again on the other side.

The shadow of the moon (called the 'umbra') only falls on a narrow band of the earth, at most about 250 km (150 miles) wide, where you will see a complete eclipse of the sun. People to the north or south of this region will see a partial eclipse of the sun and people more than 3 000 km (2 000 miles) from the band will not see anything unusual at all.

Eclipse of the moon (lunar eclipse)

An eclipse of the moon can be experienced more frequently than an eclipse of the sun, sometimes twice a year, but it is much easier to miss.

Eclipses of the moon take place when the moon is full. The sun is situated directly opposite the moon and the moon appears full as a result. If the earth moves between the sun and the moon at that moment and the three heavenly bodies are in a line, the shadow of the earth can completely cover the moon. You

---

Visibility of the phases of the moon

Phase	Rises	Highest point	Sets	When visible
☽ First quarter	12 noon	Sunset	midnight	In the evening, first half of the night
○ Full moon	sunset	Midnight	sunrise	All night
☾ Last quarter	midnight	Sunrise	12 noon	Second half of the night and in the morning
● New moon	sunrise	12 noon	sunset	Moon is not visible

do not need to go on a trip to see an eclipse of the moon. It is visible from all places on the earth that have night at that particular moment, when the moon is above the horizon during the time of the eclipse.

The moon enters the earth's shadow from the right, so that the left-hand side of the moon first becomes dark (in the northern hemisphere). The eclipse grows for about an hour before the eclipse of the moon is total. The total phase lasts up to 1 hour and 40 minutes. Then the left-hand side of the moon begins to become visible again as a thin slice, taking about an hour to fully re-emerge. Have a good look at the moon if you can: during an eclipse, the moonlight takes on a reddish glow.

The planets

The constellations that have been discussed have a fixed position in the sky and do not move in relation to one another, though they all move in relation to the horizon. The planets are something completely different. They have their own orbits and their own specific times at which they are visible. If you want to know which planets are visible, the best thing to do is to buy a star calendar. The planets, just like the sun and the moon, always have one of the constellations of the zodiac in the background.

If you know what the stars of the constellations look like, you may suddenly see a new star among the group of known ones. If you watch this constellation for several evenings (or weeks), you will see this new star moving in relation to the constellation in which it is situated. The ancient Greeks called these stars *wanderers* (*planetes* in Greek).

Besides the sun and the moon, which are not really planets, there are five planets that you can see with the naked eye. These are: Venus, Jupiter, Mars, Saturn and Mercury. They all have names of Roman gods or, in the case of Venus, a goddess. They are true wanderers; they not only move across the skies, but the time at which they are visible also changes, as does their brightness. Each of these five planets has its own pattern.

It is not easy to distinguish between stars and planets. Nevertheless, there are differences. If you look at a star near the horizon, you will see it glittering or twinkling. The star is sometimes white, then it is bluish or greenish. It is occasionally reddish. A star glistens like a dewdrop in the grass. This is not the case with a planet. It always shines in a constant way, it does not twinkle. If you have binoculars or a telescope, you will see that a star always remains a point of light, regardless of how strong your lens is. By contrast, via binoculars or

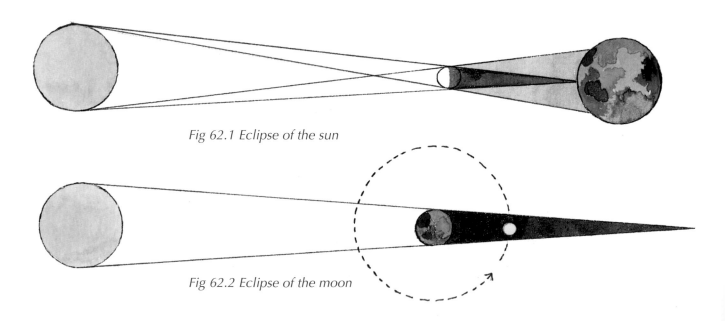

Fig 62.1 Eclipse of the sun

Fig 62.2 Eclipse of the moon

a telescope, you will see a planet as a small disc. Jupiter is an excellent example of this. Through the telescope, the planet is a small ball with a few moons close by.

Venus

Venus is the brightest planet. It shines brighter than all the stars in the sky. It is visible in the morning or in the evening, but it is never the 'morning star' and 'evening star' at the same time. As the morning star, it rises in the east just before dawn. Every day it rises a little earlier and its distance to the sun increases. After about seven months, it disappears. One or two months later, it reappears as the evening star, but now in the western sky. It is again visible for about seven months until it has reached its maximum distance from the sun. It then approaches the sun and vanishes for a few days, subsequently reappearing as the morning star.

If you look at Venus through binoculars or a telescope, you will see that it has different phases, just like the moon.

Jupiter

Jupiter is also a very bright planet. It is visible in the sky almost the whole year round. As a consequence, it is possible to follow it for a while, and you can see that it does not travel in a straight line but makes loops in its orbit. When Jupiter has risen above the eastern horizon in the early morning, it rises higher in the sky and appears a little later every day. It is at its brightest when it is visible all night. It is then brighter than all the other stars around it. If it appears in the evening or in the morning, it is less bright and thus more difficult to recognize among the other stars.

Using binoculars or a telescope, you can sometimes see four small moons around the planet Jupiter.

Mars, Saturn and Mercury

Mars can be very bright but can also diminish in strength. You can often recognize it by its reddish glow. However, there are also other stars that have a reddish flush, such as Antares in the constellation Scorpio and Aldebaran in Taurus. Like Jupiter, there are times when you can see Mars the whole night long.

Saturn is difficult to recognize among other bright stars. It is generally less bright than Jupiter or Mars, and moves very slowly across the sky. It can take as much as three or four years before Saturn has moved through a constellation.

Mercury is the most elusive planet because it is always near the sun and often invisible due to the twilight. Occasionally it is visible for a short time — perhaps only a couple of days — before sunrise or just after sunset. If you are in lower latitudes, where dawn and dusk are shorter, it is easier to see Mercury. You will be surprised by its brightness.

Which planet am I looking at?

Celestial charts and guides are published every year. These show exactly where and when the various planets are visible. Using this kind of guide will help you to search for a particular planet in the right direction.

Shooting stars

On a clear night, you may suddenly see a shooting star. It looks like a star is falling from the sky and it happens so quickly that you cannot see where the shooting star began. Shooting stars are actually meteors. At certain times of the year, you can see a great number of them, occasionally around a dozen every hour, all coming from the same part of the sky. This is a 'meteor shower.' The heaviest meteor showers take place every year on the following dates:

1–6 January
1–8 May
12–15 August
7–15 December

The best meteor showers are seen in the middle of these periods, particularly if there is no moon to brighten the sky.

Meteors are actually small chunks of iron ore and stone that fall to earth. They enter our atmosphere, become hot due to the friction with the air and start to glow. Most of the pieces of iron ore are burned up before they reach the earth. Now and again, a larger piece will reach the ground. We called these pieces *meteorites.* Although very rare, a large meteorite occasionally hits the ground with such force that it produces a crater in the earth. A well-known meteorite crater can be found in America, in the Arizona desert. It has a diameter of nearly a mile (over 1 km) and is 500 feet deep (150 metres). The crater was produced approximately 25 000 years ago. You do not have to be afraid of being hit by a meteorite if you are watching a shower of falling stars.

Make your own star chart
⊕ ✂ ✳ ⌂ ♠ ✗

See page 139.

7. Nature

When you are on vacation, it can be pleasant to get out and about, just going for a long walk. People often do not notice what is happening all around them in their own natural surroundings. Due to the noise, most animals will have hidden away, but if you walk through the woods or the countryside quietly, the stroll can become a genuine journey of discovery. There is more to see and to discover than you might imagine. You only need your senses — especially your eyes and ears, but also your nose.

* Breathe in, smell the scent of the flowers in the meadows. At the side of the road, you can also smell herbs that may grow in the garden at home or you have as dried herbs in jars in the kitchen.
* Listen to the sounds around you, the rustling of the bushes, the pecking of the woodpecker in the tree, the songbirds, the scream of the hawk.
* Above all, have a good look around you.
  The stones of the path are not just white, grey or black.

Have you ever counted how many different kinds of grass grow along the roadside? Have you seen the diversity of flowers with honeybees, bumblebees, flies and butterflies around them?

How many creatures live where you are now standing? You can see some of them, like grasshoppers and ants. You will find all kinds of beetles under the leaves at the side of the track.

You can find traces of larger animals: a deer's hoof-print, the place where a stag has rubbed the velvet off his antlers, or where a wild boar has scratched itself against the bark of a tree.

* Droppings and other excrement can tell you which animals live next to the track, even if you cannot immediately see them. In the woods, you may suddenly discover animal tracks in the grass, or a piece of churned-up ground where a wild boar has left its mark.
* Bend down and shift the leaves from the side of the track. There is a great amount of life on the ground. If you come across a fallen tree, have a look under the bark. If the wood has become soft and is rotting, you will probably encounter lots of small creatures there.

Trees

⚘ ⚘ ⚘ ✳ ♀

Trees have all kinds of shapes. They ensure that the landscape is varied and lively. Have a look around you and try to think what the surroundings would be like without trees. Can you imagine it? One large surface with only grass or sand, and only houses and roads in the towns. No shade, no fruit, no acorns or chestnuts and nowhere for the birds to build a nest. That would be a pretty bare scene.

Trees are the largest plants of all, often much taller than a house. The tallest trees are the redwoods in North America, which can grow to a height of more than 100 metres (300 feet). That is as tall as Big Ben in London.

Song of the woods

Trees do not have a mouth with which they can speak. Can they make noises?

Yes, if the wind helps them. The leaves will rustle even in the gentlest of breezes. Sometimes it sounds as if they are chatting to one another.

Keep completely silent. Can you hear what they are saying?

If the wind gets up, the branches begin to creak, and if there is a storm, you will hear the creak of the entire trunk, along with the howling of the wind. The woods sing a different song every day.

Who's the fattest?

✢ measuring tape or string

Do you want to know how thick a tree is in relation to your body?

Stretch a piece of string around a tree trunk and tie a knot to mark the circumference of the tree. How many times can this length go round your waist?

❀ You can measure the circumference of a tree by stretching a

measuring tape around the tree, or by using a ruler to measure a piece of string that you have wrapped around the tree.

❀ If you do not have a ruler, you can use other objects that you know the measurements of. For example, an A4 sheet of paper measures 30 × 21 cm, Letter size paper in 8½ × 11 in.

Looking with your hands

✢ blindfold (tea towel)

Sometimes you cannot see trees for the woods. There are so many trees

in the woods that you cannot see the individual trees. At first sight, they all look the same.

Nevertheless, most trees differ greatly from one another. You can discover this without using your eyes. You will need two people for this.

1 One person blindfolds the other and leads her to any tree.
2 The blindfolded person now begins to explore the tree with her hands, describing what she is feeling: the bark and all kinds of bits sticking out. The blindfolded

person should also rub her cheek against the bark to feel how rough it is, and smell the tree to discover if it has a special scent.

3 When the blindfolded person has discovered everything possible, she is led via a detour to another spot. In this way, she cannot remember where this tree was.

4 The blindfold is removed and she has to try to find 'her' tree.

Mini-jungle

✣ *magnifying glass*

Use a magnifying glass to look at the bark of a tree. There is a great deal to discover here. The folds in the bark form hills and valleys. Small plants (moss) and insects live in their own wilderness.

✿ There is often a green layer on a tree trunk. This is caused by algae. Algae are miniscule plants without roots and leaves.

✿ There may also be yellow, grey or green marks on the bark. These are lichens. A lichen resembles a small plant but that is not the case. A lichen is formed by an alga and a fungus that live

together. If you find lichens, that means that there is little air pollution in that area.

Making a bark rubbing

✣ *paper*
pastel crayon

Each variety of tree has different bark. Some trees have coarse bark, others smooth. You can feel this, of course, and also see it. An oak tree, for example, has rough bark while a beech tree is smooth (see Figs 67.1 and 67.2).

Fig 67.1 Oak

Fig 67.2 Beech

It is interesting to make a copy of the bark of a tree. Place a piece of paper against the tree trunk. Get someone else to hold the paper, or fix it with tape (be sure to remove this afterwards!). Rub the side of a pastel crayon across the paper until the whole sheet is covered with the print. You then have a copy of the bark on paper (see Fig 68.1).

Do this with different trees and compare the prints.

Branches

❖ *measuring tape*

Trees can become very old. They grow and grow and become thicker and higher. This is a slow process.

The twigs and branches of a tree indicate how much the tree grows in one year. Be careful that the branches do not break when you examine them. After all, it takes a tree years to grow a new branch.

Figure 68.2 shows a twig. Every winter, the twig stops growing for a time. At the end of the twig a small ring scar appears. Take a look at some low twigs and see if you can spot any ring scars.

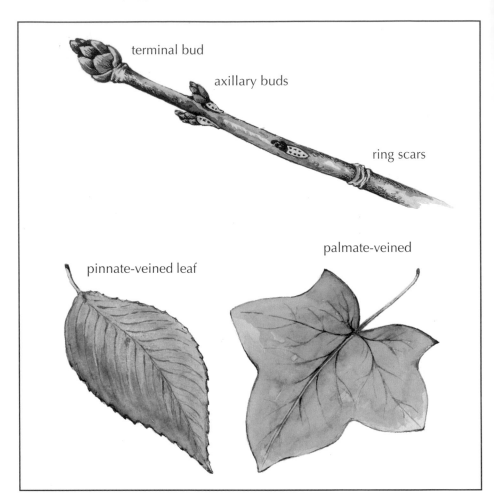

Fig 68.2

Fig 68.1

* Measure the distance between the two ring scars that are closest to the end of the twig. Now you know how much the twig grew last year. You can also measure how much the twig has grown in two or three years.
* In the summer, the tree is busy growing. The section between the last ring scar and the last bud on the branch is the amount it has already grown this year.
* With most trees, you will discover side buds next to the stems of the leaves. New leaves will come from these side buds next year. The tree is already busy with next year's growth.

Looking for leaves

Look at the leaves lying on the ground and try to gather as many different types as possible. Who can find the most?

* There are thicker lines in each leaf, called veins or ribs. They ensure the firmness of the leaf, just like bones do in people. All

the veins together form the skeleton of the leaf. Leaves can have two kinds of skeletons, depending on the kind of tree. The skeleton can be pinnate-veined or palmate-veined (see Fig 68.2). Look among your gathered leaves to see if you have both kinds.

Making a leaf print

❖ *various kinds of leaves*
paper
pastel crayons or coloured pencils

You can make a copy of leaves in the same way as you made a copy of the tree bark.

1 Lay a leaf on the table. Place a piece of paper over it and hold it down firmly so that it cannot move.
2 Take a pastel crayon and rub the side of the crayon across the paper, always stroking in the same direction, until you see the shape of the whole leaf. If you use coloured pencils, you should hold the pencil at a slight angle and not press too hard, otherwise you will go through the paper.
3 You can make copies of different leaf forms on one page. Give each of them its own colour.

The skeleton of the leaf will have become particularly visible because the veins of the leaf protrude a little. Can you see the different forms?

Lantern with leaf prints

❖ *a sheet of stiff paper or thin card*
various leaves
pastel crayons
tea-light

Create the leaf prints (in different colours) on a long piece of stiff paper. Roll the paper into a cylinder. Tape the ends together. Make a good solid bottom and tape it underneath the cylinder (see Fig 69.1).

If you place a tea-light in the lantern in the evening, the leaf forms will be illuminated.

Tree passport

❖ *pencil*
several sheets of paper or a note book
a print of bark
dried leaf

As a memento of your favourite tree, you can make a small book about it. Take a notebook or a staple a few sheets of paper into a booklet. Make a drawing of the tree on the front cover or stick a photo of the tree there.

Do you know the name of the tree? If so, write it down. Of course, you can give the tree its own name.

In this *tree passport,* you can enter data such as the height of the tree and its thickness. Paste a 'fingerprint' of the tree (the bark rubbing) and a dried leaf into the book. Write down details about where the tree grows and its surroundings. Draw or describe the plants that grow around or near the tree and which animals and birds live in the tree.

Fig 69.1

dandelion   red clover   daisy

Fig 70.1 Compound flowers

Nature in bloom

🌱 ✂ ❋ ♀

Flowers

❖ *four sticks or dead twigs per person*
  wire
  string or thread 4 metres (12 ft)
     long
  cocktail sticks

Plants are the clothes of nature. You see them everywhere. The most conspicuous parts of plants are their flowers that bloom in all colours. There are a great many different flowers.

❀ Find a place where wild plants bloom — not in a garden but in the open countryside. Watch your step and do not stand on any flowers.

❀ Use the four sticks and the wire to mark off a piece of ground 1 × 1 metre (3 × 3 ft). See how many different kinds of flowers you can distinguish in this small plot. How many different colours can you identify, and which colour do you see most? How many different flower shapes can you find?

If you do this study with several people, you can compete to see who finds the most different plants in a piece of ground. Who can find the biggest flower? Who can find the smallest one?

❀ You can use your cocktail sticks to mark out a mini-route through your 'territory,' leading to all the different flowers. You can show your discoveries to your parents!

❀ Only pick flowers that grow along the roadside or the track, and only flowers of which there are lots. However, in some countries or national parks you may not pick flowers at all.

Scent

In the early summer, the meadows with their many wild flowers have not yet been mown. Look at the flowers until you find one that you think is nice. You don't need to pick it. Just let it grow, then it can flower for a few more days. Try smelling it. Does it have a scent? Do you like it?

❀ Try some other flowers. Do they smell the same?

❀ Rub a green leaf between your fingers. Smell the leaf. What do you think smells nicer, the flower or the leaf?

Flowers in close up

❖ *magnifying glass*

You will find dandelions and daisies wherever grass grows. Some people call them weeds. It is often difficult to pull them out of the ground because they have long roots. If you pull the plant, the root will usually break. It stays in the ground and produces a new plant. So, if the plants are already growing somewhere, it is not easy to get rid of them. But this need not be a problem, because they brighten up the fields with their cheerful colours.

If you look at a dandelion, daisy or clover, at first you will see just one flower. But if you look at the flower closely, you will see that it actually consists of a great many small flowers. For this reason they are called *compound flowers*. If you want to have a better look at the small flowers, you will need a magnifying glass.

❀ Can you see any differences between the small flowers in the middle and those at the edges of the compound flower? Are they all equally tall? Are they all the same colour?

* Pull one of these small flowers out, very carefully, and suck on it. What can you taste? Now you know why bees are so happy about sitting on flowers.

* Other flowers such as pansies and buttercups do not consist of smaller flowers. In this case, each blossom is a single flower. Try comparing these to a compound flower.

The stem of the dandelion

✤ scissors
  needle
  thread
  paper

Pick a dandelion. Look at the bottom of the stem. It seems as if milk is coming out of it. Taste it. What does it taste like? Be careful not to get any of this milky juice on your clothes. The stains are difficult to wash out.

* The stem is hollow. If you can break off a piece of the stem, you will be able to look through it or suck air through, like a straw. You can also pull a needle and thread

through it. If you do it with many pieces of the stem, you will have greenish beads.

* You can also use a dandelion stem for drawing. Draw on a piece of paper using the white sap. You can hardly see what you have done. But when it dries, you can see clearly what you have drawn or written there. It is like invisible ink!

Flower salad

✤ bowl
  knife
  cup

Many flowers and leaves can be eaten. You can easily make a salad of wild flowers.

Recipe:

* lettuce
* dandelion leaves
* daisy leaves
* red or white clover flowers
* 2 tablespoons of olive oil
* 1 tablespoon of vinegar
* 2 teaspoons of the buds or young leaves or tops of sorrel
* 2 teaspoons of parsley

Method:

Older dandelion leaves are stiff and bitter. It is best to use young leaves. The bitter taste lessens if the leaves are soaked in cold water for two hours before use.

1 Wash the dandelion and lettuce leaves under the tap.
2 Cut the dandelion and lettuce leaves into pieces.
3 You can leave the daisy leaves and clover flowers whole. You must wash them before placing them in the bowl.
4 Make a dressing by pouring the oil and vinegar into a cup.
5 Add 2 teaspoons of parsley to the dressing.
6 Cut the tops, buds or leaves of the sorrel as finely as possible.
7 Add them to the dressing.
8 Stir everything together in the bowl.

Enjoy your meal!

Fuzzy balls

Flowers often only bloom for a few days then the coloured petals become weak and turn brown. At a certain moment the flower head opens again and you see a grey fuzzy ball. On

Fig 71.1

Fig 71.2

each of these pieces of fuzz is a small seed. The dandelion, thistle and hawkbit are good examples of this type of flower (see Fig 71.1).

* Have you seen any fuzzy balls yet? If so, pick one of them.
* How many times do you have to puff to blow all the fuzz away? Can you do it in one go? You can organize a small competition with other children.
* See who can keep a seed in the air the longest without touching it. Whose seed goes the furthest?
* You can also play another game. Everyone takes a fuzzy ball and blows just once. The number of seeds that remain indicates how old you are.

Decorate yourself

1 Pick a flower with a long stem.
2 Use your nail to make a small incision in the stem just under the flower.
3 Wrap the stem around your wrist with the flower facing upward.
4 Put the end of the stem through the incision and tie a small knot. You could also make a small incision near the end of the stem and insert another small twig or such-like. You now have a bracelet.

You can make a garland of flowers or a flower chain in the same way. It is done by inserting a new flower through an incision in the stem of the previous flower (Fig 72.2).

* Only pickflowers that are in abundance, such as dandelions and daisies. Pluck only flowers where lots of them are grouped together. Make sure that a few flowers are left. Remember: in the mountains and national parks there are many flowers that are protected and you are not allowed to pick these.

Fig 72.1

Fig 72.2

Grasses

✛ *magnifying glass*

You find grass everywhere. Grasses flower just like every other plant but we often don't recognize the flower as being a real flower, but take a closer look. A stalk of grass is actually a bunch of flowers.

When the grass flowers come into bloom, they give off a yellow dust: this is pollen. Some people get watery eyes and runny noses from this. They have hay fever.

Grass can grow in many places but it does not always look the same. It is often short on paths where people walk. The blades of grass lie just above the ground. Next to the path there are rougher areas with much longer grass. Tall blades reach upward and the longer stalks rise above these.

✿ Walk in your bare feet across grass that people often walk across (a path or a playing field). Then walk through a field of long grass where people or animals do not often walk. Can you feel the difference?
✿ Now look back and see where you have come from. Which type of grass shows where you have been?

With your nose in the grass

Grass flowers do not have a strong scent. Stand in the middle of a grassy field, one that has not been cut recently. Can you smell the grass? Can you smell the flowers?

Fig 73.1

a *Giant balsam with ripe seeds*
b *Seedbox of the poppy*
c *Comfrey*
d *Burr*
e *Cleavers*
f *Monkshood*

Then lie down on your stomach with your eyes closed. Can you smell it now?

If you like, you can taste a stem of grass. Then you will know why cows are always so contented.

A bunch of grass flowers

✣ *scissors or small knife*

Although they do not have large colourful flowers, grass stalks are nevertheless quite pretty. Take a good look at a field with long grass.

Gather together as many different stalks as possible. The stalks are often quite tough, so you should use a pair of scissors or a small knife to avoid pulling up the whole plant.

Now you can take a different kind of bouquet back to your mother!

Seeds

Many animals eat grass, such as cows and sheep, deer and rabbits. And people too! The grain that our bread is made from (and other grain products) is actually a kind of grass seed. Have a good look as you walk past cultivated fields. You will see wheat, oats, rye, barley and even maize. These are all plants with large edible seeds.

The dissemination of seed

Plants produce seeds and new plants can grow from these seeds. In order to grow, the seeds need enough space. For this reason, they have to be spread out or 'disseminated,' away from the mother plant. However, plants are fixed with their roots in the ground, and cannot take the seeds on a day trip somewhere else. Moreover, seeds do not have legs to get them anywhere. Some plants simply drop their seeds but there are also plants that have special tricks to disseminate the seeds as far as possible. They make use of the wind, for example. Plants

that do this create seeds with fluff or small wings. The wind then blows the seeds far and wide. The fuzzy balls are a good example of this. You have helped them in their task.

Jumping seeds

✣ *old sheet or large light-coloured towel*
clothes pegs

Although they are fixed at one spot, some plants can throw their seeds out. The giant balsam and the poppy are good examples of this. Try it. (Fig 73.1a)

❀ Find a garden balsam plant. The seed pods are at the end of the stems. They look a bit like mini-cucumbers. Touch the thickest of these. You might get a surprise!
❀ Gather together several poppies with ripe seed pods. Cut off the stems as close to the ground as possible. Use clothes pegs to clamp the stems to the sheet or towel, and hold the bottom of the stem on the sheet.
❀ Hold the stem vertically and slowly bend it using your free hand. Let go suddenly. The seeds will shoot out. Measure how far they have sprung on the sheet.
❀ You can have a small contest with poppies with equally long stems. Whose seeds jump the farthest?

Sticky seeds

You may well be familiar with sticky willows or cleavers or other plants that stick to your clothes during a walk in the countryside. This is also a method of dissemination. These seeds (that's what they are) have little spikes with barbs. They attach themselves to your clothes or to the coat of an animal that brushes past them. In this way, they can hitchhike quite a distance (Fig 73.1e).

Look and see if you can find this kind of barbed plant.

You can investigate, using old clothes, to see which materials these seeds most easily cling to. Try a raincoat, a pair of jeans, a woolly sweater, artificial fur, your socks.

Pips

Other plants make use of people or animals to disseminate their seeds. Many plants produce fruit. Some of these fruits, such as gooseberries, blackberries, wild strawberries and raspberries, are totally consumed by animals. The seeds are later excreted somewhere else. New plants can grow there next year.

❀ Towards the end of the summer, take a look at the excrement of a bird that eats berries, such as a blackbird or thrush. Can you see the seeds?
❀ Other fruits have large, hard stones or cores, such as plums or apples, for example. There is a thick layer of sweet juicy pulp around these.
❀ People and animals pick these fruits and take them with them to eat when out. They then drop the stones or the cores somewhere else.
❀ People and animals help the plants by eating their fruits. So, have a look for something delicious in the wild!
❀ However, be careful to only eat the things that you know are edible. You should also wash them first, to avoid stomach problems.

Animals in woods and fields

⚜ ✿ ⚹ ✲ ♀

If you walk through the woods with a group of people, you might imagine that there are no other creatures around. After all, you don't see any. Nevertheless, there are many different animals living in the woods.

* Rabbits, badgers, foxes and mice live in holes in the ground, but they come out regularly to look for food.
* Other animals, such as squirrels and woodpeckers, live in holes in trees. Many birds nest in trees.
* Deer and wild boar usually live in the brushwood during the daytime. You have a good chance of meeting them in a clearing in the woods or at the edge of the woods in the evening or the very early morning.
* There are also very many small creatures, which live under the bark of a tree or in moss or under leaves on the ground.

Squirrels

Squirrels spend most of their lives among the branches of trees. That is where they also build their nest. They are excellent climbers and often sit high in the trees. If you walk through the woods very quietly, you will have a good chance of seeing one.

Squirrels come down to the ground to look for acorns or other seeds that have fallen to the ground, and you can then see them close up. If you see one, don't move. If they suspect danger, they will shoot up the tree again as fast as possible.

Even if you have not seen any squirrels, you can find out if they are living in that part of the woods, by searching for traces they leave behind.

Squirrels build nests of twigs, bark, moss, grass and leaves. The nests are usually high in the tree at a point where a branch extends from the trunk.

You can check if there are any food remains. If you find a collection of pine cones whose scales have been gnawed off in a rather rough way, you will know that a squirrel has been busy here (see Fig 75.1). A rough core is all that is left. With fir cones, the squirrels do not touch the top layer of scales because they know that there are no seeds underneath. Have a look and see if you can find these leftovers.

Woodpeckers in a dead tree

On a walk through the woods, you might see a dead tree. It is completely bare and perhaps even half broken. Take a good look at this tree. All kinds of creatures live in a dead tree.

There are often round holes high up in a dead tree. These are woodpeckers' hollows. Woodpeckers prefer to make a hollow in a dead tree because the wood is not so hard, and they make their nest there.

When the woodpecker abandons the nest, other animals (birds or squirrels) take over the hollow as a nesting or hiding place. If you stand still for a time, you might be able to see who is living in this hollow. Perhaps the occupant may stick his head out to see what is going on.

Have a good look at the tree trunk. Is it full of small holes? If so, the woodpecker has been searching for food here. What kind of food is in the tree? Lift up a piece of bark to find out.

Deer

Deer usually hide during the daytime. You will only see them in the very early morning or in the evening, but you can find traces of them during the day, such as hoof-prints, for example, indicating that they do live in that area.

If you see young branches and tree stems where the bark has been stripped off from ground level to about 1 or 2 metres (3 or 6 ft) high, this means that there are deer in the area. You can occasionally find teeth marks on branches, and at the bottom of a tree where the bark has been torn loose, you will find a neat bitten edge.

Fig 75.1 Gnawed-off fir cones

Towards the end of the summer, the stags rub the velvet off their antlers. This velvet is a layer of soft hide that coats and protects the antlers as they grow. In rubbing off the velvet, they are preparing their antlers for the contest with other stags for the does (female deer).

They usually rub off the velvet against bushes or young trees. Sometimes the thinner branches break off, and the antlers leave grooves in the bark. Pieces of the velvet sometimes remain on the branches. If you find this kind of scratching place, you can feel how soft this velvet is. Or has it already dried out and become hard?

Wild boar

If you suddenly find a piece of churned-up ground in the middle of the woods, you will know that wild boar have probably been at work here (see Fig 77.1).

They root around with their snouts in the ground looking for food. They often do this under oak trees, searching for acorns.

Occasionally you will see a layer of mud up to 1 metre (3 feet) high on a tree trunk. A wild boar has scratched itself against this tree after a mud bath. You may well find a quagmire in the vicinity. Take a deep breath. Perhaps you can smell the sharp scent of the animal.

Hares and rabbits

Hares and rabbits are very similar. Nevertheless, there are clear differences. Hares are quite a bit larger than rabbits, their ears are longer and they have thicker extremities. Their back legs are much larger and stronger than those of a rabbit, which is clearly visible as they run. Hares usually appear in an open field and

< Fig 76.1

do not dig burrows (warrens) as rabbits do.

Rabbits are smaller and do not leap as far as hares. They live in woods and fields and dig burrows to live in. In contrast to hares, who live on their own, rabbits live in groups. So if you see a group of animals and you are not sure what they are, they will probably be rabbits.

Have you seen the way hares and rabbits run? Try to copy them!

Burrows and hollows

If you inspect the ground carefully, you will see holes everywhere: some very small ones, sometimes even on a path, and larger ones at the side of the track.

✿ Have you found a hole? Try to find out if something is living there. If there are spiders' webs in front of the opening, you will know that no one is living there. You can sometimes smell if an animal is living in it. Can you smell anything?

✿ Rabbits and badgers dig burrows. They often make their home under a tree or bush. The roots give the ground support so that the burrow does not collapse. Tree roots also draw moisture out of the ground so that the ground is drier. That is what most animals prefer — a nice dry house.

✿ Foxes also live in a burrow, called a 'den.' They cannot burrow as well as rabbits so they often make use of rabbit holes that they enlarge. When the rabbits have to move home, they offer little argument. A fox may also move in with a family of badgers, but they each have their own passageways.

✿ The entrances of fox and badger holes are roughly 25–30 cm (10–12 in) in diameter, and those of rabbit holes around 15 cm (6 in).

✿ The small round holes belong to mice. The entrance is as small as 2 cm (1 in).

✿ Have a good look at the surroundings of the hole. Perhaps you might find other clues indicating who is living here. These may be footprints or perhaps droppings, pieces of hair, or leftovers.

Footprints

Not all animals leave visible footprints. They must be heavy enough to make a footprint and the ground must to soft enough to take it. You can see footprints quite clearly on sandy ground but the print can easily be blown away by the wind. The best footprints are to be found in muddy ground after a shower of rain. Figure 76.1 shows several footprints. Compare these to the footprints you have found.

Casting footprints
✿ ✂ ✽ ♀
See page 171.

Fig 77.1 Wild boar were here

It's small and flies through the air

🐝 🦋 ✂ ❄ ♀

You will almost always find flowers along the edges of a path. There are often insects on them, such as flies, honey bees, bumblebees, wasps or butterflies. These are special creatures and are not difficult to observe. Try to inspect them from close by. Move slowly towards the plant, otherwise they will be frightened and fly away.

❀ Be careful with bees and wasps. They can sting if they get a fright or feel threatened. Their sting is positioned at the end of their abdomen.
❀ Look for a plant with as many different insects as possible. How many different types can you count on one plant?
❀ Can you also discover why this flower attracts so many insects? Does the flower have a bright colour? Or a strong scent?

What does a bee do on a flower?

Honey bees are the most common visitors to flowers. They extract yellow powder (pollen) from the flowers. Have a good look how they do this. Do they use their mouths or their legs?

❀ How do they carry the pollen with them? Do they go straight back to their hive or do they visit other flowers first?
❀ The pollen serves as food for the larvae, the young bees and the queen bee, who all stay in the nest. As the bees fly from flower to flower, they spill some of the pollen on the flowers of other plants. In doing do, without knowing it, they help the plants produce new seeds.
❀ Bees are mainly looking for nectar, a sweet sap that flowers make. If you examine a shallow flower (not snapdragons, for example, which the bees have to climb into)

you may be able to see how they do that. You will have to be close to the flower. Look and see how the bee extracts the nectar from the flower.

✿ Back in the hive the bees turn the nectar into honey. This is stored as food.

Bumblebees

Bumblebees are large, happy buzzers. They even look as if you can stroke them, with their black-striped coats. Still, it is better not to do so. They are not really dangerous but they can inflict a painful sting, although they hardly ever do so.

✿ There are quite a few kinds of bees with various colours and stripes. Take a good look around at a place where there are lots of bees. How many different kinds can you see?

✿ Bumblebees enjoy visiting flowers that they have to climb into. If it rains, they will take shelter there and sometimes sleep the night there. Can you find flowers that can accommodate a bumblebee?

✿ If they cannot reach the nectar (of a deep flower, for example), bumblebees sometimes break in. They gnaw a hole in the flower and steal the nectar. If you see a comfrey or monkshood flower (see Fig 73.1c and f), look and see if you can find holes in it.

Follow a bumblebee

If you follow a bumblebee on its journey, you will find out quite a lot about its life. Choose a bumblebee and follow it wherever it goes. What kind of things does it do?

✿ Does it always go to the same sort of flower? Which colour flowers does it seem to prefer?

✿ Do these flowers smell nice? When the bee has moved on, smell the flower.

✿ Perform an investigation: Is the bee attracted to the colour or the scent of a flower? You can see this by the way it flies:

Does it fly directly to a flower and land on it immediately? This will mean that it can see the flower well and goes directly to its target.

Or does it fly around a bit before landing? In that case, it is attracted by the scent. By flying back and forth, it can find out where the scent is the strongest and then it chooses a place to land.

✿ Have you observed how the bumblebee finds a flower?

Find the flower
❖ *blindfold*
something with a strong scent
Now try to discover the quickest way to find a flower, using your eyes or using your nose.

1 Hide a dish containing something with a strong scent. This may be freshly mown grass or hay or rotting leaves, but you can also use something else that you can easily smell. This is your 'flower.'
2 Someone else is the bumblebee. Blindfold the 'bee' and turn him or her around a couple of times. Move the 'bee' to within two metres (six feet) of the 'flower.'
3 Remove the blindfold from the 'bee.' He or she must now find the 'flower' as quickly as possible.
4 Now do the same again but keep the blindfold on. The 'bee' now has to find the 'flower' via his or her sense of smell. Will he or she succeed?
5 Which is the quickest way for a human 'bee' to find the 'flower'?

Watching butterflies
❖ *A magnifying glass if necessary*
Butterflies are different from many other insects. Their large wings have the most beautiful colours. They look like flying flowers. Do not try to catch butterflies because holding them will damage their fragile wings. The butterfly will then no longer be able to fly properly, will not be able to find food and will die.

✿ Have a good look at a butterfly's wings. A butterfly has two front wings and two back wings. Can you see the difference?
✿ The lower and the upper sides of the wings are also different. Which side do you like most?
✿ If you find a *dead* butterfly, you are in luck! Examine the wings with a magnifying glass. How many different colours can you see?
✿ If you look really closely, you will see that there are countless small coloured scales on each wing. What happens if you touch them?

The proboscis
Butterflies only drink nectar. They have a very long tongue, the proboscis, that they use to drink nectar from deep flowers that other insects cannot reach. If you quietly approach a butterfly on a flower, you will probably be able to see how it uses its long tongue (see Fig 80.1).

Open and closed
Butterflies are most conspicuous when they spread their wings. They frequently sit with their wings open in the sunshine, in order to absorb as much warmth from the sun as possible. Some butterflies have red spots that resemble eyes on their wings. If they are frightened, they suddenly open their wings. Two eyes glare at their enemy and often frighten it away.

✿ When a butterfly is at rest, it folds up its wings. It then resembles a dead leaf. Birds or lizards, which are very fond of butterflies, then have difficulty finding them.
✿ Have you ever seen butterflies sleeping? They hang upside down on a leaf or other shelter. At the end of the summer they may enter houses and look for a frost-free corner to spend the winter.

Caterpillars
❖ *sticks*
Butterflies grow from caterpillars. Caterpillars do not live on flowers, they live on leaves. They are much less conspicuous, but can still be

Fig 80.1

very beautiful. Try to find one! If you discover plants whose leaves have been nibbled, there will probably be caterpillars somewhere in the vicinity.

* You can have a competition to see who can find the most beautiful caterpillar, or the one with the brightest colours, or the one with the longest hair. Leave the caterpillar where you found it. Place a stick there to mark the spot.
* Pick the caterpillar up carefully. Put it on the flat of your hand and examine it thoroughly. Caterpillars seem to consist of a head and a number of rings joined together. Can you see its jaws? That is what they use to nibble at the leaves.
* Count the caterpillar's legs. How may does it have?

  Just like all other insects, caterpillars have six legs, but it often appears as if they have many more. At the front of their bodies they have three pairs of real legs. These are pointed. Further to the rear they have stumpy abdominal protuberances and at the end they have a couple of limbs that resemble suckers. The caterpillar uses these to get a good grip on its surroundings.
* Allow the caterpillar to walk across your hand or watch it moving across a leaf. Does it use all its legs?
* Place the caterpillar back where you found it.

Hover flies

Hover flies resemble bees or wasps but they cannot sting. They land on flowers to consume the nectar and the pollen. Hover flies fool you by looking like insects that can sting. In this way, they frighten away their enemies.

The art of flying
🐞 🐝 ❄ ♀

Hover flies only have two wings (one pair) whereas bees and wasps have four (two pairs). Their wings slant sideways instead of extending straight back like those of bees and wasps. Their manner of flying also makes them completely different from other insects. They can fly very fast but they can also hover in one place in the air. When they move, they move in small bursts, not in a fluid way like most other insects.

* Look for a plant with large petals. Are there any hover flies there? What are they doing?
* Go into a meadow with flowers and watch all the insects there. Can you distinguish between bees, wasps and hover flies? Now you will know which insects sting and which ones do not.
* If you can recognize them, you will see that there are a great many kinds of hover flies. They all have their own colours and patterns. How many different kinds can you find in one meadow?

Listening

Listen closely to a hover fly. Can you hear it buzzing? The hover fly makes that sound with its wings. It moves them so quickly that you cannot see them moving. You only see a slight haze.

Compare the sound of a hover fly to that of a bumblebee and a honey bee. Can you hear the difference?

Wasps

Wasps are also attracted to the sweet nectar in the flowers. They love sweet things, but they are also formidable raiders. They do not eat pollen to get their daily dose of protein, as bees do. They hunt other insects, including hover flies, and use their sting to kill

their victims. Wasps do not have a barb in their stings as bees do, so they can sting several times. It is a creature to be feared!

* Wasps have a bright yellow and black pattern, and have much less hair than bees. And they clearly have a 'waist.' This is a really thin connection between the thorax (breast segment) and the abdomen.

Ants

If you go walking in the woods (or somewhere else) you have a good chance of encountering some ants. Street ants live in hollows under the pavement slabs. Wood ants build the well-known anthills. Ants are always on the go, so there is lots to see near an anthill (see Fig 82.1).

* Ants live in colonies. Within the colony, different groups of ants have different tasks. They are all female ants. The workers that you see outside the anthill are foraging for food. There are soldiers on the

inside, protecting the nest against invaders. They can often be seen just at the entrance. The queen resides deep inside the nest. She lays eggs, ensuring that the colony continues to exist.

* Take a good long look at the anthill. Are all the ants the same size? Do they all have the same colour?
* Look for an ant that is taking something back to the nest. How does it do that? Is it doing that on its own?
* Can you find a path that the ants march across? Place a leaf or twig in their way. What do they do now?
* Can you work out what ants eat? What are they taking to the nest?
* Scatter some sugar or other food in the vicinity of the anthill and see what they do with this. Can you see what they prefer?
* Once a year you will see flying ants. These are the male ants and new queens. This often happens with several nests on the same day. This is the day of the flight of the new bride. The male ants and the young queens go out into the wide world.

* The male ants are the smallest and only live for a short time. They leave the nest for the first and the last time in their life. Sometimes they find a queen with whom they can mate, but often this is not the case. They die within one day.
* The queen ants are the largest of the ants. When they have mated with a male ant, they lose their wings. They go looking for their own home and start a new colony of ants. For the rest of her life, the queen ant stays in the nest and lays thousands of eggs.

In and around water

The creatures that live in and around water are completely different from those that live on land. If you want to examine them, you will have to find a safe place on the shore, where the bank is not too steep. Be careful: the ground around the water is wet and slippery, you could easily fall in. It is best to wear shoes with a rubber sole. Get someone to hold you, if necessary.

Dragonflies
❖ *magnifying glass*

Dragonflies are often found near water on a sunny day. You will see them hovering just above a ditch or a pool. You can recognize them by their long, thin bodies. There are many different dragonflies and can be found in all colours: green, blue, red, yellow, brown and black.

* You may occasionally see two dragonflies stuck together. These are the male and female dragonflies mating. They differ in colour. The male dragonfly has brighter colours. He grasps the female just behind her head using small hooks on his abdomen (see Fig 82.2). After mating, the female will lay eggs in the water. The young dragonflies (larvae) are true water creatures. They are small, greedy raiders, and eat all kinds of other water creatures, even tadpoles and other small fish.
* The larvae live underwater until they are as large as adult dragonflies. Then they creep up the stem of a plant, out of the water and remain just above the water

Fig 82.1 Anthill

Fig 82.2 Dragonflies mating

surface. After a while, the skin of the larva bursts open and an adult dragonfly pops out.

* When the wings have unfolded and dried out, the dragonfly can fly away. It spends the rest of its life above water. The empty skin remains hanging on the stem of the plant. You can often find the empty skin among reeds. It is light brown and transparent. It resembles a dead insect, but it is not. There is no creature inside. But you can see what the dragonfly looked like when it was a larva. If you find one of these empty skins, take it with you and look at it through a magnifying glass.

Pond skaters

There are also small creatures that live on the surface of the water. They are so light that they do not sink. They dash across the water surface and hunt small flies and other insects. The most well-known of these surface residents is the pond skater. Can you see why they are called 'skaters'?

Frogs

❖ pocket torch

You often hear croaking noises on a summer evening. The frogs are giving a concert along with the chirping grasshoppers. Listen carefully. Do all frogs make the same noise?

* Where is the noise coming from? Can you find the frogs? What happens if you get close (without falling in the water)?
* Frogs usually hide during the daytime, but if you know where they live (because you have heard them in the evening), you may be able to find them. Sit very quietly near the water. After a little while, you will see something moving. A frog! Once you have seen one, you can often see more.

Where can you find the most frogs, on land or in the water?
* A frog is a good swimmer but it cannot breath underwater. For that reason, it has to come regularly to the surface. Which part of its body protrudes out of the water? Can you see the frog breathing?

In the air
🐝🐌✂❄♀

Bird watching

❖ binoculars

You will see birds almost everywhere: in woods and open fields, in the mountains and on the beach. As they can fly, there is nowhere they cannot go.

* Would you like to know what birds do? Then you should watch them. This means that you will have to watch one or several birds over a

period of time. In that way, you will be able to see what kinds of things they do in their everyday lives.

* Go to a spot that birds visit regularly. Sit down so that the birds cannot see you easily. Keep very still. You will need to be patient because only after you have been still and unnoticed for a while is there a chance that birds will come to that spot.
* It is useful to take binoculars with you if you want to watch birds, but you can also do so without them.

Eating together

To attract birds, scatter some bird food, such as very small pieces of bread, in a quiet place.

* Choose one of the birds and watch it as it eats. Does it go for the small pieces or the larger ones? Does it eat the food immediately or does it take the food to another spot? Does it eat with the other birds, or does it prefer to eat alone?
* If other birds approach the food, watch how your bird reacts. Does it just continue eating, does it fly away, or does it chase the other birds away?
* Some birds, such as sparrows, always live in groups. They stick together and also eat together. Sometimes the group suddenly flies up and all the birds go off together.
    Does that happen while you are watching? Can you find out why they do that?
* Other birds, such as blackbirds, prefer to live alone. They eat alone and sometimes chase other birds away. You almost never see two blackbirds together, except if they are arguing or looking after their young. Check if this is true.
* Have you seen other birds that are generally alone? Or together?

Birdbath

Would you like to see how a bird takes a bath? Place a shallow dish of water in a quiet spot. The birds probably won't come straightaway. They will first have to discover that there is water in the dish and get used to a new object in their surroundings. If no birds come to the bath after a few days, you will have to try it in another spot.

* If a bird does use the bath, take a good look at what it is doing. Does it get itself completely wet or not? What does it do with its beak?
* If you are lucky, different kinds of birds may visit your bath. Do they all wash themselves in the same way? Or do some of the birds do other things too?

Watching them fly

Every bird flies in its own special way. They fly in one of three ways.

* Many birds, such as sparrows, bluetits, blackbirds and pigeons, fly forwards. They move by constantly flapping their wings and usually go directly to their target.
* Some larger birds, such as gulls and buzzards, spend much of their time gliding. They don't have to flap their wings constantly and they take their time to survey their surroundings. Birds that glide often spend much time in the air, searching for food, for example. The wings of these birds are larger than those of birds that fly straight.
* There is a third group of birds that fly in a wave pattern. They fly by flapping their wings for a short while and gliding for a bit. Woodpeckers and magpies are examples of this style of flight.

* The speed of the wingbeat is related to the size of the bird. Large birds, such as herons, use their wings much more calmly than smaller birds, such as bluetits for example. You can clearly see the wingbeats of larger birds, but with smaller birds you only see a hazy, moving picture.
* Take a good look at different birds in flight. Perhaps you can even learn to recognize them by the way they fly (see Fig 85.1).

Looking for the singer

Many people keep birds because they can sing so well. Not all birds can sing well, but most do make a sound. Well-known songbirds are the blackbird, the thrush and the nightingale. The birdsong communicates information to other birds. We cannot understand them. It is usually the male birds that sing. They try to attract females with their song and chase away other male rivals.

Go to a quiet spot and sit still for a while. Listen to the sounds around you. This works best when you close your eyes. How many different songs can you hear?

Sometimes the song of a bird will betray where it is sitting. Listen if you can hear a bird nearby. Now have a quiet look around and see if you can discover the singer. Had you already seen this bird before you heard it?

Birds' nests

Many birds build their nests in trees or bushes. They often do that on branches, well hidden among the leaves so that the eggs are difficult for ground predators to find. A pile of twigs is enough for some birds. Others weave the materials to make a firm bowl.

Fig 85.1 >

quill

shaft

barbs

styles of flight

covert

down

✤ Birds use all kinds of material to build their nests, from grass and twigs to animal hair and plastic. If you want to know exactly how a bird builds its nest, look for an old nest. Be sure to check that the nest has truly been abandoned. There should be no eggs or young birds in the nest and there should be no birds flying to and fro with twigs and other material in their beaks.

✤ Inspect the nest carefully to see which materials the bird has used and how it was built.

✤ Then look for nest material yourself, and try to build a bird's nest.

Feathers

Birds need feathers in order to fly. Feathers are light and strong. There are different kinds of feathers, they vary in form and size. Each feather has a thick and firm part. The lower part is the *quill* and this becomes the *shaft* further up (see Fig 85.1).

✤ The exterior feathers of a bird are called the *coverts*. These are smooth and give birds their streamlined shape. The coverts also protect the birds against rain and wind.

✤ The coverts at the back of the wings are larger than the others and have a long quill. We also refer to these feathers as the 'flight feathers.' These flight feathers are the support base of the wings. The birds use these to exert force during flight.

✤ The *tail feathers* are used for braking and steering. You will see this if you have a good look at the tail of a bird as it lands on the ground or on a branch. It spreads its tail feathers to slow its flight and positions them at an angle if it has to make a curve. You can see this clearly if you watch a duck landing on water.

✤ There is soft, fluffy down under the smooth coverts. This down keeps the birds warm without making them too heavy to fly. You could say that the down is the lining of their jackets.

✤ Figure 85.1 shows different kinds of feathers. See if you can find one of each type.

✤ During a walk you may find lots of feathers together in all shapes and sizes. You have discovered a place where a predator, either an animal or a bird, has captured a bird and has plucked off the feathers in order to get at the meat. Birds of prey pull out the whole feather. If the shafts have been bitten off, the predator was probably a fox or a marten.

Enlarged feather

✢ *magnifying glass*

Take a good look at a feather through a magnifying glass. The central, firm part of the feather is called the *shaft* (or *rachis*). The shaft has branches, the *barbs*. There are smaller barbs on these barbs and these have small hooks that keep the barbs together.

✤ You can make a ruffled feather smooth again by stroking the barbs softly in the same direction. With your 'fat fingers' you will not be able to make it as smooth as a bird can, but nevertheless it will look better.

✤ Compare a fuzzy down feather to a smooth covert. Can you see that the barbs of the down are not attached to one another? A covert has to be smooth and tightly closed to protect the bird against rain and wind. A down feather must be soft and fluffy to preserve warm air between the feathers to protect the bird against the cold.

Colours

Birds have plumage of all kinds of colours. Some birds have brightly coloured feathers. These are often the male birds. The beautiful colours serve to attract the females and to warn other males that they should stay away.

✤ Covert feathers can also be decorative feathers. Decorative feathers have conspicuous colours or beautiful curves. The birds only use these feathers to show off or to make an impression, such as the tail feathers of a cockerel or a peacock, for example.

✤ Keep your eyes open as you walk through the woods or the countryside. You can find the most beautiful ornaments, and if they are not attached to a bird, you can take them home for free.

✤ Many birds are not brightly coloured, they are brown or greyish. Female birds in particular look pretty dull. This is because they have camouflage, a colour that makes it easy to hide from their enemies. This is especially important if they are in a nest, sitting on their eggs. In this way, it is difficult for a cat or a bird of prey to find the eggs and the mother bird.

✤ Nevertheless, brown and greyish birds are not as dull as they may seem at first sight. Take a walk along a pond or ditch to look for duck feathers that are lying on the bank. You will hardly find a dull feather, perhaps only from white ducks. Every feather has its own particular pattern of marks, spots, and stripes. Together, the different feathers give the female duck a good camouflage suit.

✤ Take a good look the next time you go to the pond. The male birds, with their bright colours, have more smooth feathers than the 'dull' brown females.

Collecting feathers
❖ *plastic bag*
notebook or box

You can collect feathers without troubling the birds at all. They drop feathers regularly, when they have become a bit worn, and moult once or twice a year, usually just before the winter. Then they lose all their old feathers and new ones grow to replace them. You can find feathers during the rest of the year too. Take a plastic bag or a small box with you when you go out walking. You can keep your findings in it.

✿ If you want to preserve feathers, you will have to clean them carefully. Wipe them with a slightly damp cloth. Only stroke from the shaft outwards. Then allow the feathers time to dry. In that way, they will not smell bad or start to decay. The best feathers to collect are ones that are as clean as possible.

Building up a collection
❖ *notebook or album*

You can keep the feathers you have found in a box, or tape them into a solid notebook or ring folder using sticky tape. This will keep them in good shape and you can write down where and when you found them. Perhaps you can also find out who the previous owners were.

1 You can store feathers of a particular type all together. Take a good look at their shape. Tape all the decorative feathers together in an album, and all the flight feathers etc.
2 It is also possible to collect the feathers according to type of bird. Of course, you will have to know from which birds the feathers have come. You will only be able to do so if you know a lot about birds, or if you know which birds tend to sit in which particular place.
3 A third way of building up a collection is to gather feathers according to colour. Then you will be able to see how many different shapes similarly-coloured feathers can have.

When you have sorted the feathers the way you wish, tape them into your album. If you want to add to your collection as you go, it is best to tape the feathers to loose sheets of paper and to keep these in a ring folder. You can then insert new pages without difficulty.

Decorations
❖ *thin string*
thread
chain or thin leather belt
hooks for earrings if necessary

You can preserve beautiful feathers in your collection, but you can also use them straight away as decoration.

1 Take a number of beautifully coloured feathers from your collection.
2 Use thread or thin string to tie the quills together. If they come undone make a small hole in the quill and pull a thread through the quill using a needle.
3 You can now tie the bunch of feathers to a chain or leather belt and hang them around your neck (see p. 195).

✿ If you want to use them as earrings, attach them to a hook.
✿ You can also use them as decoration hanging on your jacket.

8. Orientation

In normal everyday life, you are almost always going to, or coming back from, somewhere or other. You walk, you cycle, you go by car or bus. Mostly you don't think about the route you are taking. You simply know the way.

But sometimes you go somewhere completely new and you have to orient yourself, find your bearings, in order to arrive at your destination. How do you do that?

Have you ever wondered which direction you are looking in when you gaze out of the window?

Where is your school, for example, in relation to your house?

Orientation consists of getting ready to go somewhere and ensuring that you get there safely. You must know where you are and where you want to go.

Fortunately nature can give you plenty of help.

Fig 88.1 Compass

Orientation in the wild

You are in an area that you do not know and you want to go out for a walk. An experienced walker prepares his excursion by looking at the map. He will normally take a rucksack with something to eat and drink, and a detailed map of the surrounding countryside and a compass.

❧ You have been out walking for a couple of hours and have enjoyed looking at everything around you, but now it is time to return home and you suddenly realize that you have left your map and compass at home.

What should you do? You have walked so far that it is not easy to find the way back. There are no signposts that you can follow. You are lost.

Do not panic. You now have the opportunity to test your senses, to find out the direction you have to take to reach home. In short, you will have to *orient* yourself.

In order to orient yourself, you need to know where north, south, east and west lie. These are the four main points of the compass. Figure 88.1 shows the directions and subdivisions of the compass. If you know where one of these points lies, you can easily work out the others.

❧ What do you hear?

Human voices perhaps, or a dog barking? Often you hear the noise of traffic, which means that there is a road or a railway line nearby, and possibly also houses.

❧ What do you feel?

From which direction is the wind blowing. In many places, the wind comes mainly from the west or southwest.

❧ But the most important is: what can you see in the nature around you?

You will discover that nature offers many things to help you find the correct direction.

— Above all, there are the trees. If the prevailing wind is a west wind, the trees will lean slightly toward the east.

— There is often moss on the trunk and branches of trees. It grows on the side where most rain falls, usually the west or northwest.

— Animals build their shelters away from the wind, on the south or southeast side of a tree, for example. Try to see where birds have built their nests. Which side of a tree is the anthill or spider's web on? These have been built in the lee (sheltered side) of the tree.

— You may see a kind of track in the grass or between the bushes. This may be an animal track (see photograph, p.65). An animal track usually leads to a drinking place. This drinking place is often a stream or a river. Streams flow downwards and almost always pass through areas where people live.

— The stump of a sawn tree can also tell you about the direction of the wind. You will see rings on the top of the stump, increasing in size as you go from the middle to the outside. These are the growth rings, one for every year of the tree's life. If the tree stood on its own and received enough sunlight, the central point of the growth rings will be at the centre of the stump and the growth rings will be equally thick on all sides. In other cases, the tree will have received most sunlight when the sun was high in the southern sky. In that case, the growth rings on the south side of the tree will have grown the most and will therefore be the thickest (see Fig 89.1).

❀ Finally: a satellite dish can also help you with your orientation. They are always directed toward the south, in the northern hemisphere, and to the north in the southern hemisphere.

Orientation by the sun

If the sun is shining, it will help you enormously in getting your bearings. At the beginning of July, the sun rises in the east at approximately half-past four in the morning. At the beginning of August, it rises half an hour later. At midday, the sun is high in the southern sky, and in the evening it sets in the west. Thus, you can easily get your bearings early in the morning, at midday and in the evening.

During the rest of the day, you will be able to estimate directions by the position of the sun. The compass displayed in Fig 88.1 is subdivided into twelve directions. You could write down the time that the sun appears at that point of the compass. For exam-ple: east at 6 o'clock, east-south-east at 7 o'clock, etc.

Watch as compass
❀ ✄ ✳ ♀

Take your watch in the palm of your hand and turn yourself round until the small hand is pointing toward the sun. The south is now located exactly between the small hand and 12 o'clock. Keep summer time in mind! (see Fig 89.2)

Orientation by the moon

Even though the evening sky is not clear enough to see the stars, the moon is often visible. It, too, can help you with orientation. The moon goes through different *phases* and thus has different shapes (see the chapter on 'The Stars'). There are four phases. You know that the earth orbits the sun and the moon orbits the earth. Both the earth and the moon receive light from the sun. We can see the moon and the planets in the sky only because the sun shines on them. On the half of the earth or the moon that receives light, it is daytime, and the on the other half it is night. This also applies to the moon.

If the moon is between the sun and the earth, the side that is facing the earth is not illuminated. That is why we cannot see the moon. We call this the phase of the *new moon.*

As soon as the moon moves further in the sky, a part of the side facing the earth becomes illuminated. We see a small sickle: ☽. After about five days you see a semi-circle. We call that the *first quarter:* ☽.

After approximately another seven days it is *full moon:* ○.

After another seven days the moon is in its *last quarter:* ☾.

In the southern hemisphere, the phases look the other way round.

The moon rises at a different time every night and also sets at a different time.

The sun also occupied the place in the sky where you now see the moon.

If the moon is in its *first quarter,* the sun was there 6 hours previously.

If there is a *full moon,* the sun was there 12 hours previously.

If the moon is in the *last quarter,* the sun was there 18 hours previously.

If you know the time that you see the moon in the evening, then you can calculate the time that the sun was there during the day. Then you can determine the points of the compass.

The Pole Star

If there are no clouds, you will be able to see the *Great Bear* (or *Plough*) in the northern sky at night. It resembles a kind of saucepan. Four of the stars form a square, the pan itself. The other three form a lightly curved line extending to the pan; this is the handle. Together, they are known as the constellation the Great Bear.

Draw an imaginary line between the two stars that are furthest away from the handle (the back part of th

Fig 89.1 The year rings are thicker on the sunny side

Fig 89.2 Watch as compass

pan). Extend the line upwards above the pan. At a distance that is roughly five times the distance between these stars, you will see a bright star. This is the Pole Star. Once you have found it, you will always be able to find it. It is there at the same place in the northern sky during the whole night and the whole year round. This star indicates the north (see p. 52).

Discoveries in nature

How tall is a tree?

🐚 ✂ ❋ ♀

❖ *piece of cardboard 30 × 30 cm (12 × 12 in)*
string or thread with a weight
measuring tape

It is not difficult to measure the height of a tree. You can make a tree-measurer out of a piece of cardboard.

Fig 90.1 Measuring the height of a tree

1 Take a square of cardboard of 30 × 30 cm (12 × 12 in). Cut it diagonally in half. You need one of the pieces thus produced: a triangle with two equal sides and a right angle.
2 Tape a piece of thread or string to one of the sharp corners and fix the other end of the thread to a small weight (a nail, stone, or stick, for example).
3 Hold the triangle in front of you. The corner to which the thread is attached should point upwards. Make sure that the thread hangs parallel to the vertical side.

4 Now stand at such a distance from the tree that you can see the exact top of the tree when you look along the diagonal side (see Fig 90.1).
5 Measure the distance from this spot to the tree trunk (with a measuring tape, or with steps). Add your own length and you will know the exact height of the tree.

Road and city maps

Although you can buy small GPS devices nowadays that determine your position by referring to a satellite, most people will use a map for orientation and choice of route. For this reason, we shall first discuss how to use a map.

What is a map? And how do you work with it?

A map is nothing more than a reduced picture of what you see around you. Everything has been made much smaller, but if you were to present absolutely everything that you see around you, the map would be full of details. That is why cartographers — the people who make maps — choose to represent some things and leave out others.

With a *road map,* for example, they place the emphasis on the roads. The landscape and the houses are less important. The map clearly shows main roads and secondary roads, but the buildings and natural areas are only shown simply and concisely.

With a *city map,* you want to have an exact representation of the buildings and streets. Here, the cartographers have chosen to represent the buildings, streets and green spaces in the town.

You will understand that, because of the distances involved, a road map has been reduced in scale much more than a city map.

When buying a map, be sure to check the year of publication. A map that is several years old may lack important new information.

Scale and distance

The scale of a map indicates the extent to which the picture has been reduced in size.

If everything on the map has been reduced 100 000 times, the map shows: Scale 1:100 000. With a reduction of 50 000 times, the scale is 1:50 000. The scale ratio is thus 100 000 or 50 000.

If you want to find out how far it is between two places, you can calculate this using the scale ratio. The scale is given in terms of centimetres or inches. A scale of 1:50 000 means that every centimetre on the map is equal to 50 000 cm in reality. To convert this to kilometres, simply move the decimal point 5 places to the left. In this case, this works out at 0.5 km.

So you measure the distance on the map and then multiply it by the scale ratio (in this example, 50 000). To convert to kilometres, move the decimal point five places to the left.

❀ Many maps show a *scale bar.* This resembles a short ruler divided

Fig 91.1 and 2 The map measurer

into centimetres or inches, showing how many kilometres or miles one centimetre or one inch represents. This makes calculating distances easier, but it is generally less accurate than the previous method.

The map measurer

The map measurer is a very handy device (see Figs 91.1 and 2). It has a small wheel that you can roll across the map. The display panel then shows the distance in kilometres or miles at the appropriate scale.

The aim of the excursion you want to make determines what you need and the best scale to use.

❀ Road maps showing a large area often have a scale of 1:400 000. A map of a large country, such as France for example, has a scale of 1:1 000 000. This means that 1 cm on the map represents 10 km on the ground. Maps of provinces or counties, where you wish to see more details, have a scale of 1:200 000.
Figure 92.1 (scale 1:200 000) displays the same area of land around the French town of Dole as is shown in the black frame in Figure 92.2 (scale 1:1 000 000).
❀ Cycling maps usually have a scale of 1:50 000 or 1:100 000.
❀ City maps and hiking maps mostly have a scale of 1:25 000 or 1:50 000. These maps are very detailed and often show every detached building. It is easy to find your way in a town or natural area when using such maps.

Figures 92.3 (scale 1:25 000) and 92.4 (scale 1:50 000) show the town of Cuijk in the Netherlands. On the more detailed map shown in Figure 92.3 you can see all the streets and blocks of houses.

Fig 92.1 Scale 1:200 000

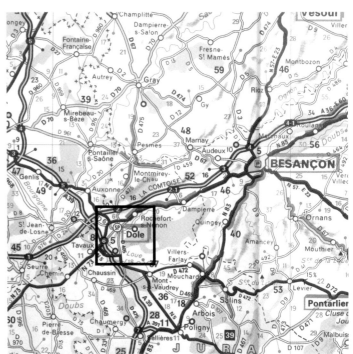

Fig 92.2 Scale 1:1 000 000

Fig 92.3 Scale 1:25 000

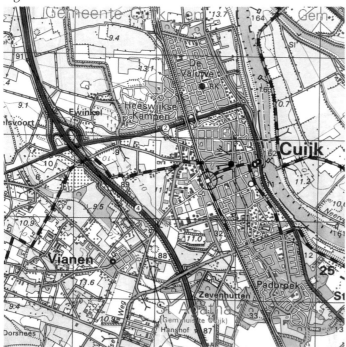

Fig 92.4 Scale 1:50 000

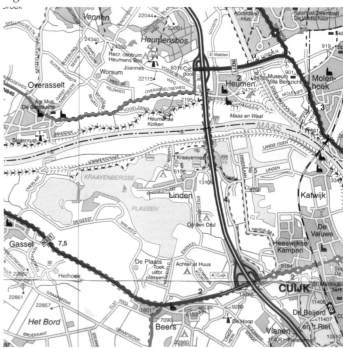

Tip:

1 cm on a large road map can thus represent 10 km (1 in — 5 or 10 miles). 1 cm on a hiking map usually represents 2.5 km (1 in — 1 mile).

In your car, you can usually drive those 10 km, or that one cm, in 10 minutes, but if you want to walk this distance, it will take around 2½ hours. So pay careful attention to the scale of the map!

❀ Hiking maps of the mountains usually have a scale of 1:25 000. It will show every individual house and also the altitude contours (see Fig 93.1).

Map legends

When making maps, cartographers use symbols and colours. What these symbols and colours stand for is explained in the *legend* of each map.

Before using a map, you should look at the symbols used. Figures 93.2 and 93.3 show that there is quite a difference between the legends used for maps in different countries. Figure 11 shows the legend of a road map. It clearly shows how motorways or secondary roads are represented. If you know which kind of road you will be taking, it is easier to work out how long it will take to travel a certain distance.

With the more detailed maps, such as hiking maps for example, the legends are equally important. Look, for instance, how a church is represented. A church is usually a conspicuous feature in the landscape and can be an important landmark during a hike. Be careful! If you interpret a map symbol incorrectly, you could easily end up taking the wrong route.

Co-ordinate system

Most maps are divided into sections by horizontal (east-west) and vertical (north-south) lines. On most maps, the sections thus created are indicated by letters or numbers at the edges of the map. The letters are usually at the top (see Fig 93.4). You can now refer to each area by mentioning the letter and then the number. If you say C2, you are referring to the area under C at the top and the area to the right (or left) of 2 at the sides.

Topographical maps, which are very detailed, give all lines a number. The first half of the group of numbers refers to the number along the top of the map and the second refers to the number at the side of the map.

If you are looking for a certain place in the index of a map, this kind of letter-number or number-number combination is often shown after the name of the place. Sometimes, several combinations are given. This means that the street, river or mountain can be found in several adjacent sections.

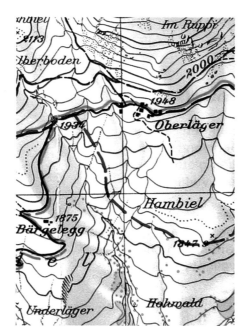

Fig 93.1 Detailed mountain map

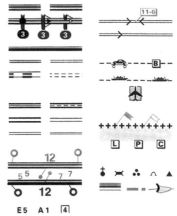

Fig 93.2 Legend of road map

Fig 93.3 Legend of topographical map

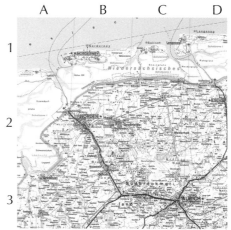

Fig 93.4 Map with co-ordinate system

In the car with the map on your lap

Begin by learning the *language* of the map you are using; in other words, what the symbols mean, because maps can differ.

If you are in the car, with the map on your lap, the driver will be expecting you to tell him or her what to look for. You must give this information in good time. The car is going quite fast and is often in a flow of traffic so it can't just stop to check the route on the map. Before you know it, you may have passed an important junction or turn-off.

Check the route in advance and know what the various symbols on the map mean. If necessary, make a few notes about the route, or gather information from the Internet.

The first part of the journey usually goes through well-known areas. Use this time to compare the map to the real world.

* Check your watch to see how long it takes to travel a certain distance.
* Pay attention to the way the various roads are indicated on the signs — by means of a certain colour and/or number?
* What kinds of signs are used? Some signs may have an arrow or pointed shape that may point to the right, for example, but the sign itself may indicate that you have to go straight on.
* How far in advance are turn-offs indicated?
* Which way are you holding the map? Are you holding it in such a way that it corresponds to the direction you are travelling in, so that left on the map also represents a left turn on the road? Or is north at the top, even when you are travelling south?

Fig 94.1 Compass

The compass

If you are walking along a well-marked path with clear signposting, or if the destination of your hike — such as the church spire of the village you are going to — is clearly visible, you will not need a compass, but there are situations in which a compass can be very handy.

As a compass is rather important, we shall deal with it in more detail. Figure 94.1 displays a Silva compass. It is very easy to use because it is made of transparent material. If you lay it on a map, you can read the information on the map through the plastic. The compass consists of two important components:

The base is the transparent, elongated base plate with the direction-of-travel arrow at one end.

The direction-of-travel arrow points towards your destination, to the place you want to go to.

The compass housing is fixed to the base plate and can rotate.

* The bottom of this case has a large red arrow with a number of parallel lines. The red arrow is called the *orienting arrow*.
* The upper part of the compass housing is the compass dial, showing a division into degrees, 0° to 360°. The main points of the compass are shown here, N(orth), S(outh), E(ast), and W(est).

North is by definition 0°. If you move clockwise around the compass, you first come to East at 90°. South is halfway round at 180°. West lies at 270°.

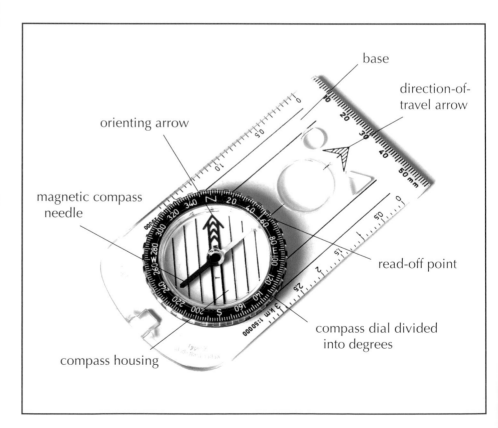

* The most important component is the *magnetic needle* within the dial. The red part of the needle always points to the north and should be able to turn freely. Keep iron or steel objects away from the compass. They can influence the sensitive needle. A steel watch strap will certainly influence it.

Getting your bearings

In order to discover the direction in which a path is going, or in which a tree or church spire stands, you can take *compass bearings*.

Fig 95.1 Pointing the compass

1 (Fig 95.1) Hold the compass horizontally on the palm of your hand, with your arm outstretched. Point the direction-of-travel arrow towards your destination.
2 Turn the dial until the orientation arrow is exactly underneath the red part of the compass needle. At the read-off point, the dial shows the number of degrees at which your destination lies in relation to magnetic north.

Every time you move right or left of the line to your destination, you will have to take new bearings.

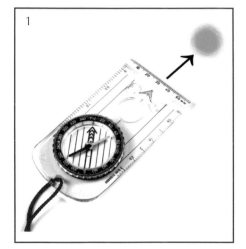

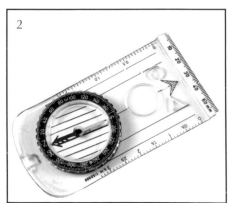

Into the unknown

In the section above, you already had a target you could see. You wanted to know the direction in which it lay.

You can reverse this process and use the compass to get somewhere that you cannot see.

* Your assignment could be something like: Walk in a **95°** direction for 10 minutes; At a junction in the road, follow **145°**; At the next junction follow **80°**, etc.

How do you do that?
1 Turn the dial so that the read-off point is at 95°.
2 Turn the whole compass round on the palm of your hand so that the orientation arrow is exactly under the red part of the magnetic needle.
3 Walk in the direction shown by the direction-of-travel arrow. When going in this direction, look into the distance to see if there is any kind of landmark there. If so, you can keep going in that direction without continually having to look at the compass.

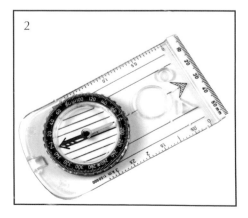

4 When you arrive at the junction after about 10 minutes, take new bearings so that the direction-of-travel arrow is 145°, etc.

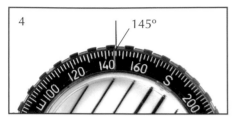

Orientation using a map

You want to use a map to find your way. Can you find your present location on the map?

Look around you and see if you can see anything that is also shown on the map: a church spire, crossroads, a sharp bend in the road, a bridge over a river. If so, you will be able to recognize where you are and then continue your journey with the map in your hand.

✿ You can also use the compass, then your route will be more exact and you are less dependent on recognizing features around you. Make sure that your map is spread out to correspond to the

surrounding countryside. On most maps, north is at the top.

1 Now turn the compass dial until the orientation arrow points to the read-off point.
2 Lay the compass with the long, right side along one of the vertical lines on the map (or along the side of the map).
3 Turn the map around, with the compass on top of it, until the arrow of orientation is exactly under the red part of the needle.

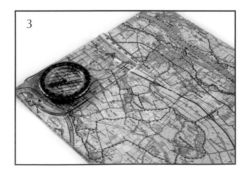

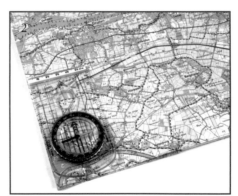

The north given by the compass is now equal to the landscape around you.

Working with the map and compass: getting directions

You want to go to a point some distance away. You have oriented your map (see the section above), so the direction of your map and the landscape now correspond.

1 Take your map. We shall call your present location A and the place you want to go B.
2 Place the compass along the imaginary line between A and B on the map that you have already oriented. The direction-of-travel arrow points towards B.

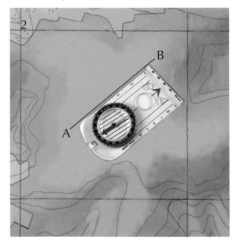

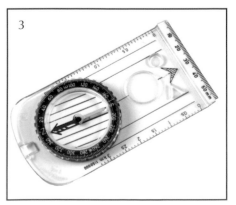

3 Now turn (only) the compass dial until the orientation arrow is exactly under the red magnetic needle.

The read-off point now shows the direction of B in degrees. Jot it down on the map or in a notebook.

Obstacles

You want to go from A to B but there is an *obstacle* in the way. It may be a lake, a swampy area, or perhaps a snowfield in the mountains (where it is better not to walk because dangerous drops may be hidden). So, as you cannot go straight on, you will have to make a detour, but afterwards, you still want to follow the route as planned.

1 Draw a line from A to B on the map.
2 You have seen that you will have to pass the obstacle on its right-hand side. Turn the whole compass (which is still on the oriented map) slowly to the right until the direction-of-travel arrow indicates you can pas the obstacle. The compass needle is now at 300°, for example.
3 You walk in the direction that the direction-of-travel arrow now indicates, until you come to the end of the obstacle on your left-hand side. We shall call this point C.

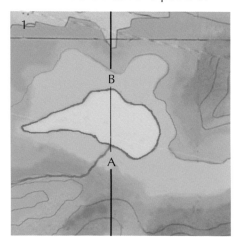

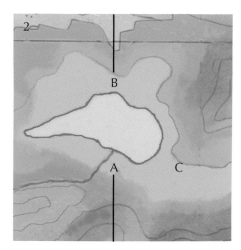

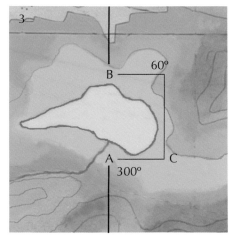

4 Now turn the whole compass so that the orientation arrow is again exactly under the red part of the

magnetic needle and follow the direction-of-travel arrow once again. You will now be travelling parallel to the imaginary line A-B. Follow this until you have passed the obstacle on your left-hand side.

5 Turn the entire compass until the magnetic needle is at 60° and follow the direction-of-travel line until your path crosses the imaginary line from A to B. Here, you can continue your original route.

Lost

You are lost, you don't know where you are.

1 Look around you for two points in the distance that are not too close together. These might be a hilltop, a church spire, etc. It should be something that is also shown on the map.
2 Point the direction-of-travel arrow at the first chosen feature.
3 Turn the compass dial until the orientation arrow is exactly under the red part of the magnetic needle.

Lay the whole compass on the oriented map in such a way that the direction-of-travel arrow is pointing to the first feature, both on the map and in reality. Use a pencil to draw the line of the direction-of-travel arrow on the map. Your present position will be somewhere along this line. You can often discover it by looking carefully at your surroundings and at the map.

4 If are still not sure about where you are, repeat the above-mentioned action with another point. When you draw the new line on the map, it will cross the first line. This is the point where you are now.

Hiking with the aid of a map

The 'In the Mountains' chapter (see p. 114) presents a number of suggestions when preparing for a hike. Do not just get up and go because you want to visit a certain place, an observation point, a lake, a waterfall, etc. First look at the map and work out how far you have to walk and what kind of ground you will be walking on — easy or difficult. Keep in mind that under normal circumstances you will walk about 4 km (2½ miles) an hour. A hiking map often shows places where you can stop for something to drink or even take public transport to get back home.

In the mountains

Altitudes

If you have to get your bearings in the mountains, the points of the compass do not play the most important role. Of course, it is important to know if you are walking on the north or the south slope. The south slope will receive sunshine the whole day and thus be quite warm, whereas the north side will lie in the shade.

* In the mountains, the altitude and the steepness of the track play a major role. Fig 98.1 shows a valley surrounded by high mountains in the Swiss Alps. In the middle there is a smaller mountain called *Schilt*. On the far side of the large valley you can clearly see that this mountain rises quite steeply about 400 metres above the valley. (The mountain is marked as 2 318 m high on the map. The road at the foot of the map is 1 938 m high.) The surrounding mountains are even higher and also very steep.
   For preparing and during your hike, you will need maps. These usually have a scale of 1:25 000 and show all the features of the landscape accurately. Every house, stream and road is shown on the map. The altitude levels

Fig 98.1

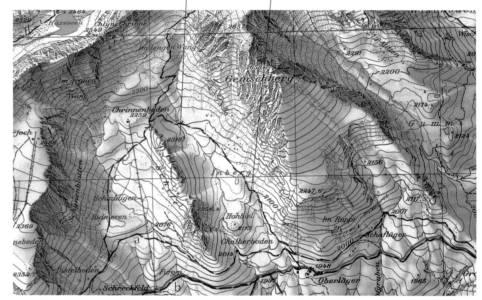

Fig 98.2

may be shown in colour. The map gives the altitudes of each hilltop and mountain top.
* If you want to go hiking in the mountains, you will have to know whether you will be walking through gently sloping areas or climbing steep faces. The contour lines give important information here. The contour lines are usually printed in light brown.
* Fig 98.2 shows a section of a topographical map of the valley shown in Fig 98.1 with a scale of 1:25 000. You will see the

mountain *Schilt* in the middle. The contour lines on this map are at 20 metres (about 60 feet) intervals. This interval may vary from map to map, depending on the scale. If the contour lines are quite far apart, the area is not so steep. If they are close together, you have a steep slope. When preparing a hike, you should watch out for such features. They determine how difficult the hike will be and therefore also its duration.
* The map shown in Fig 98.2 presents a couple of hiking routes.

If you look closely at the contour lines, you will see that the (red) hiking routes *a* and *b* run along almost the same contour line and are therefore quite flat. Mountain track *c* splits away from *a* and runs across a mountain top into the background. At the start, the track rises gradually (the contour lines lie at some distance from one another) but later it runs almost perpendicular to the contour lines, which means that it rises steeply. The chapter 'In the Mountains' provides more information, especially on how to calculate the duration of your hike.

Orientation in a town or village

When in an unfamiliar town or village, ask yourself the following questions:

- Who lived here in the past?
- What did the people live on? Fishing, mining, trade, crafts?
- Are there special buildings, such as palaces or churches? Has the town ever had fortifications and perhaps even a fort?
- What are the special attractions in this city? Museum, an extraordinary zoo, a stadium, etc.?

The shape of a town

The shape of a town often gives an indication of the history of the place and of the present situation. Old towns were often built around a church or a fort. The church spire rises high above the houses and is a clear point of recognition. This is very evident in many European towns dating from the Middle Ages.

Sometimes you can find the remains of old city walls. Within these walls, developers have had to stick to the old street plan, as in the Italian town of Sienna with its shell-shaped central square *Il Campo*. The streets radiate out from the square.

The city of Venice consists of lots of small islands with canals between them. The *Canale Grande* runs in an S-shape through the city. You have to know your way around here, otherwise you will frustrate yourself in dead-end streets.

A city like Amsterdam grew up on the waterfront hundreds of years ago. The horseshoe-shaped canals were dug in the seventeenth century. Nowadays, with their beautiful merchant houses on the quaysides, they still form the striking centre of the city.

In New York, the roads that run north-south are called 1st Avenue, 2nd Avenue, etc. while the streets that run east-west and cross the avenues are numbered and named East and West, such as 118th Street West.

The oldest part of the Swiss city of Bern lies in an elevation within a loop in the River Aare (see p. 101).

Sydney lies on an irregular bay that determines the shape of the city.

Of course you will be able to find your way in an unknown city by using a city map. But won't you be

Fig 99.1 Canal-side houses viewed from the Dom Spire in Utrecht, Netherlands

New York

Amsterdam

Bern

Sydney

paying most attention to the map and not to the unusual features that are all around you?

If you can prepare yourself in advance for a visit to a city and thus know a bit about its situation, you will enjoy the visit much more.

What should you look for in advance on atlases and road maps?

- ❀ How far is the city from where you are staying and how do you get there?
- ❀ What is the city's position in the landscape?
- ❀ Is the land flat or are there hills nearby? Are there forests in the vicinity? Does the city lie on the seashore, on a lake or on a river?

In the following section, we shall take the city of Florence as an example. However, the questions posed in this chapter can be applied to every city.

Florence lies in northern Italy, in the Province of Tuscany, roughly halfway between the border with Switzerland and Rome, the capital.

Florence lies in the valley of the River Arno, which flows from east to west through the city. It eventually

flows into the Tiranean Sea near Pisa, 70 km (40 miles) west of Florence. The hills rise gently on either side of the fertile valley. The hills become increasingly high on the north side, rising up to the *Apennine* mountain range. The city is surrounded by the typical Tuscan landscape with its narrow and elegant cypresses (see Fig 102.1).

What can a city map tell you about the city?

Piazza means square. Italian cities are full of squares. If the square is really large, it is often called *Piazzale*. A small square is called a *Piazzeta*. In Florence you will frequently see the word 'vecchio,' which means *old*. You will see it if you go to the old palace or the old marketplace, etc.

If you take a good look at the city map of Florence, you will see that the city is mainly built on the north side of the river. On the south side, the hills begin almost immediately at the river's edge. Can you see that the street layout in the old centre is very different from that of the rest of the town, where it is difficult to detect any pattern at all? The area between the River Arno and the Duomo (cathedral) is laid out like a box of square building blocks. The streets run parallel to one another and the side streets are at right angles to these. What could be the reason for this?

If you go back into the history of Florence, you will learn that, in AD 59, Julius Caesar, decreed that all Roman veterans were entitled to a piece of unbuilt land. There was a large piece of undeveloped land available in the valley of the River Arno. Not far from this spot lay the old Etruscan city of Fiesole.

Fiorentina was built up just like other Roman cities: the streets were laid out parallel or at right angles to one another, just like a chess board.

Fig 102.1 *Tuscan cypresses*

Fig 102.2 *Old city wall, Florence*

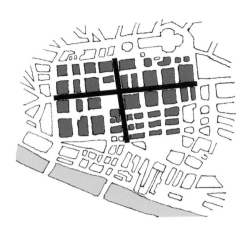

Fig 103.1 Street layout of old Roman town of Fiorentina

The central square, the Forum, lay at the junction of the two most important streets. If you look at the city map of the present-day city centre, you will see that the medieval town of Florence was built on the street pattern of the old Roman town of Fiorentina. The present-day street *Via Roma* was the *Via Calima* that ran north-south in the Roman Fiorentina. Under the *Via Strozzi* and the *Corso* lie the remains of the Roman *Decumanus maximus*, one of the two main streets. In the Middle Ages, the old market square, the *Mercato Vecchio*, lay at the location of the old Forum; this is now the *Piazza delle Republica*. You will not find many remains of the old city walls. There is a piece of city wall extending from Fort Belvedere almost down to the Arno on the south side of the river.

What is there to be seen in the city?

Let's go back to the city map. The centre lies to the north of the River

Fig 103.2 Street layout of old Roman town of Fiorentina

Arno. This is also where the most places of interest, such as the cathedral square and the old town hall (the *Palazzo Vecchio*) are to be found. Next to the town hall there is the large Uffizi Museum, which stretches down to the river. Duke Cosimo I de Medici had a passageway built from the *Palazzo Vecchio* (the town hall), over the *Ponte Vecchio*, the bridge with its many goldsmith's shops, to his new palace, the *Palazzo Pitti*.

Many buildings resemble forts. These are the city palaces that were occupied by the wealthy citizens of Florence. They are sometimes beautifully decorated on the outside. The large churches are covered with marble, they look like confectionary. There are many narrow streets and in the squares there are often large statues. It is a city that is a museum in itself, but these palaces and churches are even more beautiful inside, decorated with countless frescos, paintings, and statues.

The Renaissance

In a city that has existed for so long, it is interesting to find out which parts of history you can recognize as you walk through the streets. If you look

Piazza delle Republica   Baptistery   Duomo   Palazzo Vecchio   Museum Galeria Uffizi

Ponte Vecchio

Cosimo I passagel

River Arno

Palazzo Pitti   Fort Belvedere   old city wall

at the pictures in the travel guides, you will see that you are dealing with a late medieval town that flourished during the Renaissance (fifteenth to sixteenth centuries). This was a time of innovation in many areas. You can recognize this in the many large palaces and churches with their wonderful frescos and their paintings. Many artists worked in Florence during the Renaissance period. In those days, artists were not only painters or sculptors but masters of many artistic disciplines. Some of the artists were goldsmiths or architects as well. You may have heard of Michelangelo, Leonardo da Vinci, Alessandro Botticelli and Filippo Lippi.

Who paid all these artists?
This was mainly done by one influential family that enjoyed power for almost three hundred years, with short intermissions. This was the Medici family. Many members of this family were portrayed in paintings. Three of them were mainly responsible for a great many of the beautiful objects in the city. These were *Cosimo the Elder,* his grandson *Lorenzo dei Medici,* who was given the epithet *Il Magnifico (the Magnificent).* He helped change the political, intellectual and artistic life of the city. Finally, many decades later, there was *Cosimo I dei Medici,* who took control of the city by force. Cosimo was eventually successful in uniting the many smaller city states into the Duchy of Tuscany. One of the most important museums in the world, the Uffizi Museum, houses the many art treasures collected by the Medici family, which were later donated to the city of Florence.

However, it wasn't only the Medicis ... brought Florence renown. One of ... most important groups of the pop... tion was the Wool Guild. Wool was ...ported from England and woven ...o expensive fabrics that were sold

Fig 104.1 Sandro Botticelli: Madonna and child

Fig 104.2 Sandro Botticelli: Young man with seal depicting Cosimo the Elder

Fig 104.3 Michelangelo, Lorenzo de Medici, statue on his tomb

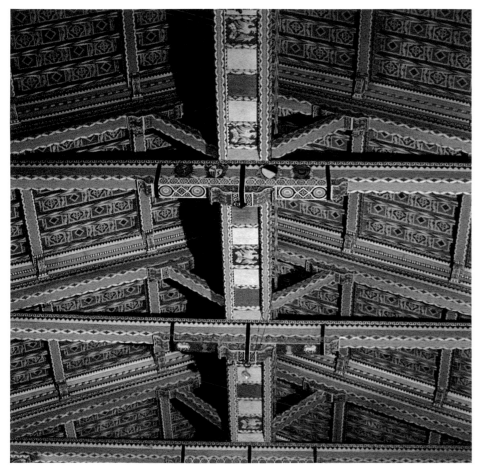

all over Europe. As a result, the Wool Guild gradually became richer and more powerful. Many Guild masters also had a seat in the town council. They wanted to show the world how important Florence was and the best way to do that was to build an enormous church. The construction of the cathedral (il Duomo), the cathedral of *Santa Maria del Fiore,* was started in 1296. The cathedral was designed to have the largest dome ever built: around 45 metres in diameter with a highest point at 114 metres. *Filippo Brunelleschi* proposed a completely new and daring way of building the dome. The entire construction took almost 150 years. The Duomo is still the highest building in the city and it determines the whole cityscape. When you walk through the city, you will see the cathedral rise above the houses wherever you go.

Fig 105.1　Interior of the roof of the Santa Maria del Monte church

Fig 105.2　Horses in the Neptune fountain on the Piazza della Signoria

Orientation when you come to the city

Is there a place where you can get a good view of the city — a tower, high building, or a hill?

In Florence, just above the Arno, is *Piazzale Michelangelo*. From the river you climb up a windy road and you can get a good view of the city from there.

The Arno flows roughly from east to west and the city lies in front of you to the north. From here you can see the main points of interest. The towers and exceptional buildings rise above the rest. This view may help you as you walk around town, so that you don't always have to consult the map.

Tips:

Go to the local tourist office just to check if the opening hours given in your travel guide are correct. They will also be able to tell you when interesting or exceptional events are taking place in the city.

Fig 106.1 Ponte Vecchio

Palazzo Pitti

Ponte Vecchio bridge

Connecting passageway from the Palazzo Vecchio to the Palazzo Pitti

Museum Galeria Uffizi

Palazzo Vecchio with campanile (tower)

Spire of Santa Maria Novella church

Fig 107.1 Palazzo Vecchio

Fig 107.2 Duomo

Fig 107.3 Procession in historical costume

Spire of Badia Fiorentina

Dome of San Lorenzo with the Medici chapel

White peaked roof of Baptistery

Campanile (bell tower)

Palazzo Bargello

Duomo

National Library

Santa Croce church

Fiesole with Roman theatre

9. At the Beach

At the beach, you have to take various factors into account: sea, wind and sun.

The combination of these three factors determines the pleasure you will have at the beach. At the same time, your safety and health also depend on them.

One important difference between the beaches of the North Sea and those of the Mediterranean Sea is that your have to pay more attention to the tides of the North Sea.

Tip:

When you arrive at the beach, you should check

* where the toilets are
* where you can get something to drink
* where you can get help if necessary (telephone number).

Lifeguards

The major beaches in Europe will have lifeguards. They monitor the beaches and warn the bathers if the sea is dangerous. Most of the rescue teamwork is done by volunteers. The rescue stations are open daily in the summer but often only at the weekend in the early or late summer. A first aid flag will be flying if they are in operation.

The sea: tides

The North Sea has a tidal cycle of lasting approximately 12.5 hours. Within that time the tide comes in (high water) and goes out (low water).

If the tide is going out (ebb), you will see the waves rolling towards

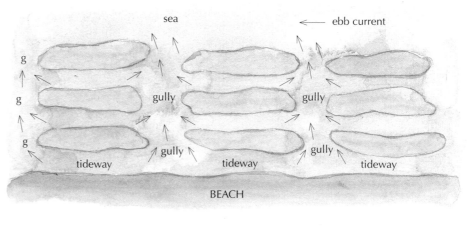

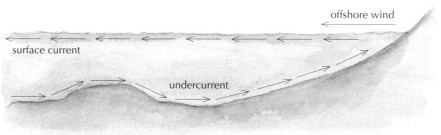

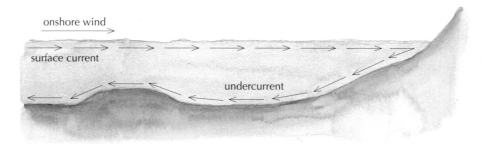

the beach, but there is an invisible flow going toward the sea just under the surface. For this reason, it is easy to swim from the beach into the sea but far more difficult to get back in again.

As the tide comes in (flow) the undercurrent is exactly the opposite. It goes towards the beach, thus reinforcing the movement of the waves, which arrive on the beach with more force.

There are often sandbanks just in front of the coast that break the waves. The working of the tides causes breaches in these sandbanks. The current through these passageways can become very strong — and is known as a 'rip tide.'

The wind

Offshore wind

When we speak of an *offshore wind,* this means that the wind is coming from the land — off the shore — and blowing towards the sea. With an offshore wind, the force of the ebb tide is strengthened. It is now even easier to swim into the sea or to drift away on an airbed, but the way back is particularly difficult because the wind also causes waves on top of the water. You have to swim or paddle against these.

Tip:
Do not use an airbed or other type of float or raft if there is an offshore wind.

If the tide is coming in, there will be a current going towards the shore, but if there is a strong offshore wind, swimming may still be dangerous.

If there is an offshore wind of wind force 2 or more (a moderate wind),

the beach services (lifeguards, police) will probably raise a yellow flag, which means: dangerous swimming, do not use floating material.

Onshore wind

With an onshore wind, the wind comes from the sea, blowing toward the beach. The situation is different to that described above. During an outgoing tide (ebb), there is an undercurrent going towards the sea. The wind makes the waves more powerful. If you are tossed about by a large wave, you may come in the undercurrent and be carried away from the beach.

During an incoming tide (flow) an onshore wind is completely harmless.

Swimming

* Do not go too far into the sea. If the sea is calm, you can go in up to your waist. If the sea is rougher and there are large waves, it is advisable not to go in so deep. Pay attention to any flags that might be flying:
  — A yellow flag means: swimming is dangerous, do not go in too deep!
  — A red flag means: swimming prohibited.

Tips:
* Do not swim too far out into the sea, away from the beach.
* Make sure that you never go in so deep that you cannot stand on the seabed!
* Never allow small children to go in the sea on their own.
* Rescue teams strongly advise you not to use airbeds, inflatable animals, boats, tyres, etc. You can easily drift away from the coast without really noticing it. If you go too far into the sea on an

airbed, it is often difficult to get back. People usually use cheap airbeds on the beach. They usually only have one air chamber. If it leaks, the airbed will sink.

In cases of trouble

If you get into trouble while in the sea, you can try to attract the attention of the lifeguards or rescue team by waving with two arms (crossing one another above your head). If they see this, they will jump into action.

Do not overestimate yourself in the water. Be sure to get back to the beach before you get too tired or too cold. You must be particularly careful if the water is cold.

If you see someone in difficulty in the water, use your mobile phone to

alert the rescue team or emergency services, or run to the nearest restaurant or beach pavilion to alert the services there.

The sun

If you are on the beach the whole day, it is advisable to use plenty of suntan lotion. The sun will get brighter as the day goes on and the chance of sunburn will be highest between noon and 3 o'clock in the afternoon.

It is actually better not to lie in the sun in the afternoon, but to do something so that the wind and water can cool you down a bit. Try to keep in the shade during these hours. It is important to drink enough liquid. The heat will cost you moisture and salt. With small children, you must ensure that their heads stay cool. Give them a sunhat that allows air through the material (see pattern for the home-made hat, p.12).

Sunburn and sunstroke

There is often a refreshing wind on the beach. As a result, you simply don't notice that you have exposed yourself to the sun for too long, and you may suffer from sunburn. The skin becomes red and painful. If you are in the sun without a sunhat for too long, you can become quite dizzy and even suffer from sunstroke.

Other problems on the beach

Jellyfish

There may be jellyfish on the beach. Be careful when walking in your bare feet, a sting from a jellyfish feels like a severe nettle sting. Red marks occur around the place of the sting. Do not rub or scratch even although it may itch. The jellyfish releases miniscule hollow arrows that stick in your skin. Rubbing breaks these arrows and makes the skin even itchier. You can also request help at the first-aid post.

Tip:
Due to certain stinging fish as well as the possibility of glass in the sand, it is sensible to get (small) children to wear (water) sandals on the beach. Make sure they fit well and are not too big, otherwise the sea will wash the shoes off their feet.

Lost children

Children can easily get lost on a crowded beach. For this reason, you should try to settle in at a spot that is easily recognized. Some beaches have posts with signs of animals on them. Others have clearly recognizable features. As soon as you settle in, show your children where you are. If there is a feature they can use, they will easily be able to find their way back. You can also mark your own spot by hoisting a small flag or by flying a small kite (if there is enough wind). If your child gets lost, contact the lifeguard or rescue team. They will help you in your search. If a child has been found and has been brought to the rescue station, a white flag with a blue question mark will be raised.

Tips:
* A child that wanders off usually goes off with the sun and/or the wind behind him or her. This is the first direction in which you should go searching.
* Give small children a name plate with their name and an address where the parents can be contacted. On some beaches, the beach pavilions will issue 'hospital' bracelets for young children.
* You can also write your mobile phone number on the back of your child's hand.

What not to do

On some North Sea beaches, you are not allowed to fly kites or walk dogs. Pets may be refused by the lifeguard. Flying kites is sometimes only allowed in certain places.

There are often signs at the entrance to the beach stating what is (not) allowed on the beach and what the various flags mean.

Beach flags

These will vary from place to place, but many codes are common all over Europe.

Green flag: Everything is safe. Swimming allowed.

Yellow flag: It is dangerous to go into the sea; it is better not to go for a swim.

Red flag: Swimming prohibited.

Red flag with blue square: No floating items allowed; the offshore wind will make it difficult to get back to the beach.

White flag with a blue question mark: Child found.

10. In the Mountains

Guests in nature

When in the countryside, try to behave as a proper guest and be careful with everything around you. Take all leftovers and other garbage with you as you go, and put it in a garbage bin. Many flowers are protected species. Do not pick them, even if there are lots of them.

You should only light fires at places where this is specifically allowed.

Do not allow children to roll stones down the slope, even if it is an exciting game. It could dislodge more stones and someone lower down might easily be hit.

There are 'rules' for going hiking in the mountains. The most important of these are:

* Prepare well for your hike. You should know where to go if you encounter difficulty.
* When you get back, think about whether or not there were differences between your plans and the actual hike. Learn from your mistakes or from things that went differently than you expected.

Be careful!
The situation in the mountains and the climatic circumstances are different from those to which you are accustomed. Do not underestimate a hike in the mountains.

With or without a guide

Hiking in the mountains is a fantastic experience, especially for families that live in the city or in an area without hills. If you go walking in the mountains with your children on several consecutive trips, they will soon learn how to cope in an exceptional part of nature. Every year you will be able to undertake longer hikes and explore new mountainous areas. Such hikes will usually involve marked routes so that you will not need a guide.

Going on a day hike with a guide may be a special experience for children of eleven years and older who can walk well. The guide may take you into the high mountains, over rocks, snow and ice. He or she will know the surroundings and can take you to places where you would normally never go. The guide will also give you a few basic pieces of information that you should know before setting out on this kind of trip.

Tips:
* If you are going with children, take it easy with them at the start and slowly build up their fitness as the vacation progresses.
* Always adapt your hikes to the youngest and/or the weakest. Be careful about going on a hike with other people if you do not know from experience what you, or they, are capable of.

Gentians: do not pluck these!

What are children capable of?

Experienced mountain guides always issue the same warning: do not force children beyond their limits. They regard children of twelve to fourteen years old — not younger — as being capable of completing a full day's hike.

Children up to five years old

Children that you can take with you in a papoose or backpack are happy with a small walk, especially if they get the chance to romp around. The stones on the path, a small waterfall or rocks that they can climb on often provide enough challenge for them. It is better not to take them in a lift that ascends or descends too much in a short time.

* Even slightly older children should not be encouraged to go on a hike at high altitude; do not ascend more than 1 500–1 600 m (5 000 ft). For these children, too, it is better not to ascend or descend too much in a short time, as in a lift for example. Allow them to acclimatize gradually to higher areas. Do not expose them to too much sun in the mountains.
* With children aged 3 or 4, you can embark on a hike on not-too-steep ground for about an hour. Be sure to take enough breaks and allow them enough opportunity to play as they go. Telling a story during the last stages may help in conquering the fatigue. The strongest parent may have to carry them occasionally.

From five to seven years old

You can begin to undertake real hikes with kids of five to seven years. One or two hours of good walking are

possible, but they may have to take a break regularly and play as they go. To them, the hike should be interesting and variable. You should stay under 3 000 metres (10 000 ft).

Eight and nine years old

Children are very enterprising at this age. You can go on whole-day hikes, depending on their age, as long as you ensure that there are enough breaks. They should also have the opportunity for playing, such a building a dam in the river, etc. You should realize that a hike that normally takes four hours will occupy the whole day. Stay under 3 000 metres (10 000 feet). To these kids, following a path into the unknown is an exciting challenge. Let them lead the group and look for the markings or signs. Tell them that them should always wait at forks in the road or track and that they should always be within the parents' hearing range.

Ten years and older

You can embark on serious day hikes with children of 10–12 years and older. You can also go above 3 000 metres (10 000 ft). However, you should gradually build up their fitness over the vacation. Do not go on hikes that are too long in the first few days

of the vacation. This will demand too much effort and they may develop an aversion to such activity. Remember to adapt the hike to the youngest member of the family, and take into account that children do not have the stamina of adults.

What should you wear?

* Solid mountain boots (that support the ankles) with a good sole underneath. Trainers, gym shoes and other light shoes are not suitable. The chance of a twisted ankle or sprained foot is too great. Mountain boots give much better support, especially when descending. Children usually walk well in light mountain boots.
* When buying mountain boots, make sure that the upper part is waterproof, otherwise you will get wet feet if it rains. Goretex mountain boots will keep your feet nice and dry. The boots should not be too tight.
* Absorbent socks.
* Comfortable but strong trousers, which also dry quickly after a shower of rain. Denim jeans take a long time to dry.
* Clothes that absorb moisture eas-

ily. You can wear a thermal vest under your shirt.

It might be pleasant and warm in the valley but rather chilly up in the hills. Moreover, the weather in the mountains can change rapidly. A fleece jacket is not heavy and can provide enough warmth. If you depart in good weather, you can still end up with rain later on. So be prepared with a windcheater or raincoat. It is better to wear several thin layers than one thick layer.

What should you take with you?

Rucksack

Choose a rucksack that is not too large or heavy. An interior frame is important because it ensures that the weight is spread evenly across your back, and also allows ventilation. Belts that keep the rucksack in position are good for longer hikes.

Do not fill the rucksack too full and place the heavier objects (thermos flask) as close to your back as possible. Children are often pleased to carry a backpack. Give them a small one and do not make it too heavy. Three kg (7 lb) is quite sufficient for a child of five; a ten-year-old can carry 5 kg (11 lb).

In addition

* Sunglasses and something to protect your head (with peak).
* Suntan lotion.
* A good hiking map (with a scale of 1:25 000 or 1:50 000)
* A compass.
* An altimeter if desirable.
* Binoculars.
* Guide to animals, plants, and/or mushrooms.
* Cash, telephone number of the emergency services, a mobile

phone (which may not always work in the mountains).

* Pen and paper.
* First-aid kit (see p. 18), insulation foil (thin aluminium foil) for survival if caught out by weather.

Food and drink

* Tea or fruit juice. It is important to have enough food and (especially) liquid with you. Let every member of the family carry his or her own flask.
* Sandwiches with a hearty or savoury filling.
* Fruit that will not burst open.
* Something tasty for the children.

Preparations

* You must realize that 95% of the success of your hike, and certainly your safety, depends on your own preparations. Examine the map before you set out and pay particular attention to:
  — the differences in altitude: it best to climb first;
  — the length of the hike;
  — how much time is required for the various of the hike;
  — alternative routes;
  — in cases of emergency, can you turn and go back again?
  — whether there is a restaurant or a mountain hut available?
  — is there a place where you can take a bus or train home back?
* Ask about the lie of the land at the local tourist office or climbing centre. There may be snow at the top, even in the summer.
* Ask advice from a local guide if you wish to hike from hut to hut with children.

Rules

* Try to do the hardest part on the outward leg of the journey. As the hike progresses, the walking speed will gradually drop. If you want to ensure that there are enough breaks for the children, note that four hours of hiking will take the whole day.
* If you want to cross a section of snow-covered ground (do not do this with children), you should start out as early as possible. On warm days the snow will become soft and could be dangerous.
* Study the map regularly as you go.
* While you are walking, pay particular attention to road markings and forks in the road/track. You can place your own marking, such as small cairns for example.
* Can you recognize other particular features?
* Stay on the paths. Only leave the path if you can view the whole area you are to cross.
* Do not cut off any curves or zigzags to shorten the route. A steep descent will cost extra energy.
* Make sure you and the children take sufficient breaks but also that you have enough leeway to complete the hike comfortably, even if the children are tired or the hike takes longer than expected.
* Always keep an eye on the weather. This can be done by checking the altimeter at each point marked on the map. An altimeter works on air pressure, so any change in air pressure will show a deviation in relation to the value shown on the map.
  A change in air pressure indicates a change in the weather. In that case, shorten your hike and turn back if possible when the weather changes, or when you notice that you have taken longer

than expected to complete a particular section.

* Walk or climb directly under your child if you have to ascend a difficult path. If necessary, take some rope with you. Tie it around your child's waist and hold a loop firmly in your hand.
* Be careful about getting too much sun. In the mountains, the UV effect is reinforced, although you will not notice this due to the lower temperatures and stronger wind.

How long will it take?

In general, it will take you 15 minutes to walk a kilometre on a flat track. So in an hour, you will about 4 kilometres (2½ miles).

* But if you have to ascend or descend, allow yourself more time. Every ascent of 100 m (330 feet) needs an additional 20 minutes more
  You may need to add a bit of time for breaks.

Fig 117.1 A little cairn

Contour lines

In the figure on the right, the brown lines indicate the contours. The distance between the lines is 20 m (65 feet).

The solid black line represents a footpath that runs mainly along one of the contours. This means that this path will not ascend or descend very much.

The dashed line represents a mountain track that runs almost at right angles to the contours, showing it rises steeply.

The closer the contour lines are, the steeper the ground.

The weather

Many inexperienced people have been caught out by bad weather in the mountains because they had not prepared for their hike properly, or because they did not take possible weather changes into account.

Even if the weather forecast is good, the weather in the mountains can be very changeable. If you are planning a hike, check the weather forecast the evening before and ask about the local weather conditions before you go. Even if the weather forecast is good, it can still be damp

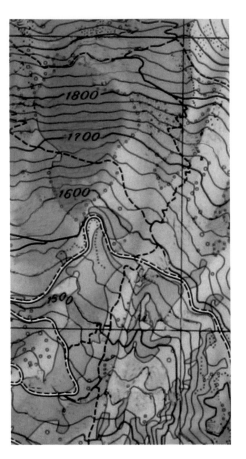

in the valley in the morning. The television pictures from the mountain station will show what kind of weather there is in the mountains. Pay attention to the sky and the temperature as you go. Good weather will not change very rapidly if:

* there is dew in the morning;
* it is clear and cold in the morning;
* there is a strong breeze;
* there are woolpacks in the sky in the afternoon.

There is a chance of poor weather or a change in the weather if:

* it is warm and clammy in the morning;
* the surroundings appear very sharp and the sun is already burning your skin;
* you see feathered clouds in the sky;
* you can see woolpacks expanding upwards rapidly.

There is a big chance of thunder if you see clouds that resemble an anvil and the air is sultry.

How far away is the storm?

Count the number of seconds between the flash of lightning and the sound of thunder. Divide it by three and this will tell you how far away the storm is in kilometres (divide by 5 for miles). If you do this a few times, you will know how fast the storm is approaching.

Plan a short hike if bad weather is on the way.

What should I do if ...?

Accidents

* Do not move the casualty unless it is dangerous to leave them where they are.
* Keep the casualty warm and dry.
* Apply first aid if necessary.
* Try to get help by using your mobile phone. Try to describe where you are as accurately as possible. Note it on the map.
* Never leave a wounded person behind on his or her own. Only do so if your own life is in danger.
* Be very careful if you have to go for help; you are already a little tense due to the accident. If possible, go back the way you came and do not look for a new path across unknown terrain.
* A helicopter needs a piece of flat open ground of approximately 20 metres (70 feet) across to land. If possible, mark this area with a coloured jacket. The signal for *I need help* is standing straight up with your arms raised diagonally, the letter Y.

Bad weather: mist

* You will be able to see a slowly approaching mist and you can prepare yourself for it. Determine where you are. Keep to the road or path. Only continue if you know where you are going. Otherwise go back the way you came.
* If you are suddenly surrounded bymist and you are not on a track-kyou may lose your bearings. In cases of emergency, wait until the visibility improves.
* If necessary, seek shelter, for example under an overhang, and try to keep warm.

  A piece of rope 25 m (80 ft) long can help: the group can remain at one spot while one person takes one end of the rope along the track until he or she reaches another safe spot. A jerk on the rope or a yell lets the others know that they should follow the rope.

Heavy weather with lots of rain

* Seek shelter, perhaps under overhanging rocks.
* Do not go too close to a stream. If there is much rain, it may suddenly burst its banks.

Thunder

* You will probably be able to see or hear a thunderstorm coming well in advance. Seek a safe place to shelter immediately.
* Lightning may strike near protruding rocks or trees standing alone. Avoid mountain tops, a rocky ridge or a rocky plateau and try to find a spot that is as dry as possible not too close to the top.
* Water and moisture conduct electricity from lightning. Stay away from lakes and streams and do not stand under overhanging rocks, where the ground is moist.
* Keep your feet together; in that way no current will pass between your feet.
* Make sure that there is no iron in the vicinity; check your own equipment. Place rucksacks and other iron objects at some distance from the group, as they may attract lightning.
* If the ground is flat all around you, lie down.

11. Games Along the Way

In this section, to keep the explanations short, we shall use 'he' to represent both boys and girls.

Visual games

Who sees the first ...
♟ ✿ ✳ ⌂ 🚗

Decide what you are going to look for. It may be something easy, such as the colour red for example. It will become more difficult if you decide on an object as well: *red* and *a coat*.

But you can, of course, decide on unusual things, such as a weathervane on a spire.

11 or 22
♟ ✿ ✳ ⌂ 🚗

First agree on who is to start and who is next. The first person looks for a car number plate with two consecutive 'ones' in it. The next person looks for a number plate with two 'twos.'

Variation:
You can give children several number or letter combinations. Then they have to try to find these combinations on the number plates of cars.

Alphabet on your travels
♟ ✿ ✂ 3⁺ ✳ ⌂ 🚗

You can go through the alphabet as you travel by car or train.

Take the first letter of the alphabet. The person who first sees an object beginning with the letter 'a' should shout it out. This could be an automobile, an ape, the Adriatic Sea, an apple, etc. When 'a' is done, you go

on to 'b.' Continue like this until the entire alphabet has been covered. If it takes too long before something comes up, you can simply decide to move on to the next letter.

Counting cars
♟ ✿ ✂ ✳ ⌂ 🚗

How many cars:
* are red
* have the same letters on the number plate

* have four passengers
* have a trailer, etc. ?

How many ... can you count?
♟ ✿ ✂ ✳ ⌂ 🚗

Every child chooses his own object, a red car, a farmhouse, a junction, etc.

Each child counts the number of times he sees this object during the journey. The winner is the person who first reaches ten or twenty.

Animal, vegetable or mineral?
♿ ♾ ⚔ 3⁺ ⌂ 🚗

One of the players thinks up a word. The others now ask if it is an animal, vegetable, or mineral.

The first player answers which of the three. After this, he may only answer 'yes' or 'no' to all other questions.

The person who first guesses the right answer thinks up the next word.

Tongue-twisters
♿ ♾ ✺ ⌂ 🚗

This involves a number of difficult words spoken consecutively. Try to say one of the following sentences as quickly as possible without making mistakes:

- She sells sea shells on the sea-shore.
- A box of biscuits, a batch of mixed biscuits.
- Red lorry, yellow lorry, red lorry, yellow lorry.
- Unique New York.
- Six thick thistle sticks. Six thick thistles stick.
- Mrs Smith's Fish Sauce Shop.

I'm going on a journey and I'll take ...
♿ ♾ ⚔ 3⁺ ⌂ 🚗

Someone says: I'm going on a journey and I'll take a suitcase with me. The second person says: I'm going on a journey and I'll take a suitcase and a toothbrush (or any other object). The third person repeats this and adds another object. The next person repeats what the last person said and adds another object. Everyone has to repeat all the objects and add one to the list. If someone makes a mistake, he is out.

What didn't I say?
♿ ♾ ⚔ 3⁺ ⌂ 🚗

Think up a story. Tell it but leave out part of it. Now the others have to fill in the missing piece. Everyone gets a turn and can think up anything, even if it is nonsense.

ABC
♾ ⚔ 3⁺ ⌂ 🚗

One of the children starts by repeating the alphabet. He deliberately leaves out one letter. When he has finished, the next person repeats the alphabet and leaves out two letters — the letter the previous person left out and one of his own choice.

The next person repeats the alphabet and leaves out the previous two letters and any other letter of his choice. When someone makes a mistake, he is out. The game goes on until there is a winner.

Variation:

You can also train your memory by talking about something that really happened a while ago, and then asking if anyone knows exactly what happened.

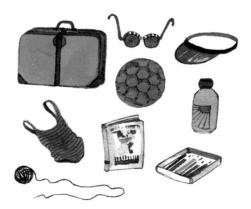

Just a minute
🐞 ✂ 3⁺ ⌂ 🚗

Choose a subject (what I am going to do tomorrow, for example) and have one of the others talk about that for a minute.

With older children, you can make it more complicated by choosing another subject in addition to the first one, such as

1 *what I am going to do tomorrow* and
2 *water.*

No ... without
🐞 ✂ 2⁺ ⌂ 🚗

You say, for example: 'No house ...' One of the others has to answer: '... without a roof.' You can think up lots of variations:

* no car ... without wheels.
* no shoes ... without soles.
* no face ... without eyes.
* no plane ... without wings.

Continuing story
🐞 ✂ 3⁺ ⌂ 🚗

✤ cards with random pictures

Before you go, make a number of cards on which an object has been drawn or cut out from a magazine, etc. Shuffle the cards and get the children to pick one without looking at it.

One of the children begins telling a story about what is shown on his card. Then the first child says to the next: you can continue the story. This child should try to continue the story but the contents of the story should fit in with what is shown on his card.

You cannot say 'eh ...'
🐞 ✂ 3⁺ ⌂ 🚗

Choose a subject and get one of the children to talk about it for a minute.

During the talk, he is not allowed to say either of two words: 'eh..' and another word that is often associated with the subject. If he says *eh* or the other word, he is out and it is the next child's turn.

Guessing games

Riddles
🐞 🐞 ✂ ✳ ⌂ 🚗

What talks without a mouth?   (echo)

When is the best time to have lunch?   (after breakfast)

When should you strike a match?   (when it gets violent)

What makes a man bald-headed?   (lack of hair)

What always ends everything?   (the letter g)

What does one need most in the long run?   (your breath)

What animal keeps the best time?   (a watchdog)

Why should you always carry a watch when crossing a desert?   (because it has a spring in it)

There are countless riddles, books full of them. If your children like riddles, buy a book for the journey.

Who are you thinking of?
🐞 🐞 ✂ 3⁺ ♀ 🚗

By asking questions, everyone tries to find out who the quizmaster is thinking of. He can only answer 'yes' or 'no.' If the answer is 'yes' the person asking the question may ask again. If it is 'no,' it is the next person's turn. The person who guesses correctly then thinks of someone else.

Odd man out
🐞 🐞 ✂ 3⁺ ♀ 🚗

Someone mentions things or people that apparently belong together, but there is one that doesn't quite fit.

Examples:
House-door-roof-knife-stairs
Painter-carpenter-bricklayer-plumber-teacher
London-Birmingham-Paris-Liverpool-Edinburgh
Get the children to say which is the odd man out. Then one of the children can think up another series of five.

Counting blind

Give everyone an equal number of matchsticks, ten for instance. Everyone hides a certain number (this can also be none) in a closed hand. The players have to guess how many matchsticks there are in all the hands added together. The person who guesses correctly gets the matchsticks from the other hands. The game is repeated until finally one of the players has no matchsticks left. He is out. You can continue until someone has all the matchsticks, or you can stop at this point and the one with the most matchsticks is the winner.

Who is it?

A guessing game for children who know one another. Everyone is given a piece of paper and he must write down a number of his favourite things: favourite meal, hobby, future job, etc. You must agree in advance what kinds of things are to be written down.

Then everyone folds up his piece of paper and they are all put together and mixed up. Everyone takes one and reads what is written there. They have to guess, one by one, who the owner of the paper is.

Guessing a number
3⁺

Someone thinks of a number under 100. The others ask questions to try to find out what this number is. The first person may only answer 'yes' or 'no.'

Questions may be, for example: *Is it an even number, does it consist of two digits, is it part of the five-times table?*

Whoever guesses right can then think up a number.

Pass on the song!
4⁺

Someone thinks of a song and taps the rhythm of the first line on his neighbour's back. He then has to tap this rhythm on the next person's back, even although he or she does not know what the song is. This process goes on until the last person is reached. The last person has to guess which song it is.

Variation:

One of the adults claps the rhythm of a song and the others try to guess which song this is.

Counting money
various coins

Take a number of coins with different values. Pass them on one by one. Everyone can see them for just a moment. When all the coins have been returned, the others have to say how much money has gone through their hands.

What do I look like today?
blindfold

Someone puts on a blindfold or holds a hand in front of his eyes. Then he tries to describe what one of the others looks like, the clothes he is wearing, etc.

How long is a mile?

Give the children a sign when they have to close their eyes. This is when the game begins. When they think that they have travelled one mile (or kilometre), they should say 'yes' and open their eyes. The milometer will indicate how accurate they were.

Variation:

You may see a bridge or a spire in the distance.

Get everyone to guess how many seconds it will take until the car reaches that point.

Games with pencil and paper

Drawing a story
♟ ❀ ✻ ⛪ 🚗 ✎

Tell a short story and get the children to draw it as you go.

Head, body and legs
♟ ❀ 2⁺ ⛪ 🚗 ✎

The first person begins at the top of the paper. He draws a head and neck and everything else that belongs here. The neck ends with two small vertical lines.

The paper is folded over exactly at these lines so that no one can see what has been drawn. Only the two small lines are visible and the next person has to draw the body attached to these lines. He draws what he wants, down to the hips. When he is finished, the paper is again folded so that the next per-son can see where the last person stopped. The next artist then has to draw the legs.

When this has been done, the paper is opened and a rather remark-able figure will appear. Of course, if there are more players, you can divide the body into more pieces to be drawn.

Hangman
❀ ✂ 2⁺ ⛪ 🚗 ✎

One person thinks of a word and jots down a dash for each letter. The other player asks if a certain letter, 'o' for instance, occurs in the word. If yes, the first person writes 'o' in the appropriate place in the word.

If a letter is mentioned that does not occur in the word, the first player can draw the first line of the gallows. After guessing wrongly a number of times, the asker will be faced with a fully-drawn gallows and he or she is out.

Noughts and crosses
♟ ❀ 2 ⛪ 🚗 ✎

Draw two vertical and two horizontal lines, thus creating nine boxes.

Agree who is to start. One of the players begins by placing a cross in one of the boxes. The other player places a nought in another box. The winner is the first person to place three noughts or crosses in a row: horizontally, vertically or diagonally. Of course, each player has to prevent the other player from doing this first.

Variation:
It is much more difficult if you draw three horizontal and three vertical lines, thus producing sixteen boxes.

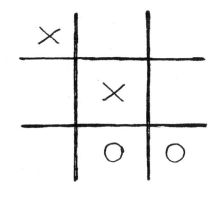

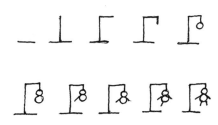

Initials
☗ ☻ ✕ 2⁺ ⌂ 🚌 ✎

Draw eleven horizontal and eleven vertical lines on a piece of paper, thus creating a square with 10 × 10 boxes. You can also use squared paper.

Each player places his or her initial in one of the boxes. He is not allowed to place two initials from the same player in boxes next to one another. Every box is worth one point. The person who gains the most points is the winner.

Hiring a room
☗ ☻ ✕ 2⁺ ⌂ 🚌 ✎

Place a horizontal row of ten dots (it may be more if you like) at a regular distance from one another. Place a new row exactly under the first row. Do this until you have ten rows.

The game can now begin. The first player can join two dots, either vertically or horizontally, by drawing a line between them. Then it is the other player's turn. They take turns to draw lines.

After a while, if two horizontal lines have been joined by a vertical line, it will only take one more line to make a complete square. If a player does this, he can claim this box by putting his initial in it. It has become his room. Each time someone has claimed a room, he gets an extra turn. The person with the most rooms is the winner.

The bus is full
☗ ☻ ✕ ✳ ⌂ 🚌 ✎

Draw a bus with lots of windows. Draw one or more people behind these windows. Tell a story about the people you have drawn. Then the next person can draw someone at the window and talk about him or her.

Finishing the drawing
☗ ☻ ✕ ✳ ⌂ 🚌 ✎

One of the players draws a random shape on a piece of paper. This may be a square, a circle, the outline of a house, etc. The other players should now try to convert this shape into something else. A square can become a box, a circle can become a clock, etc.

How many names do you know?
☻ ✕ 3⁺ ⌂ 🚌 ✎

Take a first name and let the children write down as many names as they can think of that begin with the same letter.

Trailer
☻ ✕ 2⁺ ⌂ 🚌 ✎

The *trailer* is the next word that you can attach to the first word. The idea is to create a term that is as long as possible:

Bicycle
Bicycle clip
Bicycle clip holder
Bicycle clip holder polish
The person who can make a term
    with the most trailers is the winner.

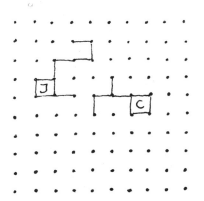

Back to front

One of the children thinks up a word that can be said backwards. He or she can use pencil and paper if necessary.

Then the word is said and whoever is the first to say it properly gets to think up the next word.

Advertisement

Fold a number of sheets of paper into four, six or eight strips. Agree on the order that the information in the advertisement is to be placed: object, size, colour, quality, etc. Each player gets a sheet of paper and can fill in the first strip — the object for sale (or hire). Then the strip is folded over so that the next person cannot see it, and the sheet is passed on to the next player. He or she fills in the information for the advert. When all the strips have been filled in, all the advertisements are read out.

Variation:

You can play the same game with a story. Everyone writes a sentence without the last word. Then the paper is folded over and the last word is written on a new strip in such a way that the previous strip cannot be read. The sentence written by the next person must begin with this last word. And so on.

An animal with nine points

❖ *blank cards*

Place nine clear points or dashes on the cards in advance. Deal out the cards. Give everyone instructions what he or she should draw. Each drawing has to pass through all the points or dashes. When everyone is finished, you can compare the drawings.

Secret language

The are lots of ways to make a secret language. The easiest way is to give all the letters a number, such as A=1, B=2, etc.

It is more complicated if A=5, B=6, etc.

Another possibility is A=E, B=F, etc.

You can also make a combination of both, where the vowels are given a different symbol from the consonants.

You can also give every letter a small symbol, a kind of hieroglyph.

A= a plate, B= a cup, C=a fork, etc.

How many words with ...

Take a word, such as *sun,* for example.

The children should write down as many words as they can think of in which the word *sun* occurs.

I have 100

Everyone should try to as quickly as possible to create a sum that gives 100 as the answer, or as close as possible.

For every sign (+ − × ÷) in the calculation you get a point.

$(9 \times 9) + 20 - 1 = 100$ produces 3 points.

$(6 \times 6) + 9 + (5 \times 8) + 7 - 2 = 100$ produces 6 points.

Variation:

You can give the children five numbers and ask them to combine these to make 50 or any number of your choice. For example: 8, 7, 6, 5, 4. This could be: $(5 - 4) \times (7 \times 6) + 8$

My sentence rhymes

Say any short sentence. Now the others have to think of a sentence where the last word rhymes with the last word of the first sentence. Give

the children plenty of time. They can use pencil and paper if they like. The child who first thinks up a rhyming sentence can think up the next sentence.

With older children, you can try if they can think up a second or third rhyming sentence.

Making new words
🌼 ✕ ✳ ⛫ 🚗 ✎

Give the children a word, such as *mountain* for example. With these eight letters, the children have to think up as many new words as possible. This can be *mount,* or *man,* or *ton,* etc.

See who can make the most words. You can give extra points for difficult words.

Compound words
🌼 ✕ 3⁺ ⛫ 🚗 ✎

See 'Indoors and / or Outdoors Games,' p.172.

Counting to one hundred
🌼 ✕ ✳ ⛫ 🚗 ✎

Write down the first two numbers from the number plates of cars on the road. Make a list and add them up as you go. The first person to reach one hundred is the winner. This obviously works better on less busy roads.

Battleships
🌼 ✕ 2 ⛫ 🚗 ✎

Both players draw two squares consisting of 10 x 10 boxes on a sheet of paper. That means eleven vertical and eleven horizontal lines. Place numbers along the vertical edge (1 to 10) and letters along the horizontal edge (A to J).

Each player has his or her own navy:

1 battleship, covering 4 boxes
2 cruisers, covering 3 boxes
2 destroyers, covering 2 boxes
3 submarines, covering 1 box.

Now each player places his or her navy in this square in such a way that the ships are parallel to one of the edges (they cannot lie diagonally).

Now the battle begins. Agree on who is to start. The first player fires on the enemy. In other words, he or she names a box, such as B7, for example. The other person must say whether or not he or she has been hit, in other words, if a ship is located at this place. But he or she need not say which kind of ship has been hit, so that the attacker does not know if he or she has hit a destroyer or has hit a battleship. A battleship only sinks if it has been hit four times.

The attacker notes down the box in which the stricken ship lies. He or she also jots down the shots that missed. In this way, he or she can try to find out in which boxes his enemy's ships are located.

After a hit, the attacker can shoot a second time. If a ship has been sunk, this must be stated.

The aim is to sink the enemy's ships as soon as possible.

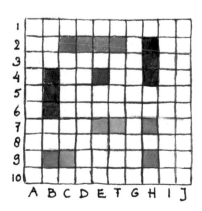

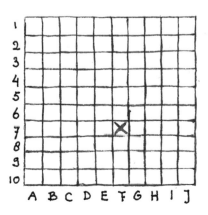

Games to stretch your muscles

Hands and feet
♉ ♒ ♒ ✕ ❄ ♀ 🚗

When you stop at a parking place, step out and get your limbs moving.

First your hands: clap twice with your hands above your head. Then twice in front of your body, then twice against your thighs.

Now it's time for your legs: stamp each of your feet twice on the ground, then make two jumps using both feet. Do this again using one leg, then the other.

You can repeat this exercise several times and vary it as you please.

A quick lap
♉ ♒ ♒ ✕ ❄ ♀ 🚗

Look for a suitable spot and jog around it together. You can vary your arm and leg movements as you jog.

Shoulder charge
♒ ♒ ✕ 2⁺ ♀ 🚗

A very simple game to get the blood flowing. Two players stand at a distance of two metres from one another on grass or soft ground. They lift one of their feet off the ground and cross their arms. They hop towards one another and push against one another, shoulder to shoulder. Who is first to lose his or her balance?

Jumping roundabout
♒ ♒ ✕ 3⁺ ♀ 🚗
✤ A piece of rope

Someone turns around holding a piece of rope about 20 cm from the ground. The others stand around and have to jump over the rope as it comes round. If the rope hits them, they are out.

Leapfrog
♒ ✕ 3⁺ ♀ 🚗

This is a very old game. You can even see it on old paintings from the seventeenth century.

One child bends over. The others take a small run and jump over him or her with their legs apart. The child that is first in line stops a few metres further on and bends over so that the others can jump over his or her back. And so on.

Hopping
♒ ✕ 2₌ ♀ 🚗

The children should hop to a certain point and back again. Depending on their age, you can choose a point nearby or further away.

Skipping
♒ ♒ ✕ ❄ ♀ 🚗

Page 158 has a number of skipping possibilities. The idea is to get your child moving.

Backwards
♒ ♒ ✕ 2⁺ ♀ 🚗

Make two children stand back-to-back and then take twenty steps forwards. Then they walk backwards towards one another without looking. They may collide, but they will probably completely miss one another.

12. Living and Playing in the Countryside

Treat nature properly

Imagine that every passer-by were to break off one branch of a tree or a bush. The countryside would be ruined. So treat nature with respect.

It sometimes appears as if foresters just leave a tree lying around after it has been cut down, but this is not the case. They leave it lying there for the small wild animals. It helps them survive.

Have a good look at where you can borrow something from nature for temporary use.

Building a hut
❀ ✄ ❋ ♀
✢ *Rope*

If you are staying in one place for some time, it is good fun to build a hut that you can visit every day. Sometimes you can find a hut that someone else has built. It may need finishing or improving, just like the hut on the adjoining photograph, which was probably made by a whole group.

You can also build your own hut. Begin with three or four thick branches that you tie to one another at the top using a piece of rope (see 'Tying and lashing,' p. 134). Then you will have a frame against which you can place other branches. If there are thin branches available, you can weave them into the thicker branches. If the hut has to be rainproof, you can cut open some large plastic bags and attach them to the roof of the hut.

When you leave to go home, take everything with you that does not belong to nature itself.

Wigwam

⚘ ✄ ❄ ♀

✤ *Rope and fabric*

If there are long branches or thin stems in the woods, you can make an wigwam. The frame is formed by six or eight long branches that are placed in a circle on the ground. To make a good circle, take a piece of rope approximately 1metre long. Tie each end to a stick. Shove one stick into the ground and use the other stick to draw a circle while walking around, keeping the rope taut.

Just as when building the hut, the first thing to do is tie the top ends together. They now form the frame against which you can lean and fix the other branches. You then need some large pieces of cloth to cover the wigwam. You can leave a small opening right at the top. Native Americans leave a space here so that the smoke from their fires can escape.

Building a dam

⚘ ✄ ❄ ♀

In a hilly landscape, you will find lots of streams with running water. Mostly there are plenty of stones that

you can use to build a dam. Check that the water is not too deep and that the current is not too strong. During a walk in the mountains on a warm day, it is good fun to play in the water and build a dam so that the water has to look for another way around.

Building a waterwheel
❀ ✂ ✳ ♀ ⚒

❖ *Orange box*
twigs
paint if desired

Where is the waterwheel to be placed? The answer determines the kind of waterwheel you should make. In a gently flowing stream, you will need broad blades on the wheel. If there is a lot of rapidly running water, narrow blades will be sufficient.

Look for a straight piece of a branch about 3 cm (1 in) thick. Drill holes about 1 cm (½ in) wide in both ends. Shove the axles in here (see Fig 132.1). The water will cause the wood to expand and the axles will remain firmly in place.

The blades of the waterwheel shown in Figures 132.3 and 133.4 are made of slats from an old orange box. They have been fixed with a few nails, overlapping one another like roof tiles, to a piece of branch. If you like, you can paint the blades to make them more colourful.

Now look for two sturdy twigs that are forked at one end. Push them into the bed of the stream and place the axles of the wheel on them.

If the ground is too hard, look for some squarish stones and fix the

Fig 132.1

Fig 132.2

Fig 132.3

Fig 132.4

Fig 132.5

Fig 132.6

twigs to them with thick string (or wires). Then place the whole thing in the water.

The waterwheel in Figures 132.1 and 132.2 has small blades. The wooden axle has four grooves that the blades fit into. They can be fixed there using nails if necessary. As the waterwheel turns quickly, you should place stops at the ends of the axles (see Fig 132.1).

Figures 132.5 and 132.6 show a small waterwheel with eight blades. They are clamped in grooves in the axles, which is around 2.5 cm (1 in) thick. The axles of the waterwheel rests on two pieces of branch in which a hollow has been carved.

Lighting a campfire
🌿 ✕ ❄ ♀

If the countryside is very dry, you will have to be very careful with fires. At many places you won't actually be allowed to light a campfire. However, there are also places where everyone is allowed to light a fire to toast bread or barbecue sausages etc.

If you want to light a fire, and it is allowed, you must take care that the fire cannot spread. Look for a suitable place where any sparks will not land on bone-dry leaves on the ground.

1 Use some large stones to make a circle in which the fire can burn without spreading. Dig a small hollow inside the circle.
2 Look for twigs of differing thickness: very thin dry twigs and also some quite thick ones. Dry pine cones with thin scales are very good for the heart of the fire. You begin to build up the fire using the thin twigs or some splinters from a thicker branch. You can add the pine cones. You can also use several sheets of newspaper if you like.

3 Place the twigs in a pyramid shape at the middle of the fireplace.
4 Use some thicker branches to build up the fire around these twigs.
5 Set fire to the inside of the pyramid you have built. As soon as the fire is burning well, you can add some thicker pieces of wood if you wish.

Make sure that the fire is completely extinguished when you leave. Cover the ashes with some earth and place the stones on top.

Tying and lashing

♔ ✄ ✳ ♀

Knots are primarily used in sailing. You will recognize that by the names of the various knots, such as the *reef knot,* but you also need to be able to tie some good knots if you want to build a hut or suspend a hammock for example.

Reef knot

1 – 4 The reef knot is perhaps the simplest and most frequently-used knot. You can use it to tie together two pieces of rope (or string) of similar thicknesses. Most people use this knot to tie up a parcel. If you tie the knot too tight, you will find it very difficult to untie.

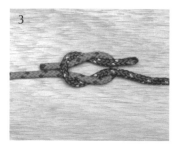

Two half hitches

1 – 2 You use this knot to tie a rope to a ring, for example.

Carpenter's hitch

1 – 2 A hitch is actually just another name for a knot that is used to fasten something with a rope. If you want to fasten something quickly, the carpenter's hitch is a handy knot. But if you want to fix it really well, you would be better to use a *clove hitch.*

Single sheet bend

1 – 4 If you want to tie together two ropes of differing thicknesses, you should use the sheet bend.

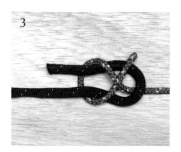

Two sweet lovers

1 – 5 This knot is also called the 'fisherman's knot.' Fishermen used it to tie together two threads when tying their nets.

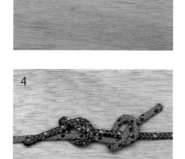

Clove hitch

1 – 4 The clove hitch is used to tie a piece of rope tightly to a mast or tree. You can also lay the clove hitch as two loops around a pole.
5 – 6 To prevent the knot becoming loose if the rope moves back and forward, you can put a half-hitch in the rope when you are done.

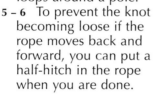

Lashing

Lashing together means tying things together, like two or more branches for example. Begin with the *carpenter's hitch*. Wind the rope tightly around the branches, depending on the way they are to be kept together.

1 – 2 The illustrations show how two branches are lashed together at right angles. Finally fasten the rope using a *clove hitch*.

Folding techniques

Paper boats
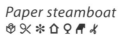
✣ *paper*

1 Fold an A4 (Letter) sheet down the middle lengthwise, open it up and now fold it across the middle.
2 Hold the closed side upward and fold both ends of the closed side to the middle of the paper.
3 / 3b Fold the open ends upwards.
4 When you push the ends inwards, a square is formed. The *bottom* is open.
5 Fold these corners up on both sides, so that a triangle is formed.
6 Repeat 5.
7 Now pull the two loose corners outwards at the top, and you have your boat.

Paper steamboat
✣ *paper*

1 Cut a square 30 × 30 cm (12 × 12 in) from a piece of wrapping paper or a large paper bag. Fold the paper along both diagonals and open it up again.
2 Fold the four corners to the middle so that a new smaller square is formed.
3 Turn the folded square over and fold the new corners to the middle again.
4 Repeat step 3.
5 Turn the folded paper over, pull two opposite corners outward. These are the chimneys.
6 Now pull the other two sides outward, and the steamboat is completed.

Aeroplane 1

🐛🌼❄☖♀🐘✂

✣ *paper*

1 Fold an A4 (Letter) sheet down the middle lengthwise.
2 Fold one of the corners toward the closed side. Repeat this with the other side.
3 Repeat step 2 on both sides.
4 Repeat step 2 once again.

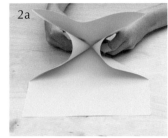

Aeroplane 2

🐛🌼❄☖♀🐘✂

✣ *paper*

1 Take an A4 (Letter) sheet and fold one of the corners to the opposite side. Do the same with the other corner.
2 Push both sides inward.
3 Fold a triangle at the top of the paper.
4 Fold both corners upward.
5 Repeat the fold as in 4.
6 Fold the aeroplane double lengthwise.
7 Make a fold on either side in the other direction.
8 Repeat 7.

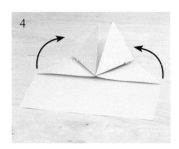

Carving a walking stick
❀ ✂ ✳ ♀ ✂

Look for a firm stick with thin, dark bark, and cut it to the right length for your walking stick. Now use your pocket knife to carve shapes in the stick. Cut the bark deep enough that you actually go through it and you can see the light wood. At home, you can make your walking stick even better by colouring in the figures you have cut.

Houses from a slice of tree
⬡ ❀ ✳ ♀ ✂

If you are lucky, you will find a slice of a tree near a sawn-down tree or at a sawmill. Figures 138.1 and 138.2 show how you can build a whole village of houses from this disk. The bark on the outside is the roofs.

Draw the houses on the disk before you start sawing. If necessary you can sandpaper the houses to make them nicer.

Villages of branches
⬡ ❀ ✳ ♀ ✂

A child does not always have to have model houses in order to play with his or her toy cars. You can build a village out of some old branches. Saw off various lengths. Don't make them too large. See Fig 139.1.

Fig 138.1

Fig 138.2

Fig 138.3

Sundials

☿ ✕ ✳ ♀

❖ *pieces of a branch and/or stones*
perhaps a flowerpot
orange box

A sundial is actually a natural clock and if you are living in a hut, you will want to be able to see the time.

Old houses often have a sundial on the wall that faces the sun. These were placed there according to the position of the sun in the south at noon. Nowadays we use the same time across a large part or whole of a country and even adjust it for daylight saving (summer) time, and so these sundials no longer show the time that we use.

However, with the help of your watch, you can create a modern-day sundial. On a sunny day, insert a stick into the ground and look where the shadow of the sun falls on the ground. Place a stone or a twig there and write down the time.

In this way, you can mark the time according to your watch and the sun (Figs 138.3 and 139.2).

The next day, if the sun is shining, you will no longer need your watch!

Simple rotating star chart

☿ ✕ ✳ ♀ ⚹

❖ *white card*
fastening pin (see 139.4)

Pages 212 and 213 show two parts of a star chart, each measuring 20.5 × 20.5 cm (8 × 8 in). Cut these figures out.

1 Take a piece of white cardboard, fold it in two, and cut it to the same measurements.
2 Stick the first figure to the front of the cardboard. Cut the oval out of the front page and cut the notch on the right-hand side out of both pages.
3 Make a hole in the middle of the back page (at the place where the two diagonals intersect).
4 Stick the printed round chart of the stars to a piece of cardboard and cut it out. Make a hole in the middle; that is the Pole Star.
5 Insert a fastening pin through the holes in the round chart of the stars and the back page, and bend the lips back. You can also make your own fastening pin from a piece of wire (see Fig 139.4).
6 Stick the corners together.

Fig 139.1

Fig 139.2

Fig 139.3

Fig 139.4

Your own weather station

Pine cone to show humidity
🌸 ✄ ❋ ♀

The simplest hygrometer (measure of humidity) is the pine cone, because it reacts strongly to moisture.

1　If humidity is high, it closes up tight.
2 / 3　If it is very dry and sunny, the pine cone opens up completely.

A home-made barometer
🌸 ✄ ❋ ♀ ✂

❖ *a large mug or a tin*
a straw
a balloon
an elastic band
paper and tape

Cut a balloon in two. The mouthpiece is no longer needed. Stretch the other piece until it becomes more flexible. Place it over the open end of the mug or tin and fix it there with the elastic band.

1　Tape the straw to the middle of the balloon membrane in such a way that one end sticks out and almost touches the wall.
　　Tape a piece of paper or white wood against the wall so that the end of the straw almost touches it. The barometer is now ready.
2　The air pressure outside the barometer will do the rest. The air in the tin cannot change. If the air pressure is high, the balloon membrane will be pushed down and the end of the straw near the wall will rise. If there is low pressure, the reverse process will occur.
　　By setting stripes on the paper to mark the various positions of the straw, you will be able to read your own barometer. The barometer shown here displays a reading of approximately 20 mm (3/4 in).

Windvane
🌸 ✄ ❋ ♀ ✂

❖ *plywood (orange) box*
thin twig
wire
paint

It is important that the weather vane can turn around freely.

1　Cut out or saw two identical arrows and a few small pieces that can be stuck between the two arrows.

high

low

2 Stick the first small piece to the sharp end of one of the arrows. Then seek out the centre of gravity of the arrow and mark it.

3 On either side if this mark, place two pieces of wood with approx. 2 mm ($^1/_{16}$ in) space between them.

4 Stick the two arrows together and paint them. Make four small arrowheads showing the four major points of the compass.

5 Use a slender branch to make a cross and make a small incision in the ends. Use a few beads to enable the windvane to turn around easily.

6 Make a loop at the end of a piece of iron wire and thread it through the cross and the beads.

Hang the windvane on a tree. A stone underneath will ensure that it hangs straight.

Rain gauge

❀ *glass jar and funnel*

You will need a funnel that is as wide as the glass jar. Draw a millimetre (or tenth of an inch) scale on the outside of the jar.

Place the jar with the funnel on top of it in an open spot and wait until it rains. The millimetre scale will indicate how much water has come into the jar. Empty the jar again for the next time.

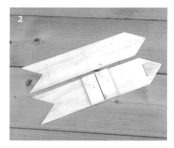

Playing with boats

Walnut boats
⚒ ✤ ✂ ✳ ♀ ✗

✤ empty walnut shells
  cocktail sticks
  paper
  glue

Walnut shells are very light and therefore cannot bear too much weight.

1 Cut a sail out of a piece of paper and push the cocktail stick (the mast) though it.
2 Cut off the sharp end of the cocktail stick. Fix the mast to the shell with a little glue or a piece of plasticine or wax. Walnut boats are soon knocked off balance. Control whether or not the boat stays the right way up. If necessary, stick some plasticine to one of the sides as ballast (see Fig143.1).

Bark boats
⚒ ✤ ✂ ✳ ♀ ✗

✤ a piece of bark
  a thin but strong twig
  large leaf

Figures 143.2, 143.3 and 143.4 show three boats that have hulls made of bark.

Look for a fine thick piece of bark. You can often find bark at places where trees have been felled.

1 Use your pocket knife to cut the bark into the right shape, with sharp bows at the front.
2 Now you have to decide if your boat is to have one sail or perhaps it is to be a two or even three-master.
3 Look for thin, straight twigs for the mast. Decide how high the mast is to be and cut the twig to the right length. Shape a blunt point at the bottom. Use an awl to make a hole in the bark hull.

4 Make a sail out of a piece of stiff paper or take a large leaf. Fix the sail to the mast and insert the mast into the hull. If necessary, use some glue to fix the mast.

Small wooden raft
⚒ ✤ ✳ ♀ ✗

✤ twigs with a diameter of 1–2 cm (¹/₂ in)
  thin rope
  piece of cloth

Look for a few twigs that are equally thick.

1 Saw the beams of the raft from the twigs. Make sure that they are all approximately the same thickness. Lay the beams next to one another, so that you can see how broad the raft will be.
2 Now saw a beam that is just as broad as the raft. Cut it in two lengthwise so that you have two half-round twigs. Lay them flat across the beams of the raft and fix them to the other beams. You can nail them down, but you can also lash them together (see Fig 143.5).
3 Now cut the mast and two twigs to which the sail will be attached. You can use a small piece of cloth or a piece of a plastic bag for this. Tape it to the twigs.
4 You can drill a small hole in the top of the mast and insert a matchstick. You can attach a flag to this.

Jam the mast between the beams and fasten it by lashing.

Cargo ships
✤ ✂ ✳ ♀ ✗

✤ 18 mm (³/₄ in) thick wooden plank
  string

For these boats, you should go to the timber yard for a plank measuring around 7 cm (3 in) wide and 18 mm (³/₄ in) thick.

1 First draw the shape of your boat on a piece of stiff paper. Fold it in two lengthwise, draw half of the boat and cut it out. Fold the paper open and trim it to make it equal if necessary.
2 Lay the paper on the wood and trace around it on the wood. Saw out the boat shapes. You can also give the boat an extra deck if you like.
3 If you want to join several boats together, drill a small hole at the front and the back. Insert a piece of string in the holes with some glue, and fix it there by jamming a matchstick in. Cut off the extra piece of matchstick.

Paper boats
⚒ ✤ ✳ ♀ ✗

To make the boats shown in Figures 143.6 and 143.7, see 'Folding Techniques,' p. 136.

Fig 143.1

Fig 143.4

Fig 143.2

Fig 143.5

Fig 143.7

Fig 143.3

Fig 143.6

Fig 143.8

A

C

E

B

D

Playing with the wind

Windmill
🐞🐢✂✳⛺📕✄
✢ thin card
  twig (beads)
  piece of wire
  hand drill

Look for a thin, straight stick. We assume that you cannot get large beads and long pins, so we shall make them ourselves. To begin with, drill a hole in the top of the stick with a small drill.

1 Now cut a number of beads from the top part of that stick.
2 / 3 Drill a hole through the top part of the stick and insert the wire through it.
4 Take a square piece of cardboard measuring 21 × 21 cm (8 × 8 in) and draw the two diagonals. Cut along the diagonals until you get to about 4 cm (1½ in) from the middle.
5 Make five holes at the places shown (middle and just next to the four corners).
6 Bend the corners with the holes to the middle, and insert the wire through all five holes.
7 Thread the wire through a wooden bead, use pliers to bend the wire into a 'knot,' and cut off the extra wire.

Tip:
It is sometimes good to tape an extra card strip at the back of the windmill (Fig 146.2) to make sure it does not rub against the stick.

< Fig 144.1

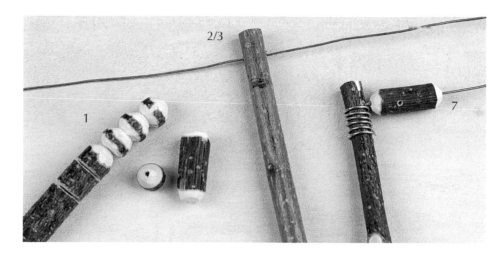

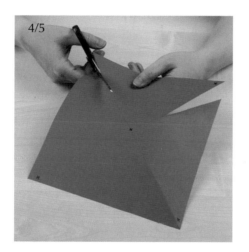

Fig 146.1

Fig 146.2

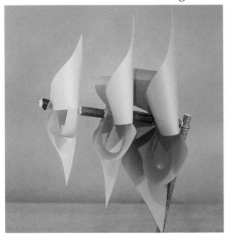

Fig 146.3

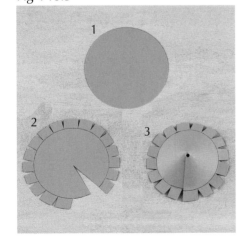

Three in one

🔧 🖐 ✂ ✳ ⌂ 🐚 ✂

✤ thin card
   twig
   (beads)
   piece of wire
   hand drill

On the left of page 144 (A) you can see a combination of three windmills of different sizes, which together make one windmill. If you make this type, you should place 3 cm (1 in) beads between them to ensure they don't rub against one another.

Flower windmill

🔧 🖐 ✂ ✳ ⌂ 🐚 ✂

✤ thin card
   twig
   (beads)
   piece of wire
   hand drill

1 The six blades of this windmill (page 144, C) are 12 cm (5 in) long. Cut the blades out of coloured cardboard.
2 The separate petals need a heart to hold them together and to allow the windmill to turn.
3 Cut a card circle of around 5–6 cm (2 in) (see Fig 146.3). You can attach the separate petals to this.
4 Draw a slightly larger circle and make small incisions around the edge. Cut a small section out and join the ends together again. The middle will now rise up a little (see Fig 146.3, 2 and 3). Attach this whole unit to the front of the mill.

Windmill with blades

🔧 🖐 ✂ ✳ ⌂ 🐚 ✂

✤ firm card
   twig
   (beads)
   piece of wire
   hand drill
   pair of compasses

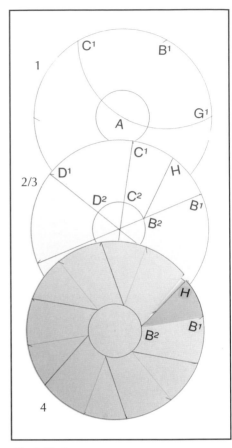

Fig 146.4

You will need a pair of compasses for this windmill.

1 From point A (Fig 146.4), draw two circles with diameters of 4 cm and 15 cm (1½ and 6 in).
2 Take point B^1 on the larger circle. Divide this circle into six equal parts as follows: Choose point B^1 and use the compasses to draw a circle with the same diameter as A-B^1. You now have points C^1 and G^1. Draw circles from these points in the same way, and so on. Connect these points to A so that points B^2, C^2, etc. are created on the smaller circle.

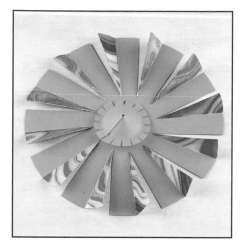

Fig 147.1

Fig 147.2

3 Divide the distance between the points on the larger circle and you now have points H to N. Draw the lines N-B², H-D², etc.

4 Use a knife to crease the lines B¹-B², C¹-C², etc. so that it will be easy to fold along these lines. Cut out the lines N-B², H-D², etc. Fold open the triangles thus created.

5 Finish the windmill by following steps 3 and 4 of the flower windmill above (Fig 146.3)

Variation:

Instead of dividing the circle into six, you can divide it into twelve by halving the distances between the points on the outer circle. You will then have twelve blades. You can cover these with different coloured paper to make it more attractive (see windmill E, p. 144).

Hanging windmills

✿ ✂ ✳ ⌂ 🛋 ✄
❖ firm card
    twig
    (beads)
    piece of wire
    hand drill
    pair of compasses

Make eight windmills (or any number of your own choice) with blades of various colours and thread a long piece of string through them. You can then hang these from a branch. Thread a *wooden bead* (Fig 147.3) behind each windmill and tie a knot in the string to keep the mill in place.

Making a parachute

✿ ✂ ✳ ⌂ 🛋 ✄
❖ *cloth handkerchief*
    pieces of string

Take a handkerchief and tie a piece of string to each corner. Take the loose ends of the string and tie them to a stone or stick.

Fold the handkerchief and throw in as high as you can into the air. The handkerchief will open up and slowly fall to the ground. You will have to try to find the best weight for your handkerchief.

Folding aeroplanes

✿ ✂ ✳ ⌂ 🛋 ✄
See 'Folding techniques,' p. 137

Wind-chime

✿ ✂ ✳ ⌂ 🛋 ✄
See page 198

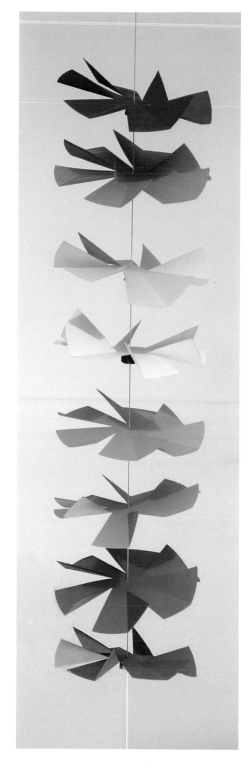

Fig 147.3

13. Tig and Other Outdoor Games

(In this section, to keep the explanation brief, we shall use 'he' to represent both boys and girls.)

Selection games

Eeny meeny
♟ ⚘ ✳ ⛫ ♀

An old game. One child says the rhyme while the others stand around in a circle. With each syllable, the first child points to each of the other children in turn: ee-*ny* mee-*ny.* The last word 'mo' determines who is to be 'it.'

> Eeny meeny miney mo,
> Catch a tiger by the toe,
> If it growls let it go
> Eeny meeny miney mo.

Spuds up
♟ ⚘ ✳ ⛫ ♀

All the players will stand in a circle with both hands in front of them, clenched in a fist. The counter goes round the circle, counting the fists as he recites 'One potato, two potato, three potato, four. Five potato, six potato, seven potato MORE!' and the 'spud' (fist) struck on 'MORE' is put behind the back. The rhyme continues round the circle — two 'spuds' and you're out, and the last one left in is 'it.'

Drawing lots
♟ ⚘ ✂ 3⁺ ⛫ ♀
✤ *matchsticks*

This is an easy way of choosing a child. Take the same number of matches as there are children and break a piece off one of the matches. Hold all the matches in your hand in such a way that the ends stick out but no one can see which is the short one. All players pull out a match and the child with the short match is 'it.'

How many do I have in my hand?
♟ ⚘ ✂ 3⁺ ⛫ ♀

You can use this selection game if there are not many children and you need to have a leader. Take a number of stones, matches or other small objects in your hand and get the children to guess how many there are. The child who guesses correctly, or is nearest, can begin or be the leader. In this way you can also determine the order of sequence of the children (for example, order of turns on the swings) if necessary.

Who closes the bridge?
♟ ⚘ ✂ 2⁺ ⛫ ♀

A good game to decide which of two children gets first choice. Two children stand facing one another at a distance. In turn, they place one foot right in front of the other. After a few steps, the open space between the children has been considerably reduced. The child who places the last foot, the bridge, can choose.

Tig and other outdoor games

Tig
🐊 🕸 5⁺ ♀

One child is 'it' and tries to touch the other children. If they are touched, they have to try to tag the other children. It is advisable to mark out the area of play in advance.

Clothes peg tig
🐊 🕸 3⁺ ♀

✛ clothes pegs

In this game, the aim is not to touch the others, but to get a clothes peg stuck to their clothes, which is slightly more difficult.

Ball tig (dodge)
🐊 🕸 3⁺ ♀ ⚭

In this game, one child has to try to hit the other children with a ball. You must mark out the play area in advance otherwise the players will be too far away to give the thrower a chance.

Cross tig
🐊 🕸 5⁺ ♀

If one of the children crosses the path of the chaser, the chaser must stop chasing the child he was after and has to chase the child that crossed his path.

Shadow tig
🐊 🕸 5⁺ ♀

Tig in which the chaser can catch the others by standing on their shadows and calling out Got you!

Thieves
🕸 ✂ 4⁺ ♀

Draw a circle of approximately 2 m (6 ft). The seller lays out his wares in this circle. These may be pine cones, or stones or shells from the beach, etc.

The thieves walk around the circle and try to steal the wares. If the seller sees this, he can touch the thief if he is partly in the circle. The caught thief is out. The seller has to stay in the circle. The game is finished when the thieves have stolen all the wares or when all the thieves are out.

Fox's den
♟ ♙ 5⁺ ♀

✛ *handkerchief for each player*

In this game, there is the fox and a number of other animals. Each player has a handkerchief with a knot in it. That is the animal. Mark out the fox's *den* by drawing a circle with a diameter of 3 metres (9 ft) on the ground.

The fox is safe in his *den,* that is his territory, but he can touch the other animals with his handkerchief if they come into his den. A player who has been touched must hand over his handkerchief and is out.

Outside the fox's den, there are other *animals* that try to entice the fox out of his den by going into his den for a moment. As soon as the fox is outside his den, the others can touch him with their handkerchiefs. The child that tags the fox can take over his den for the next game.

Catching fish
♟ ♙ ✂ 5⁺ ♀

✛ *newspaper, string*

Each child cuts or tears a fish shape out of a newspaper page. These fish are tied to each child's waist with a piece of string so that they hang down on the ground behind the child like a tail.

All the children now go fishing. You catch a fish by standing on someone else's fish so that it is torn off the string. At the very moment that one player is trying to stand on a fish, someone else may be trying to stand on his fish.

Tree-hopping
♟ ♙ ✂ 4⁺ ♀

A well-known game that is best played in the woods, for obvious reasons.

All the children except one have their own tree where they are safe. The children try to swap trees with one another, but only one child can stand at one tree at one particular time. As soon as one child leaves his tree, the child without a tree tries to get there first. If he succeeds, there is a new child without a tree. He has to try to get someone else's tree.

Blindman's buff
⚘ ⚘ 3⁺ ♀ ✎
⁜ blindfold

For this game you need a piece of ground 4 × 4 m (12 × 12 ft) in size. It may be a little larger if there are lots of players.

Someone is blindfolded. He tries to catch the others. The others can try to run away but are not allowed to go out of the marked area. If they do, they are out. If the blindman catches someone, the caught person is blindfolded.

Variation:

If there are five or more players, the blindman can only take off the blindfold when he has correctly guessed who has been caught.

Hands and feet
⚘ ⚘ 4⁺₌ ♀
⁜ 4 shoes
  boots or slippers for each child

You can make two groups if there are more than four children. If there are less than four, you can set up a contest between the individual children.

Each child has shoes on hands and feet. The child must go as quickly as possible on all fours to a given place and back again.

If there are two groups, the first two children run to the given spot and back, then the shoes are passed on to the next pair who then set off. You can do a number of relays in this way. If the children are competing against one another, you can measure the time they take.

Sumo sitting
⚘ ✄ 4⁺ ♀

Draw a circle on the ground that easily accommodates two children. The children sit in the middle back to back. At a given sign, they try to push one another out of the circle. They have to remain seated while doing so.

Knocking down the pyramid
🌷 ✂ ✳ ♀ ◐

❖ *10 or 15 empty cans*
   3 small balls

Place the cans on top of one another in a pyramid shape on a raised plank. You will need at least four cans for the bottom row. The second row will have three cans, and so on. In this instance you will need 10 cans. If you have 15 cans, you can place five on the bottom row, etc.

The children throw the balls one by one from a distance of around 4–5 metres (12–15 feet) away. After each throw, the cans left standing are set neatly on top of one another again. The number of cans knocked down represents the number of points gained. The child with the most points after a few rounds is the winner.

If you don't have any balls, you can bundle together some old rags and tie them in a ball with a piece of string. You can even use wet newspaper.

Hoops
🐞 🌷 ✳ ♀

See 'Beach games,' p. 164.

Leapfrog
🌷 ✂ 3⁺ ♀

See 'Games to strech your muscles,' p. 128.

Over the line
🌷 ✂ 2₌ ♀

Mark a line on the ground with a piece of tape, rope or chalk.

Two children stand back to back on either side of the line. At a given sign, they bend down and clasp one another's hand between their legs. Then they pull in an attempt to pull the other one across the line.

Pebble football
🌷 ✂ 2⁺₌ ♀

❖ *pebbles*

Draw a playing area on the ground measuring 3 × 6 m (9 × 18 feet) and mark the halfway line. Mark goals of 1 metre (3 feet) in width at each end.

Divide the children into two groups.

Place three pebbles on the halfway line. Choose who is to begin. The children have to hop and try to kick the pebbles into the goal using their supporting (hopping) leg. Then the other group gets a turn.

Rules:

- The pebbles should not go out of the field of play.
- The player must not cross any of the outside lines.
- The player must not stand on two feet.
- As soon as one player has had his turn or is out, the other team gets an opportunity.
- The team scoring the most goals within a certain time is the winner.

Hit the can
🐞 🌷 ✳ ♀ ◐ ✦

❖ *blindfold*
   empty can
   stick

One of the children is blindfolded and given a stick. He is taken somewhere and turned around a couple of times. Then he has to try to hit the can with the stick. Of course, he cannot see the can. If he succeeds, he receives the reward that is under the can. Make sure that the can has no sharp edges.

Carrying water

♟ ♙ 2⁺ ♀

✤ *four buckets*
pans or large tins
two small plastic cups

This game is actually a relay race for two groups, but two or three children can compete against one another.

You have two buckets with equal amounts of water. They are placed at a distance of three metres (nine feet) from each child. Next to each of the children is an empty bucket. At a given sign, they run with their cup to the bucket, fill the cup and run back to the empty bucket and pour the water in. Then they go off to get more. The child that has the most water in the empty bucket within a certain time is the winner.

If there are enough children to form two groups, the first child goes and gets water, then passes the cup to the second child, and so on. You can keep the game going by getting the children to refill the original bucket as part of the game.

Potato dropping

♟ ♙ ✂ 4⁺ ♀

✤ *potatoes*
2 boxes

This is a relay race. Each child is given an equal number of potatoes. Two boxes or buckets are placed at a distance of three metres (nine feet) from the starting line. The children have to hold the potatoes between their legs and run or hop to the box or bucket and drop the potato in there. Then they run back and get a new potato or, if you are playing in groups, it is the next child's turn.

Catch

♣ ♙ ✂ ✳ ♀ ◐

A relaxing game where the players throw the ball to one another at random.

Wall ball

♟ ♙ ✳ ♀ ◐

✤ *ball*

Draw a line about 2 metres (6 feet) from a wall and get the children to stand behind it. They take it in turns to throw the ball against the wall. But before they catch it again, they have to perform an assignment. This may be:

❀ turn around once
❀ hop around once
❀ sit down
❀ clap three, four or five times, etc.

Variations:
You can also vary the way the ball is thrown or caught.
❀ throw the ball against a certain area (number) drawn on the wall
❀ let it bounce a certain number of times before catching it, etc.

Earth, water, air

♙ ✂ 3⁺ ♀ ◐

✤ *ball*

Someone throws the ball to one of the players and shouts out one of the following: *Earth, water* or *air*. If the thrower shouts *air*, the catcher has to reply within ten seconds with the name of an animal that can fly. Then he throws the ball back. The same applies to *earth* and *water*. Each animal can only be used once. If a player cannot reply, he loses a life, or is out completely.

Water ball
🏵 🏵 3⁺ ♀

❖ *balloons*

A game for a hot day. Fill some balloons with some water. You can use these 'balls' to play ball games. It is very refreshing if the balloon bursts and one of the children gets a shower.

Defending the tower
🏵 ✂ 5⁺ ♀ ◎

❖ *ball*
  cans

Build a tower of tin cans within a circle. The size of the circle depends on the age of the players (and how well they can throw).

Two players in the circle try to defend the tower against the other players who stand around the outside of the circle and try to knock down the tower with the ball. They have to pass the ball to one another until they see an opening. The ball can be thrown across the circle.

If the tower is partly knocked down, the defenders are allowed to build it up again. The person who knocks the tower down gets to defend it in the next round.

Stand ball
🏵 🏵 4⁺ ♀ ◎

See 'Beach Games,' p. 164.

Piggy in the middle
🏵 🏵 3⁺ ♀ ◎

❖ *ball*

Two children stand at some distance and throw the ball to one another. Another child stands between them and tries to catch the ball. If he does so, the child that threw the ball then goes in the middle.

Who's got the ball?
🏵 🏵 3⁺ ♀ ◎

One child with the ball faces away from the rest of the children. He throws the ball backwards over his head towards them. One of the children grabs the ball and holds it behind his back.

The thrower then turns around and tries to guess who has the ball. The other children pretend that they too have the ball. If the thrower guesses correctly, he gets another turn. If he is wrong, the child with the ball gets a turn.

Red light
♟ ♙ 6⁺ ♀ ◐

One player has his face to the wall or stands facing a tree. The other children are behind a line. The distance from the line to the wall depends on their ages: between 3 and 10 metres (10 and 30 ft).

The child facing the wall counts to ten as quickly or slowly as he pleases. The other children move towards him. The first child then shouts 'red light' and turns around quickly. The other children have to stand absolutely still. If they are caught moving, they have to go back behind the line. First to the wall is the winner.

Bottle ball
♟ ♙ ✄ 2⁺ ♀ ◐

✣ *empty plastic bottles*

This is a wet game. Two children stand at a distance of 4–13 metres (10–40 ft). They each have a full bottle of water. If there are three children, you can place them in a triangle.

Throw the ball among the children. The child that gets the ball tries to knock down the other bottle(s) by throwing the ball. If a bottle is knocked down, the owner has to run after the ball and pick it up. During this time, the thrower can hold the knocked-down bottle upside down so that the water runs out. When the ball has been recovered, this bottle must be put down properly. At the same time, the child with the ball can try to knock down his opponent's bottle. The child whose bottle is empty first has lost.

Hide and seek
♟ ♙ ✄ 4⁺ ♀

A particular spot is marked as the home base. One child covers his eyes and counts to one hundred in fives: he then shouts: *Hundred! Ready or not, here I come!* Very young children can count to ten.

In the meantime, the others have hidden. The playing area should be agreed in advance, otherwise the game will take too long. The first child goes looking for the others. Each time he sees someone, he calls out his or her name and runs back to the base to mark him or her out. The found child has to come to the base.

Every child can try to get free by getting to the base before the seeker and shouting *Free!*

When all the children have been found and captured, the child that was caught first has to count to one hundred and find the other children, but if all the children have managed to free themselves, the first child has to start all over again.

Waving

♟ ✿ ✂ 4⁺ ♀

This is a variation of Hide and Seek. The children who have been caught stand at the base. A child who has not yet been caught appears to the caught children and waves to them. The caught children can then run away and hide again. If the seeker sees them running away, he can call them back. By waving, the waver also runs the risk of being seen. Each waver can only free two children (the longest captives), otherwise the game lasts too long.

Kick the can

♟ ✿ ✂ 4⁺ ♀

In this game, the home base is a tin can. The seeker marks a capture by placing his foot on the can. If one of the hidden children gets the chance to kick the can, the seeker first has to run after it and put it back at its original place by walking there backwards. In the meantime, all the captured children have been freed by the kick, so the seeker has to look for them again. The others can only kick the can twice, otherwise the game takes too long.

Skipping

Skipping
♟ ♧ ✄ 1 3⁺ ♀

✣ *long piece of strong (skipping) rope*

You can go skipping on your own. You hold the ends of the rope in either hand, swing the rope over your head and jump over it when it comes to the ground. You can vary this in lots of ways: change feet, hopping, etc.

You need at least three people if you want skipping to be a joint activity. Two children turn the rope at a distance of three metres (9 feet) from one another. The other children jump in from one side and jump out on the other side. The children can take it in turns to jump in and out, but they can also jump together if they wish.

I had a little puppy
♟ ♧ ✄ 2⁺ ♀

✣ *long skipping rope*

I had a little puppy,
His name was Tiny Tim,
I put him in the bathtub, to see if he could swim,
He drank all the water, he ate a bar of soap,
The next thing you know he had a bubble in his throat.
In came the doctor, *(person jumps in)*
In came the nurse, *(person jumps in)*
In came the lady with the alligator purse *(person jumps in)*
Out went the doctor *(person jumps out)*
Out went the nurse *(person jumps out)*
Out went the lady with the alligator purse *(person jumps out).*

I like coffee
♟ ♧ ✄ 3⁺ ♀

✣ *skipping rope*

I like coffee
I like tea
I like (person's name)
To jump with me

You can make the jumping more difficult by making an extra turn after every call.

Teddy bear, teddy bear
♧ ✄ 3⁺ ♀

✣ *long skipping rope*

Teddy Bear, Teddy Bear,
Touch the ground.
Teddy Bear, Teddy Bear,
Turn around.

Teddy Bear, Teddy Bear,
Show your shoe (foot in the air).
Teddy Bear, Teddy Bear,
That will do.

Teddy Bear, Teddy Bear,
Run upstairs (running)
Teddy Bear, Teddy Bear,
Say your prayers (on haunches)

Teddy Bear, Teddy Bear,
Blow out the light.
Teddy Bear, Teddy Bear,
Say good night (jumps out)

With each verse, the jumper has to perform the actions mentioned.

How old am I?
🌸 ✂ 3⁺ ♀

❖ *skipping rope*
A child jumps in and each skip is counted. How long can the child keep on skipping?

Marbles

Marbles
🎲 🌸 2⁺ ♀
Although most games of marbles aim at winning as many marbles as possible, we have chosen a system where the children win points instead of marbles. It is always easier to find new marbles when you are at home than when you are on vacation.

In the game, you can try to roll the marbles into a hollow, or you can try to hit the other player's marbles.

The first player rolls a marble a good distance. Then the next person tries to hit this marble with one of his own. If he does so, he wins a point and the marbles are returned to their owners. The players take turns in trying to hit the other person's marble.

In a hollow
🎲 🌸 2⁺ ♀
Look for a flat piece of ground and draw a line. Make a small hollow in the ground about 3 metres (10 ft) from the line.

Determine in advance how many marbles each person can use in the game. The marbles have to be rolled into the hollow. The aim is to gain as many points as possible. If the marble is rolled into the hollow in one go, the player gets 10 points and another turn. If he knocks a marble that is lying in the playing area into the hollow, he gets 8 points. If he needs several shots to get the marble in the hollow, he gets two points less (than 10) for each shot taken. When the players have used up all their marbles, they take their own marbles from the hollow. The player with the most points is the winner.

Marble arch
🎲 🌸 ✳ ♀

❖ *piece of cardboard*
Cut a number of round holes of different sizes in a piece of firm cardboard, such as a box from the supermarket, for example. Place this piece of cardboard at a distance of 1 metre (3 ft) from a line on the ground. If the children are not very experienced with marbles, cut three arches that the marbles can easily pass through. Write the assigned number of points above each arch.

Of course, you can cut five or seven arches. If a child manages to roll a marble through the arch, he gets another turn. If not, he can take the marble back and use it for his next turn.

Marbles in a row
🐚 🌼 2⁺ ♀

A number of marbles are set up in a row, so that there is some space between them. The children stay behind a line about two metres (6 feet) away. They now take turns to try to hit the marbles in the row with another marble. Each time a marble is hit the player gets a point.

Variation:
You can also play this game with pebbles. Lay a number of pebbles in a row. The players use small stones to try to hit the pebbles in the row.

Wall tig
🌼 ✂ 2⁺ ♀

The children sit about two metres (6 feet) from a wall. They roll or throw their marbles against the wall. If the marble rolls back within arm's reach, the player can pick it up again, otherwise it stays where it is. Each player tries to hit one of the marbles in the playing area via the wall. If he does so, he gets as many points as there are marbles in the playing area.

Hopping games

Hopscotch
🐚 🌼 ❄ ♀
❄ *chalk*
  flat stones

Hopscotch games are very old. Each hopscotch game consists of a number of squares that are usually numbered. You can use chalk to draw the court on the pavement, or a stick to scratch it in the ground.

The easiest hopscotch court consists of eight squares plus one that is called 'death.' The squares are around 40 × 40 cm (16 × 16 in). You can only put one foot in each of the squares. You must hop over the court but you can land on two feet in squares 4 and 5 and 7 and 8. If you put a foot in *death* you are out.

* You throw your marker into square 1 and you hop over square 1 to square 2 and then to square 3 and so on. At squares 7 and 8 you jump up and turn in the air, landing again in 7 and 8 facing the other way. You then hop

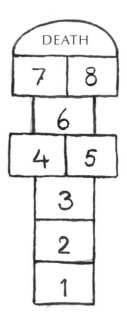

back, hopping over the square containing your marker but picking it up as you go. If you do this successfully, you then begin all over again. This time you start by throwing the marker into square 2. If your marker lands on a line or if you touch a line as you hop, you are out.

* More complicated hopscotch courts can have two unnumbered squares at the end. One is death, the other is life. You have to hop over *death* and land with both feet in *life*. Otherwise, you are out.

Variation:
You can determine in advance how you are going to jump from one square to the next. For example, you hop to square 1, land on 2 feet in square 2, cross your legs as you land in square 3, etc.

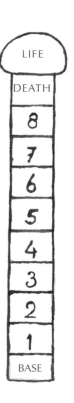

You jump from the last numbered square over *death*, turn in the air and land on two feet in *life*, facing the other way. You then go back.

Boy, girl

♟ ♧ ❀ ♀
❖ *chalk*
  flat stone

This is a different kind of hopscotch. While you are hopping, you have to think of something. The hopscotch court has six or eight squares. You can land just once in each square.

You hop to the first square and say *Boy*. Then you hop to the next square and say a boy's name. You do this in all the squares. If you land on a line or if you get stuck for a name, you are out.

Then you start again and this time you say *Girl* and go through the court. Then you can go on to other categories, such as food or cars or tennis players, and so on. If you have exhausted all the possibilities, you can hop with a hand in front of your eyes. After each jump you have to ask *Am I dead?* In other words, *Am I on a line?* If so, you are out.

Earth, water, air and fire
✿ ❋ ♀

✤ chalk or a stick

This version of hopscotch is geared to getting to heaven. To get there, you have to hop the whole hopscotch court four times. Each time, you get a more difficult assignment. In the first round, you pick up your marker on the way out. If you complete this round successfully, you are Lord of the Earth.

In the second round, you have to pick up the marker and keep it in the hollow behind your knee for the whole round. If you succeed, you are Lord of the Water. In the third round, you have to throw the marker into the air and catch it when you hop into every square. Then you are Lord of the Air. Finally, if you can kick your marker from box to box while hopping, without it coming on to a line, then you are Lord of Fire. Then you can get into heaven.

Days of the week
♟ ✿ 2⁺ ♀

✤ chalk
    flat stone

You start in the home box and you have to throw the marker into the Monday box. Then you hop over Monday into Tuesday and to the rest of the boxes. You land on Sunday with two feet. You turn around in the air and go back. You cannot stand on a line, otherwise you are out. At the end of the game, the marker is in Sunday. Because this is a free box, you can stand there on two feet and pick up the marker. You then have to throw the marker into Base and hop back before you are completely finished.

Of course, you can also use any other hopscotch variations during this game.

Treasure Hunts

Treasure hunts in general
⬡ ♟ ✿ ✄ ❋ ♀

Points to note:
You should always organize a treasure hunt with two adults. One of them should set out the route in such a way that outsiders do not move the clues or even take the 'treasure.' The other adult should accompany the children and make sure they do not take the wrong direction, or get into other kinds of trouble. The children should know where they can find you if they get stuck of if anything unusual happens.

* Choose an area that is clearly marked off, such as a park, a meadow, the campsite. A treasure hunt can take five to ten minutes in a small park. If the treasure hunt is to take longer, you will need a larger area or a piece of ground with many bushes or trees.
* Take the children to the starting point and tell them where the boundaries of the playing area lie. This avoids you having to look for a (lost) group later.
* Get the children to agree to keep together in their group.

Simple treasure hunt for children of five to seven years old
♟ ❋ ♀

An adult should lead a simple treasure hunt with these young children in one group. They follow a route that you have set out and they come to an endpoint. You can set out the route by drawing arrows on the ground, or you can also hang things on branches. The final goal could be some kind of *treasure*. You should hide it in such a way that the children can see a bit of it if they look hard. The end

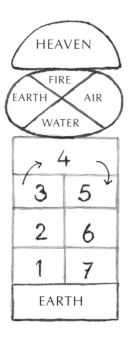

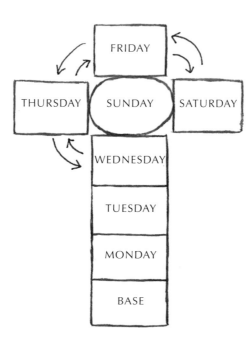

will be exciting if the last sign leading to the treasure is small and at an unexpected spot, so that the children can easily miss it. Chocolate coins in gold or silver foil are ideal treasure. Of course, it is even better if you can hide the coins in a box or 'treasure chest.' The final goal can also be a picnic or a playground.

Treasure hunt with instructions
❀ ✂ ✽ ♀

You can get children of this age to answer questions or do assignments. It is best to take seven-year-olds in a single group with adult supervision. For older children, it is more exciting for them to go without supervision and to introduce a competitive element, by having two groups, for example.

You can use a fairytale or saga or even one of your own stories as a starting point for the assignments. In this way, you can also provide information on the area. For example, your great-grandfather was captain of a large ship. He was chased by pirates and left a number of instructions behind that lead to the place where the treasure is hidden. In your story you can mention the material that you use for setting out the route. For example, your great-grandfather always wore a hat with feathers. Set out the route with feathers (or cut paper feathers) and hang them on branches.

Points to note:
Make sure that the instructions cannot be blown away or rained on.

Jot down the time you need to get from one clue to the next.

❀ First explore the area and draw out the route on paper. Use your notes and the assignments to work out how long the treasure hunt will last. Keep in mind that the children will be running half of the time and thus may not need too much time.

❀ Mark out the trail with material that will decay within a few days and does not leave any litter. Make sure that the clues from a previous treasure hunt are not visible otherwise the children may take the wrong route.

❀ If the route is complicated, draw a map of the area. Jot down information on the starting point and on the places where you can hide the clues, instructions or the treasure. Give them a number on the map. Indicate on the map the time it takes to go from one spot to another.

❀ Get the children to bring any instruction cards back with them so that no litter is left behind. A missing instruction card could mean a penalty point.

Treasure hunt in a town
❀ ✂ ✽ ♀

To older children, a treasure hunt in a town can be very exciting. You are not working with a route that you have to invent. You begin straight away by writing down the instructions that lead the children from one place to another. At each point, they must answer a question, such as *Whose statue stands in the middle of the square?* or *How old is the Town Hall?*

Keep in mind that this kind of treasure hunt requires a lot of preparation. You can do part of this at home, before you go on vacation. For example, the Italian city of Florence was used as an example in the chapter on *Orientation*. This kind of city lends itself to setting out a treasure hunt. However, a small village with fewer points of interest can also work quite well. Of course, you should not let the children go off alone in a large city like Florence.

14. Beach Games

Stand ball
♟ ♤ 3⁺ ♀ ◐

A child throws the ball into the air and shouts: *Stand in the sand, the ball is for* (a calls out a name). While all the others run away, the named person has to catch the ball as quickly as possible. If he catches the ball in the air, he throws it into the air again and shouts out *Stand in the sand, the ball is for ....* But if the ball has rolled across the ground, the named person must hold it and shout *Stop!* The others have to stop where they are. The person with the ball tries to hit them with the ball. They can move, but their feet have to remain fixed to the ground.

A child who is hit becomes *feeble.* If he is hit again he becomes *ill.* A third time means he is *dead* and out.

The last one left is the winner.

Water tig
♟ ♤ ✕ 3⁺ ♀

You should only play this game if the tide is coming in. Playing tig in the sea has an extra dimension especially if there are high waves that can hide you temporarily. Agree in advance that you cannot go in deeper than waist-deep. Adults should keep an eye on all the children.

High tig
♟ ♤ ✕ ✳ ♀

This is a kind of tig in which you cannot be touched if both your feet are off the ground.

Toe tig
♟ ♤ ✕ 3⁺ ♀

This is a barefoot variation of tig.

Mark out a playing area of around 14 × 14 metres (45 × 45 ft). If 5 or 6 bigger children are playing, the area can be a bit larger.

Agree who is to start. The chaser has to touch the others by standing with his bare feet on the bare foot of one of the others.

Jumping carousel
⛀ ✿ ✕ 3⁺ ♀ ⛟

See 'Games to stretch your muscles,'
p. 128

Thieves
✿ ✕ 4⁺ ♀

See 'Tig and Other Outdoor Games,'
p. 150

Hoops
⛀ ✿ ✕ ✤ ♀

✤ a number of sticks
   large rings or hoops (diameter
   around 20 cm, 8 in)

Push an uneven number of sticks (5, 7 of 9) into the ground at various distances from one another. Draw a line at a distance of around 2 metres (6 ft) from the nearest stick. The children stand behind this line and try to throw the rings over the sticks. A ring over the nearest stick is worth one point, the next one is worth two, etc. The child with the most points is the winner.

If you cannot find any rings, go to the local supermarket and get a few firm cardboard boxes. You can cut rings out of these.

Kites
✿ ✕ ✤ ♀

It is tricky to keep your kite in the air. It is not always easy and depends mainly on the strength of the wind. Kites can often be bought cheaply. Be careful, you cannot fly kites on all beaches.

Your own shell collection
⌘ ✄ 2⁺ ♀
✤ *shells,*
   large cardboard box or orange box

You cannot really build up a good shell collection in one vacation. The collection shown on this page was brought together during different vacations and comes from different beaches.

But you can make a start. You can sort your collection according to colour (see the 'Shell pictures,' p. 199) or shape.

You can create a kind of 'type' case from firm cardboard or from thin wood from an orange box, for instance. You can find both of these at the local supermarket.

Shell game

☗ ⚘ 3⁺ ♀

❖ shells

Go in a small group to look for shells. Each child looks for three kinds that he can easily recognize. You can do this according to the kind of shell, the colour or the shape. Mark the shells if necessary. You also need a large, neutral shell.

Rules of the game:
Draw a line in the sand.

The neutral shell is thrown forward from behind the line.

Now all the players throw their shells one by one to see who can get nearest to the neutral shell. The nearest shell gets a point.

The shells are gathered up again and the same procedure happens again. Agree in advance how many rounds are to be played.

Making words with shells

⚘ ✗ 3⁺ ♀

❖ shells or stones
    pencil

Look for shells or some pebbles. Write a letter on each shell or stone.

Divide the shells among the players. Everyone has to try to make words using his own shells. They can be swapped if necessary.

Gobang

⚘ ✗ 2 ♀

❖ stones or shells

Originally a Japanese game.

Draw at least ten horizontal and ten vertical lines that cross one another in the sand.

Each player has the same number of shells or stones that are clearly different from one another in shape or colour.

The players take it in turns to place a shell or a stone at an intersection of the lines. They have to try to make a row of five of their own shells, either horizontally, vertically, or diagonally. Of course, each player tries to prevent the other from completing a row of five by placing his own shells in the way.

The player who first creates a row of five is the winner.

Building a tower

☗ ⚘ ✗ ✳ ♀

Sandy beaches are not found everywhere. There are places where the beaches only have stones.

Due to the strong sea currents, the stones on the beach have become rounded. You can use these to build splendid towers. See who can build the tallest tower or one with the most stones.

Invasion

⚘ ✗ 2/4 ♀

❖ pocket knife

Look for a flat piece of ground and draw a square on it, 50 × 50 cm (20 × 20 in). With 2 players, this area is divided into two halves. If there are four players, then it is divided into quarters.

Agree who is to begin.

The first player drops the open knife on to the area of the square belonging to the other player(s). Be careful: there should be no hands or feet in the square. If the knife sticks in the ground the person who dropped the knife can draw a line from one side of the square to the other, through the knife mark. The first player now owns his own area plus the part he has just invaded. The land of the other player is now much smaller.

If he drops the knife into a piece of ground that does not border on his own land, nothing happens.

The next player now gets his turn. In this way, a new border is drawn.

In the course of the game, the land of one of the players will be completely occupied by the others.

The game is finished when one of the players has all the land.

Building with shells
🐚 ⚘ ✄ 2⁺ ♀ 🚩 ⚒
See 'Working with shells,' p. 198.

Cutting sand
⚘ ✄ 2⁺ ♀
✣ sand
  matchstick or cocktail stick
  spade or stick
Make a hill of wet sand and stick a matchstick or a cocktail stick into the top. The children now have to cut away the hill bit by bit until the matchstick falls. When that happens, the child causing the fall gets a penalty point.

Sandcastles
⚘ ✄ ✽ ♀
✣ sand
  bucket
  spade
  knife
First find out when it is high tide and how high the water will come. You don't want the castle to be washed away.

You sometimes see magnificent works of art in sand that have been made by real artists. It is usually river sand that is used for these. The grains of sea sand are relatively round due to the ebb and flow and therefore they do not make such a compact mass as the grains of river sand which are more angular.

To build a good sand castle, the sand has to be really wet so that the grains of sand stick to one another. First make a compact hill of wet sand. You can then use your knife and a spade to shape the castle. Don't forget to place flags on top of the turrets.

Sand sculptures
🐚 ⚘ ✄ ✽ ♀
✣ sand
  bucket
  spade
  knife
You can also create other shapes in the sand besides sandcastles. You can make animals, for instance. You can also turn this into a small contest.

Ball mountain

🝔 🝕 ✕ ✳ ♀ ◐

✛ *small balls*

A fine pastime on a sunny day. First find out when it is high tide and how high the water will come. You don't want the castle to be washed away.

Make a large, solid hill of wet sand. Beat the sand so that it is firm. Dig tunnels and holes and make channels along which the balls can roll.

Shadow puppets

🐚 ✂ ❋ ⌂ ♀

You can do this indoors in the evenings but it is also easily done on a sunny day on the beach. The figures on the left show how to hold your hands to create shadow pictures of animals.

Plastercasts

🐚 ✂ ❋ ♀

❖ *plaster*
 water
 a small bowl
 a spade
 a stick

Look for a piece of the beach where the sand is wet and also firm, such as a section that is wet as the tide goes out.

1 Make a small hollow in the sand, 2 cm is deep enough. You can use a stick to sharpen the corners. This is your 'mould.'
 You can also lay some shells in the hollow so that they will be embedded in the plaster.
2 Make a firm paste of plaster and water. Do not make it too thick, because you will have to be able to pour it into the sand mould. You can use the stick to push the plaster into all the corners, if necessary. The plaster will become firm quite quickly, but it will take around 12 hours to become really hard.
3 Let the plaster dry sufficiently. You can then take it out of the sand. If you do this carefully, you can use the mould again. You will probably not be able to do it a third time, because sand sticks to the plaster each time you take it out and the mould loses its sharpness.

15. Indoor and Outdoor Games

Rules that always apply

In all the games, it is important that the rules of play are clear before you begin.

* *Who begins?* This will sometimes be self-evident. On other occasions it will be useful to do a selection game (see p. 149).
* During the vacation, other children will take part in the game, even although you do not know them (well). It is then important to establish in advance *how many rounds* or *how long* the game will last.
* This also applies to the way points are earned and when someone is declared the winner.

Penalty points
⚜ ✤ ✂ 5⁺ ⬆ ♀

Penalty points refer to moments when children who have lost a game, don't know the answer to a question, or do something else wrongly, have to incur a penalty. They may have to relinquish something: a handkerchief, comb, hairgrip, pencil or do a chore, etc.

Lots of games in this chapter can involve penalties or pledges, such as:

* Earth, water, air, see page 154
* All birds fly, see page 179
* Who sinks the ship, see page 183
* Watch the plate, see page 183

If there are children who have not yet incurred any penalties, you could play the Yes/No game, in which the children have to respond to a number of questions without saying *yes* or *no.*

Redeeming pledges
⚜ ✤ ✂ 3⁺ ⬆ ♀

After a whole afternoon playing games, the children may have incurred a number of penalties or pledges. They will have to try to redeem these by doing something positive.

A game can be played to redeem objects. For example, one of the children turns around and hold her hands in front of her eyes so that she cannot see the objects that have been relinquished. One of the others points to an object and asks the child with her hand in front of her eyes what the owner has to do to redeem the first object. The child has to think up an action or a chore without knowing who has to perform it.

* Things that the children can do:
  — hop around a specific circuit
  — clear the table
  — run an errand
  — feed one of the others
  — kiss one of the others, etc.

Quiet table games

Gathering sweets
⚀ ⚜ 3⁺ ⬆ 🔔 ▦
✤ dish
  knife (not sharp)
  sweets (candies)
  dice

There is a dish of sweets (candies) in the middle of the table. The dice is passed around and each child throws once. As soon as a child has thrown a six, he can try to get sweets out of the dish using only the knife. He continues to do so until the next six is thrown. Then a new child tries his luck with the knife.

Raisin
⚜ ✤ 3⁺ ⬆ 🔔
✤ raisins
  plate

One child goes out of the room. A plate of raisins is placed on the table and one of the children points to one of the raisins. Now the other child can come into the room. She eats the raisins from the plate one by one until she gets to the chosen raisin. Then the other children shout *Stop!* The plate is filled again and one of the other children leaves the room.

The game goes on until everyone has had the same number of turns. One of the children may have been unlucky and could only get one or two raisins. Give them some extra to compensate.

Who has the most squares?
🎲 🎯 2-6 ⌂ 🏃 ✎ ▦

❖ *dice*
   sheet of paper
   coloured pencils or felt-tips

Draw seven horizontal and vertical lines on a sheet of paper so that 6 x 6 boxes are created.

Place one dot in each of the boxes in the top row, just like on the dice. Place two dots in each of the boxes in the second row, etc. If the children are not yet good in counting, you can give each box a colour. In that case, you should use a dice with colours instead of dots.

Give the children a number of tokens (or sweets, for instance), each in their own colour. Each child throws the dice and then lays his token on a box with the same number of dots (or colour). If a child cannot lay a token because all the boxes are full, he misses a turn. At the end, the child with the most boxes is the winner.

Variation:

Of course, you can get the children to colour in a box. Each child has a coloured pencil in a particular colour. The child with the most boxes in their colour is the winner.

Another variation is to allow a child to colour in a box only when he has thrown a six.

Playing cards for candy
🎲 ✂ 3⁺ ⌂ 🏃

❖ *pack of cards*
   sweets (candies) or bar of
   chocolate

There is a dish full of goodies in the middle of the table — small chocolate bars, etc.

Shuffle the cards and give each child four cards. The rest of the pack lies face down on the table. Each child looks to see if his four cards belong together: four jacks, four twos, or three-four-five-six of one suit, etc. If this is the case, the player lays her cards open on the table, takes four new cards, and chooses something from the dish.

If no one has a set, one of the players takes a card from the pack and throws one away, next to the pack. If he then has a set, he can show it and take a sweet. Then it is the next player's turn.

Determine in advance when the game is to finish.

Pursuit
🎲 ✂ 2 ⌂ 🏃 ✎

❖ *a white and a grey stone*

Take a chessboard or draw 11 horizontal and vertical lines on a large piece of paper so that 10 × 10 squares are created.

The first child begins by laying his stone in a box somewhere in the middle. Then the second child does the same. The first child tries to get to one of the edges as quickly as possible. He can move his stone in all directions, even diagonally, but only one square at a time.

The second child tries to prevent the other child reaching his goal. He places his stone in such a way that the first child cannot go any further in the direction he wanted to go. The second child can move his stone two squares at once, if he wishes, but he cannot move his stone diagonally.

Agree in advance about the number of moves to be made.

Kim

❂ ⚒ ✿ ✳ ♀ ⚑ ✎

✢ *small objects*
   cloth
   pencil
   paper

Place a number of different small objects on a table under a cloth. Take the cloth away and let the children look at the objects for a certain time.

You can make this game easy or difficult according to the age of the children. You can vary the number of objects (ten to twenty) and also the length of time they get to view the objects (twenty to thirty seconds).

With small children, you should go round in a circle and ask each child to name one of the objects under the cloth. The other children then say whether or not they have seen that object too.

Older children can write down the objects they remember.

Variation:
Instead of looking at objects, the children can feel what is under the cloth and write down they think what it is.

Natural kim

⚒ ✿ ✳ ⌂ ♀

✢ *a number of small objects from*
   nature
   cloth

Look for around ten natural objects: a twig, a pine cone, a stone, etc. Lay a cloth over them, then remove it and get the children to look at them for twenty seconds. Then the children have to look for the same objects in nature. Who is quickest to complete the set?

How many things fit into a matchbox?

⚒ ✿ ✂ 3⁺ ⌂ ⚑

✢ *lots of small items*
   such as paperclips
   matches
   stones
   peas
   grains of rice, etc.

Look for lots of different things and lay them in small piles on the table.

Give all the children an empty matchbox. Then they try to place as

many small items in the matchbox as possible without it overflowing.

Who can get the most items, or the most different items, into the matchbox? You will not win if you only fill the matchbox with grains of rice.

Variation:
You can get older children to look for things in nature to put into their matchboxes. Of course, they will need more time for this. It can produce some surprising results.

Winning the treasure
♟ ♘ 3⁺ ⬛ ⬛ ⊞

❖ *a treasure (a small present or something tasty)*
  cocktail sticks
  dice

A tower of cocktail sticks is built around the treasure. The children begin by throwing the dice. The first child to throw a six starts. The children then remove from the tower the same number of cocktail sticks as the number on the dice they have thrown. When the tower has been completely demolished and all the cocktail sticks have been divided among the children, the child with the most cocktail sticks is the winner. He wins the treasure. Then the game can begin again, offering the other players the chance to win.

Blow dice
♘ ✂ 4⁺ ⬛ ⬛ ⊞

❖ *three dice*
  cup

Two dice are shaken in a cup that is then turned upside down on the table. The third dice is placed on the bottom of the cup, with the two facing upwards and the 1 on the edge of the cup. The player blows the dice from the edge of the cup and multiplies the number gained by the total number shown on the dice under the cup. The player with

the most points is the winner. Agree in advance about how long you are going to play.

Run
♟ ♘ 2-5 ⬛ ⬛ ⊞

❖ *three dice*

This game aims at creating a run of three, such as: 1-2-3 or 2-4-6, etc. Each player can throw twice. If someone has thrown 1-5-6, he can throw the 1 again in the hope of getting a 4. A penalty point is given for each number that is not in a run. The player with the least penalty points after an agreed number of rounds is the winner.

Threes
♘ ✂ 4⁺ ⬛ ⬛ ⊞

❖ *three dice*

Each player has to try to get three equal dice (each showing the same number) in a maximum of three throws. He can leave dice lying if he wishes. A player can throw 2-2-5, for example. He leaves the 2-2 as they are, and tries to throw a two with the third dice.
— Two equal numbers in three throws = 1 point
— Three equal numbers in three throws = 3 points.
— Three equal numbers in two throws = 4 points.

— Three equal numbers in one throw = 15 points.

Throwing dice for matches
♘ ✂ ✳ ♀ ⬛ ⊞

❖ *matchsticks*
  dice

All players have 10 matchsticks. There is a bowl at the middle of the table. The dice goes round and the person who first throws a six begins. He places the same number of matches in the bowl as are shown on the dice. In the second or third round, it may happen that a player throws a five but only has two matches left. In that case, he has to take three matches from the bowl. To win, the player must throw exactly the same number as he has matches.

The 'Games Along the Way' chapter, beginning on p. 120, includes the following games:

Games with pencil and paper

Drawing a story
🎲🌼 ❄ ⌂ 🚗 ✎
Head, body, and legs
🎲🌼 2⁺ ⌂ 🚗 ✎
Hangman
🌼✂ 2⁺ ⌂ 🚗 ✎
Noughts and crosses
🎲🌼 2 ⌂ 🚗 ✎
Initials
🎲🌼✂ 2⁺ ⌂ 🚗 ✎
Hiring a room
🎲🌼✂ 2⁺ ⌂ 🚗 ✎
The bus is full
🎲🌼✂ ❄ ⌂ 🚗 ✎
How many names do you have?
🌼✂ 3⁺ ⌂ 🚗 ✎
Trailer
🌼✂ 2⁺ ⌂ 🚗 ✎
Back to front
🌼✂ ❄ ⌂ 🚗 ✎
Advertisement
🌼✂ ❄ ⌂ 🚗 ✎
An animal with nine points
🎲🌼✂ ❄ ⌂ 🚗 ✎
Secret language
🌼✂ ❄ ⌂ 🚗 ✎
How many words with …
🌼✂ 3⁺ ⌂ 🚗 ✎
I have 100
🌼✂ ❄ ⌂ 🚗 ✎
My sentence rhymes
🌼✂ ❄ ⌂ 🚗 ✎
Making new words
🌼✂ ❄ ⌂ 🚗 ✎
Counting to 100
🌼✂ ❄ ⌂ 🚗 ✎
Battleships
🌼✂ 2 ⌂ 🚗 ✎

Matching dice
🌼✂ 2⁺ ⌂ 🚗 ⊞
❖ *three dice*

In this game, the total number shown on two dice is equal to that shown on the third. You can add, subtract, multiply and divide. Points are given for a correct throw. Agree in advance how many rounds you are going to play.

Left, right or middle
🌼✂ 2⁺ ⌂ 🚗 ⊞
❖ *three dice*
   matches as tokens

If there are two or three players each player is given five matchsticks. The person throwing the highest number in a preliminary round gets to start. After that only the 1, 2 and 3 count.

If you throw a 1, you have to give the neighbour on your left-hand side a match. If you throw a two you get a match from your right-hand neighbour. If you throw a three, you lay a matchstick on the table. If you throw three ones, for example, you have to give your left-hand neighbour three matches, etc.

If you have no matches left, you cannot throw the dice but you are still in the game because you might get matches from your neighbours. Agree on how long you are going to play. The person with the most matches is the winner.

Trumps
🌼✂ 3⁺ ⌂ 🚗 ⊞
❖ *three dice*
   matches

Each player gets nine matches and places them in front of him on the table.

One of the players throws one of the dice. The number he throws is 'trumps.' This number is fixed for the rest of the game.

If three is trumps and you throw a three, you can lay one of your matches in the middle of the table. You then get another turn. If you throw three threes, you can put in an extra match, thus four matches in total. If you throw any other number except for a three, your turn is over and it is the next player's turn. The player that first gets rid of all of his matches is the winner.

House dice
🎲🌼 2⁺ ⌂ 🚗 ✎ ⊞
❖ *pencil and paper*
   dice

A (drawn) house consists of twenty lines. Each player throws the dice and draws his own house by drawing the number of lines he has just thrown with the dice. The first person to complete his house is the winner.

Chicago
⚘ ✂ 4-8 ⌂ ♞ ⊞
❖ *three dice*

This game aims at getting a certain number of points agreed in advance. It may be 500 points or 1000, for example. Points are given according to the number thrown with the dice.

1 = 10 points,
2 = 20 points, etc.
6 = 60 points.

Each child throws three times.

How many matches?
⚘ 3 ⌂ ♞
❖ *matches*

Make a pile of matches on the table. Each of the children guesses how many matches there are on the table in total. The person who has guessed correctly, or is the nearest, gets three points, the next best guess earns two points, etc. Agree in advance how many rounds you will play. The child with the most points is the winner.

Variation:

You can play a variation of this game. All the children are given a certain number of matches. Then they give a certain amount to the games master without the other players seeing how many. After this, they all have to guess how many matches the games master has. The player who guesses correctly gets the matches from the games master. When someone has no matches left, he is out.

Remembering names
⚘ ✂ ❋ ⌂ ♀

This is a good game to play when there are children who don't know one another. The children stand in a circle and say their first name, one by one.

Then one child goes into the middle of the circle and points to one of the children, saying at the same time *left* or *right*. The person pointed to must then say the name of her left or right-hand neighbour. If she cannot do this, she has to go into the circle and point to someone. You can also give the children points if they remember the names correctly.

Zero
♙ ⚘ 2⁺ ⌂ ♞
❖ *matches*

Place sixteen matches in four rows, as shown below. In turn, the players remove one or more matches from one of the rows. The person who has to take the last match has lost.

Twenty-five letters
✂ 3⁺ ⌂ ♞ ✎
❖ *pencil and paper*

This game resembles a crossword puzzle. Each player receives a sheet of paper and draws six horizontal and six vertical lines, thus creating twenty-five squares. One by one the players say a letter that each player writes down in a square of his own choice.

The aim is to make as many words as possible, both horizontally and vertically. The same letter can be used in a horizontal word and in a vertical word.

After twenty-five turns, all the squares have been filled. The player with the most words is the winner.

Writing blind
⚘ ✂ 3⁺ ⌂ ✐
❖ *pencil and paper blindfold*

One of the children is blindfolded. She gets a piece of paper and a pencil between her fingers. Now one of the other children takes the blindfolded person's hand and writes a word. The blindfolded person does not know which word this is, as her hand was guided by the other child. The blindfolded child then has to guess which word he has written.

This is not an easy game. Don't allow the guessing to go on too long. Encourage the children by saying they are getting warm, hot, etc. when they are getting closer to guessing correctly.

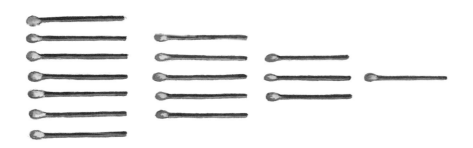

Musical games and listening games

Sing a song
♡ ♟ ♙ ✳ ⇧ ♀ 🚗

Singing a song is often a good way of getting the children to relax.

Guessing songs
♟ ♙ 3⁺ ⇧ ♪

✛ *musical instrument or CD player*

In this game, one adult has to supply the music, while another keeps the score.

Play a song, and give points to the child that guesses the name of the song first. The quicker the correct solution, the more points the children score.

Adapting the melody
♙ ✄ 3⁺ ♀ ♪

Someone hums the first part of a line in a song. As soon as he stops, the other children try to complete the line. If the song is not guessed correctly after the first line, you can repeat the first line and go on to the next line.

Variation:

The quiz-master reads out one line of a well-known song. The players then have to say the next line. You can also play this game in two groups.

Which song is that?
♙ ✄ 3⁺ ⇧ ♪

One of the children begins by clapping the rhythm of a well-known song. The children then try to guess which song this is. The child who guesses correctly claps the rhythm of the next song.

Clapping the rhythm of a song is difficult for younger children. Older children usually have no difficulty. You can award points for every correct guess.

Bottle music
♟ ♙ 2-3 ♀ ♪

✛ *bottles*
  strings
  wooden sticks

Hang a piece of strong string or rope between two trees. Take eight glass bottles and hang them with thin string on the piece of rope.

If you hit the bottles with a stick, they will make a sound. You can change the tone they produce by pouring some water into the bottles. The more you put in, the higher the tone they produce. Pour a little bit in at one time and listen to the sound the bottle makes. If you do this carefully, you can make a scale and then learn to play tunes on the bottles.

Guessing sounds
♟ ♙ 3⁺ ⇧ ✎ ✐ ♪

✛ *pencil and paper*
  blindfolds
  'instruments'

The *musical instruments* in this game can be random objects, as long as they make a noise: a block of wood, a glass (perhaps filled with water), a tin can, a paper bag, etc.

All the children are blindfolded except for one, who makes a number of consecutive noises. With younger children, there should not be too many in one go. Older children can make six or eight.

When all the sounds have been heard, the blindfolds are removed and the children have to write down the sounds they remember.

Word games and guessing games

Occupations
⚅ ♘ ✄ 5⁺ ⌂ ♀ ◍
✥ *ball*

The children sit in a circle on the ground and one of them has the ball. She rolls the ball to one of the others and calls out an occupation. The receiver has to name three things that are concerned with that occupation (younger children only need to mention one thing). For example, if the first child calls out *gardener,* the receiver of the ball could mention *spade, rake* and *wheelbarrow.*

If a child takes too much time to mention three items, or makes a mistake, he loses a life or incurs a penalty point.

Then the child with the ball rolls it toward another child and calls out the name of another occupation, and so on.

Where is it?
⚅ ♘ 5⁺ ⌂
✥ *a small object*

The children are shown a small object and then they all go out of the room. The object is placed at a spot in the room where it is hardly noticeable. The children come into the room and look for the object. If one of the children sees the object, he does not say anything but simply stops looking. The game goes on until the last child has found the object. In the meantime, the children can gain pleasure from the fact that the others are apparently not smart enough to find the object.

All birds fly
⚅ ♘ 3⁺ ⌂ ♀

You begin the game by calling out: *all birds fly* and stretching both arms in the air. The children have to do this, because all birds fly. Then you can name lots of birds that can all fly and the children have to raise their arms. Then you mention an animal that cannot fly. Anyone who (partially) raises his arms is out, or gets a penalty point.

If older children are participating, let them take turns to call out the names.

Simon says
⚅ ♘ 3⁺ ⌂ ♀

This game is a variation of *All birds fly.* One of the players tries to confuse the others. She says, for example: *Simon says: Raise your right arm,* but raises her left arm. The others have to follow her instructions and raise their *right* arms. She can use all her limbs.

She can also mislead them in another way. If she says: *Fold your arms,* the others do not need to do this because it was not Simon who gave the order.

Travelling shop
♟ ♞ 2-4 ⌂

I have a travelling shop
I'm on my way and here I stop.
I do not sell black or white
Yes or No are not right,
What will you buy?

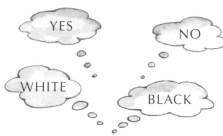

While the shopkeeper is out of the room, the other children decide on an object. The shopkeeper comes back in and asks one of the buyers what he wants to buy. The shopkeeper tries to find out what the object is, but the questions may be about anything; they are also intended to confuse the buyer. The buyer must give an answer but, as said in the rhyme, he cannot mention the words *yes* or *no* or *black* or *white*. If the buyer makes a mistake, he is out. If he always answers correctly, he can be the next shopkeeper.

What have I bought?
♟ ♞ 3⁺ ⌂ ♀

One of the children imagines that he has bought something. If necessary, the games master can help him here. Then the child says: *I was in the shop and there I bought, I've forgotten what it's called.*

Now the other children try to guess what the article is. The buyer can only answer with *yes* or *no*. The child who guesses correctly becomes the new buyer.

I spy with my little eye
♟ ♞ 3⁺ ⌂ ♀

One of the children says: *I spy with my little eye something beginning with ... (a letter of the alphabet).*

Now the other players look around and try to guess which object this could be. The child that guesses correctly then gets to say a letter.

You've got it, you haven't!
♟ ♞ 5⁺ ⌂ ♀

The games master (or one of the children) walks past all the children and says *You've got it.* At the next child he can say *You've got it too.* At the next child he may say *You haven't got it.*

He has a particular object or feature in mind, which some children have and others haven't. It may be a sandal, a T-shirt, or an earring. After the games master has said something to all the children, they have to guess what the object is. The child that guesses correctly is the new games master and the game starts again.

How many matches 2
♟ ♞ 3⁺ ⌂ ♀

⚘ *matches*

All the players are given an equal number of matches. If there are three or four players, this can be ten matches, if there are more players this may be fifteen.

All the players have their hands behind their backs. Each player decides how many matches he will hold in his closed fist (this may also be none). The players stretch out the fists holding the matches. One of the players guesses how many matches each of the other players is holding in his fist. If the player has guessed correctly, the player with the matches has to place his matches in the middle. Then the game starts again with a different child guessing. When a child has lost all his matches, he is out.

Variation:
You can also agree that a player who guesses correctly gets the matches from the other player. The player with the most matches at the end is the winner.

The Games Along the Way chapter, beginning on p. 121, includes the following word and guessing games:

Word games

Animal, vegetable, or mineral?
⚃ ✿ ✂ 3⁺ ⌂ 🚗
Tongue-twisters
⚃ ✿ ✳ ⌂ 🚗
I'm going on a journey and I'll take …
⚃ ✿ ✂ 3⁺ ⌂ 🚗
What didn't I say?
⚃ ✿ ✂ 3⁺ ⌂ 🚗
ABC
✿ ✂ 3⁺ ⌂ 🚗
Talking for a full minute
✿ ✂ 3⁺ ⌂ 🚗
No … without
✿ ✂ 2⁺ ⌂ 🚗
Continuing story
✿ ✂ 3⁺ ⌂ 🚗
You can't say 'eh…'
✿ ✂ 3⁺ ⌂ 🚗

Guessing games

Riddles
⚃ ✿ ✂ ✳ ⌂ 🚗
Who are you thinking of?
⚃ ✿ ✂ ✳ ⌂ 🚗
Odd man out
⚃ ✿ ✂ 3⁺ ⌂ 🚗
Counting blind
⚃ ✿ ✂ ✳ ⌂ 🚗
Who is it??
✿ ✂ ✳ ⌂ 🚗
Guessing a number
✿ ✂ 3⁺ ⌂ 🚗
Pass on the song
✿ ✂ 4⁺ ⌂ 🚗 ♪
Counting money
✿ ✂ ✳ ⌂ 🚗
What do I look like today?
✿ ✂ ✳ ⌂ 🚗
How long is a kilometre?
✿ ✂ ✳ ⌂ 🚗

Compound words

✿ ✂ 3⁺ ⌂ ♀ 🚗 ✎
❖ *pencil and paper*

Write down a word on a notepad. You must be able to make a compound word from this. Pass the notepad on to the next person. This person tries to make a new word by taking the last part of the original word and adding a new part. If this is successful, he passes the notepad on to the next person. If someone cannot go any further, he loses a life or gets a penalty point and the notepad is passed on to the next person. If it is not possible to make any new words, the game starts again with a new word.

Example:
  Fire
  fireman
  manpower
  powerplay
  playground
  groundhog
  hogwash
  washday
  daytime
  timeline, etc.

Whose suitcase?

✿ ✂ 3⁺ ⌂ ✎
❖ *pieces of paper*
  pencils

One of the players leaves the room and the others agree for whom the suitcase is to be packed. They each take some pieces of paper and write down items that have something to do with this person. All the pieces of paper are placed in a dish.

The first player comes back into the room and reads what is written on the pieces of paper. He has to guess for whom the suitcase has been packed. Everyone gets a turn. The child who reads the least number of papers before guessing correctly is the winner.

Adjective charades

✂ ✳ ⌂

One of the children leaves the room and the others choose an adjective, such as passionate. The child comes back into the room and asks the other children to act out this word. This can be: giving a kiss, showing lots of emotion, etc. The emphasis lies on how the child acts out the word, rather than on what he does.

When the word has been guessed, another child leaves the room. If the word is not guessed, the first child can leave the room again and a new word is thought up.

Variation:
The players are divided into two groups. Each group thinks up a word for each player in the other group. Each player is given his word in turn and has to act it out for his own group, which has to guess the word

as quickly as possible. This can be easy, such as footballer, or penguin, or more difficult, such as milk bottle, or mountain, or custard, etc.

More games

Blowing bubbles
🔲 🐞 ✳ ♀

✦ soapsuds
  thin wire

Take a piece of thin wire and make a circle with a diameter of 2–3 cm (1 in), with a handle. Make some soapsuds (a little sugar in the mixture helps make good bubbles). The children can dip the wire in the soapsuds and blow bubbles into the air.

Car race
🔲 🐞 🐞 ✳ ⌂ ♀

✦ thin string or wool
  small cars

The string can be long or short depending on the children's ages. It should be 3–5 metres (9 to 15 feet) long.

Tie each of the cars to a piece of string. Every child gets a car on a string

and has to roll up the string as quickly as possible to draw the car toward himself. With younger children, it is better to fix the string to a piece of cardboard.

Balloons
🐞 🐞 ✳ ⌂ ♀

✦ balloons
  gifts

There is sometimes a good reason to give all the children a small present. Wrap all the gifts in advance and give them a number or a picture.

Take the same numbers or pictures and stick them to a piece of paper and put them inside a balloon.

At the right time, the balloons are inflated and thrown into the air. Each child grabs a balloon and bursts it to get the piece of paper out. He then knows which present is for him.

Bite the cake
🔲 🐞 ✳ ⌂ ♀

✦ thick string
  several pieces of thin string with a
    piece of cake attached

Stretch a piece of thick string from one side of the room to the other, or between two trees.

Attach some cake to several pieces of thin string which are then tied to the thick string. The cake should hang at around mouth height for the children.

The children now keep their hands behind their backs and try to bite the cake without using their hands (of course, the games master will have to help younger children if they have too much difficulty).

Fishing
🔲 🐞 🐞 4⁺ ⌂ ♀

✦ fishing (rod) with a magnet
  fish with iron rings (washers)
  paper

The fish swim in a large cardboard box. They all have an iron ring (or a paperclip) in their mouths. There is a magnet at the end of the fishing line. The children are not allowed to look into the box as they go fishing. The box also contains old rubbish (old shoes, for example) that you have also cut out of paper. They can catch these too. You can give the fish a number to represent their weight if you are organizing a competition, or the number can correspond with the number on a present waiting for them on the table.

Eat and whistle
❀ ✄ 3⁺ ⚲ ♀

✛ *cream crackers*

This is a difficult game.

Hand out some cream crackers. When you give the sign, the children begin to eat the crackers. The child who first finishes his cracker and then whistles the first line of a well-known song is the winner.

Variation:

You can play this as a contest between two groups. The second person in the group can only begin eating his cracker when the first person has finished his cracker and whistled his song.

Who can sink the ship?
♟ ❀ 3⁺ ⚲ ♀ ⚙ ⊞

✛ *basin*
jam pot lids
spoon
dice

The lids are the ships. Float them in a basin of water.

The dice goes round. If someone throws a six, he has to use a spoon to put a little water in one of the floating lids. If too much water goes in, the lid may sink. The person who causes a ship to sink loses a life.

Watch the plate
❀ ✄ 5⁺ ⚲ ♀

✛ *plastic plate*

The children sit in a circle. One of the children goes to the middle and sets the plate spinning on its side. He now calls out the name of one of the other children. This child has to jump into the middle and grab the plate before it falls. Then he sets the plate spinning, and calls out the name of another child. If the plate falls before the player can grab it, he loses a life.

Hot or cold?
♟ ❀ 4⁺ ⚲ ♀

✛ *any object*

While one of the children is out of the room, the other children choose an object. When the child comes into the room, he has to seek out that object. The other children can help him by shouting *hot* or *cold*. If necessary, an agreement can be made in advance on how long the search should take.

Pin the tail on the donkey
⚘ ⚘ 4⁺ ⌂ ✎

❖ *blindfold*
drawing of a large donkey (without a tail)
separate piece of firm paper in the shape of a donkey's tail
drawing pin

Draw a large donkey without a tail on a large piece of cardboard (from the supermarket). The donkey does not need to be perfectly drawn. Fix it to the wall at a position where the children can easily reach it. Draw a separate tail.

One by one, the children are blindfolded and have to go to the donkey and try to attach the tail in the right place. You can use a drawing pin for this or a piece of double-sided tape.

You may get a donkey with a tail on its nose.

Dropping the nail
⚘ ⚘ ✳ ⌂ ♀

❖ *empty bottles*
thin string
nails

All the children get a string tied around their waists. A piece of string with a nail at the end is tied to this waist belt.

At a given sign, the children stand in front of the bottles and try to drop the nail in the bottle without using their hands. They can only do so by bending their knees.

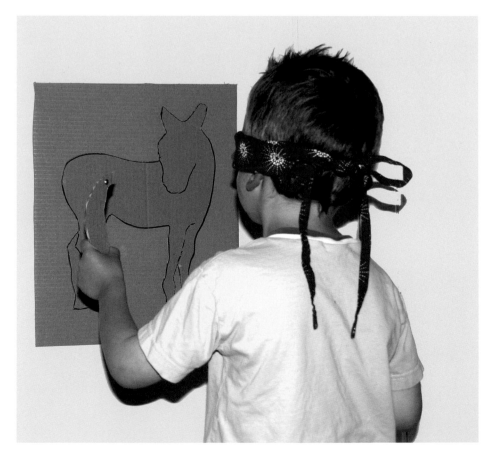

Who has the longest string?
⚘ ⚘ ✳ ⌂

❖ *many short pieces of string or wool*

Cut some thin string or wool into lots of pieces with varying lengths and lay the pieces at different places in the room. The children have to look for the pieces of string and tie them together. Who has the longest string?

Who has the longest snake?
⚘ ✂ ✳ ⌂ ♀ ✄

❖ *newspapers*

All the children get a quarter or half of a newspaper page. They now have to tear it into one thin strand without it breaking. The longest strand of newspaper is the winner.

Cup-catching
⚘ ✂ ✳ ♀

❖ *plastic cup*
piece of string
small ball

Make a small hole in a plastic cup. Thread a piece of string about 1 metre long through the hole and tie it to the cup. Now tie the other end to the small ball or, if the ball is made of polystyrene, push the string through it with a needle.

The rules of play:
Throw the ball up and try to catch it in the cup.

Bobbing for apples
♣♕✳⌂♀

✤ *basin of water*
an apple for each child
several towels

Float several apples in a basin of water. One by one, the children try to grab one of the apples using only their mouths (hands behind their backs). The younger children may need some help.

Travel tickets
♕✂4⁺⌂♀

One of the players leaves the room to think up a travel story. In the meantime, the other children left in the room agree on a number of words that they will mention when the storyteller points to them. The storyteller comes back in and starts on his story. When he points to someone, he is given a word that he has to include in his story. In this way, the story can consistently take a new turn.

Blow football
♣♕6⁺⌂♀🔨

✤ *ping-pong ball*
thin cardboard
sellotape
straws

Tape a small vertical board around the table but leave open a space of around 15 cm (6 in) to function as goals at either end.

The rules of play are the same as in real football, but the ball is not kicked or headed. The children use the straws to blow the ping-pong ball into their opponent's goal. They are not allowed to push the ball with the straw.

Throwing hoops
♣♕✂✳⌂

Although this is an ideal beach game, you can also play it indoors with a number of empty bottles.

Begin by making a line on the floor. The children have to stand behind this line. Place a number of empty bottles at varying distances from the line. Each bottle is given a certain number of points. If someone manages to throw a hoop over a bottle, he gains the number of points shown on or under the bottle. The child with the most points is the winner.

16. Being Creative with Natural Materials

What tools do you need?

This question can be answered in different ways, depending on your skill and what you want to make. If you want to make complicated things, you will probably need more tools.

For the more simple jobs, you will probably only require:

* a good pocket knife with a blade, a serrated edge, and an awl (see Fig 187.1).
* two pairs of pliers
* a ball of thin wire
* strong string
* a piece of sandpaper.

You can add to these with:

* a hand drill. The small gimlets are very handy.
* a pair of pincers
* a normal saw, smallest size
* a small file
* a small hammer
* a small wood clamp

Fig 187.1

You can get all kinds of *glue*. It is important that the glue dries reasonably quickly. Use all-purpose glue in a tube with a thin nozzle. We advise you not to use the really fast-drying glues (super glue, for example), certainly not with young children. With most do-it-yourself glues, both sides have to be coated, allowed to dry a little and then pressed together. The glue is only really dry after a few hours.

If you are using wood, then original wood glue is the best. So-called fast-drying wood glue takes more time to dry than normal all-purpose glue.

You could also take with you:

* a tube of acrylic paint and a brush
* a little transparent (acryl) varnish

Acryl paint and varnish are water-based. Paint or varnish that has not yet dried can be washed off with water.

Gnomes from branches

⚒ ⚘ ❋ ♀ 🏹

❖ saw
  pocket knife
  sandpaper
  glue
  form sticks
  dried moss
  a leaf

These gnomes can be made by children without any help from the adults. The size of the gnome depends on the thickness of the branches and also on the length of the saw.

You can make all sizes. If you have a stick 2 cm (1 in) thick, you will need a length of 8–9 cm (4 in).

Fig 187.2 shows that the length of the long pointed hat is equal to the rest of the body. The gnomes pictured on page 186 are 5 cm (2 in) thick and around 20 cm (8 in) long. With the gnome on the left-hand side, the

Fig 187.2

hat has been sawn off and used as a peaked cap.

First saw the slanting end because it is easier to hold on to the longer branch. As you are sawing diagonally, you can easily make two gnomes at once. Make the bottom as flat as possible. If necessary, sandpaper the sawn ends. If you have small gnomes, it is easiest to paint the gnomes' faces. For larger gnomes, you can use all kinds of material for their faces.

Fig 188.1

Fig 188.2   Fig 188.3

Wooden snake

❀ ✄ ✳ ♀ 🐘 ✄

❖ thick sticks
  thinner sticks or wooden beads
  red wool or string
  drill

The snake shown in the Figure 188.1 is around 45 cm (18 in) long. To make this, you will need: 17 large and 17 smaller wooden disks.

A thin disk is inserted between each pair of thick disks to allow the snake to move better.

Because the snake gets thinner towards its tail, you will need different sticks to cut the appropriate thicknesses.

1 Saw the disks and drill a hole through the middle. Saw a larger piece for the snake's head and shape its jaws. Drill a hole through the disk.
2 Lay all the disks in the proper sequence Take the red wool or string and thread it through all the segments of the snake. Figure 188.2 shows how you can make a kind of needle from a thin piece of wire. If you do not have any wire, you can dip the end of the string in a little glue and allow it to dry so that the end becomes hard.
3 Tie a good knot in the jaws and at the tail so that the disks cannot become loose. Leave a lengthy piece sticking out of the jaws as the tongue.

   Give the snake enough space between the disks so that it can writhe like a real snake.

Giraffe from branches

🐘 ❀ ✳ ♀ 🐘 ✄

❖ saw
  pocket knife
  sandpaper
  glue
  thick and thin sticks
  piece of thick string for the tail

First look for a suitable branch for the body and saw this to size. Then determine how thick and how long the neck and the legs ought to be.

1 Cut a piece the right size for the head. Round the snout off and flatten the underside.
2 Now use all-purpose glue to fix the head to the neck. If it will not stay on, drill a small hole through the head and the top of the neck and use a matchstick as a *nail*. You can cut eyes in the bark.
3 Drill two small holes where the horns are located. Take two very small sticks, sharpen one end and insert them into the holes. Then stick two ears to the back of the head.
4 Flatten the lower part of the neck so that it can easily be fixed to the body. Glue or nail (with matches) the neck to the body.
5 Flatten the place where the legs are stuck to the body, and cut the legs diagonally at the point of contact (see Fig 189.2). Glue the legs to the body and allow the glue to dry thoroughly.
6 Drill a small hole at the back for the tail and insert a piece of string.

Dog from branches

⚗ ✤ ❀ ♀ ♠ ✄

✤ saw
    pocket knife
    sandpaper
    glue
    solid branches

You can make many different kinds of animals in much the same way you made the giraffe. See the figure of the dog on this page. (see Fig 189.3)

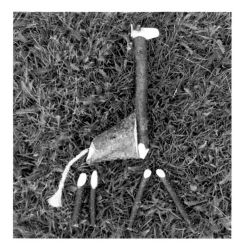

Fig 189.1

Fig 189.2

Fig 189.3

Fig 189.4

Snail

⚗ ✤ ✂ ❀ ♀ ♠ ✄

✤ snail's shell
    stick
    glue and pocket knife

You will find an empty snail's shell somewhere in the countryside. You can also use a shell from the beach. It is quite easy to make the snail itself. Look for a short stick, preferably one that is slightly curved. Round one end (the head) with a knife and make the other end pointed. Prick two holes in the head and glue two matchsticks in these holes. Then glue the shell to the back of the snail.

Puppet dog

✿ ✂ ✳ ♀ 🐕 ✂
✥ saw
  pocket knife
  sandpaper
  glue
  thick and thin branches
  matches
  strong
  thin string

1 Look for suitable pieces of branch
   for the separate components: the
   body, neck, head, ears, four legs
   and the tail, as well as a stick to
   hold up and control the puppet.
   Saw everything to size.

2 Because all the parts have to be
   able to move, the pieces have
   to be attached to one another
   with string. The adjacent picture
   shows where the holes have to be
   drilled. The body has four holes
   for the legs, a hole for the string
   that goes through the neck and
   the head and is attached to the
   control stick itself. There is one
   hole for the tail and another at the
   rear for the string that goes to the
   control stick. There are two holes
   in the head for the ears.

3 Drill the holes in the neck and the
   head all the way through, ena-
   bling the head to move.

4 Thread a piece of string through
   the holes in the limbs. Cut the
   ends, press them together and
   smear a little glue on them. Insert
   them into the appropriate holes
   and push in a piece of matchstick
   to clamp them in.
     You can make the string to the
   control stick as long or short as
   you wish, depending on the size
   of the children.

Pine cone mouse

⚜ 🐚 ✳ ♀ 🐐 🦌

⁘ *pine cone*
  all-purpose glue

Under a tree, you will often find a pine cone that squirrels have only half consumed. These cones already resemble mice with their pointed snout, tapering body, and long tail. You only need to stick two pointed ears on the cone and the mouse is complete. If you place the mouse in a warm spot, it will become really fat: the scales of the pine cone will open up.

Pine needle hedgehog

🐚 ✂ ✳ ♀ 🐐 🦌

⁘ *long pine needles*
  gnawed-down pine cone
  all-purpose glue
  thin wire

In a pine wood, the ground is often covered with long, brown pine needles that have fallen from the tree and with pine cones gnawed by squirrels. The pine needles occasionally have a beautiful red-brown colour.

1 Tie a sizeable bunch of pine needles together with a piece of wire. They may be attached to some small twigs. This makes it easier to give the bunch a sharp point with a knife.
2 Look for a piece of gnawed-down pine cone that can function as the snout of the hedgehog and to which you can glue the bundle of pine needles. Use a small drill or a knife to make a hole in the gnawed-down pine cone.
3 Glue the bunch of pine needles in the hole. Before you go any further, wait until the glue has become dry (it is best to use quick-drying glue). You can now cover the hedgehog by gluing double pine needles to the pine cone around the bunch that you have already glued on. Make sure that the needles stick up

Fig 191.1

Fig 191.2

vertically as much as possible. You can trim any pine needles that are too long.

Pine cone tortoise

⚜ 🐚 ✂ ✳ ♀ 🐐 🦌

⁘ *pine cone*

Look for a solid, round pine cone and saw it in half. You need the rounded part, the part that was attached to the tree. Pull six scales from the other half: one for the head, four for the legs, and the last one for the tail, which you will have to cut into a point.

Glue the legs under the half pine cone and the tortoise is completed.

There is one problem, however. It is usually cool and damp in the woods, and as a result the pine cone stays closed. As soon as it comes into the warmth, all the scales will open up and you will get an extraordinary tortoise. (see Fig 191.3)

Pine cone duck

🐚 ✂ ✳ ♀ 🐐 🦌

⁘ *pine cones*
  all-purpose glue

This duck is made from two small pine cones. The neck and the legs are formed by several loose scales. The whole creation has been glued together.

Fig 191.3

Fig 191.4

1

How do you work with natural materials?

This chapter will cover around forty natural materials, all of which you can pick up from the ground in the countryside. The grasses, the maize kernels and the seeds are perhaps an exception. You will be able to find this material the whole year round. If it lies on the ground for a lengthy period, the bright colours will disappear and it will become a little grey.

❀ How does it start?
    Your enthusiasm is often aroused during a walk or a hike when you see an unusually-shaped branch or suchlike. You can see an animal's head or other features in this shape. You take it with you, but when you want to make something you realize that other materials may be necessary.

❀ If you have had this kind of experience, you walk through the countryside with a different attitude. On the ground you suddenly see all kinds of objects that you can use to make things. From that moment on, you should take a bag with you to collect material in.

    When you get back to base, you can pick up a cardboard box from the supermarket. You can make compartments in this box to store all the separate items. You can also make such boxes yourself (see p. 204).

    Working is easiest when you have gathered quite a big collection and you have everything at hand when you start on your do-it-yourself projects.

Note:

In contrast to activities with paper and glue, making things from natural materials demands more time and patience because you often have to

2

3

wait until the glue has dried properly before continuing. If you glue too many things together at once, there is always the danger that the object will collapse and you will have to begin all over again.

People and animals from natural materials

☘ ❀ ✂ ❄ ⌂ 🐎 ✄

Which materials are used for the dolls and animals shown on this page?

Twigs, hanging moss, maize kernels, the white bark of the birch tree, hazelnut and hazelnut shells, pumpkin seeds, small stones, acorn cups, grasses, birds' feathers, various kinds of pine fruits such as pine cones.

Around the Mediterranean you will find different pine cones from those you find further north. They have very hard scales (see dolls 2 and 4) that only open at very high temperatures (with forest fires), releasing their seeds to the earth.

Doll 1 is made from various sawn off pine cones. A hollow has been made in the *dress*, into which the body has been inserted. The arms, made of thin twigs, have been glued between the scales. The hands are made of scales. The head is attached to the body by

means of a matchstick. The hair is a kind of moss that hangs down from coniferous trees.

Doll 2 is made from a Mediterranean pine cone. It has grass for hair. Maize kernels function as hands.

Bird 3 has feathers. The legs are made of kernels from Mediterranean pine cones.

The hair of **doll 4** is made from the top layer of birch bark.

The hair of **doll 7** is made from shells of the hazelnut.

4

5

6

7

Pictures made from natural materials

❀ ❀ ✄ ✳ ⌂ 🐘 ✂

✥ plank
  the bottom of an orange box or
    solid cardboard box
  natural materials
  glue

These pictures demonstrate that you can make all kinds of things from the simplest materials: dried grasses, leaves and maize sheaves. Even the youngest children can make this kind of objects if they receive some assistance.

The woman is made of the thin scales of a pine cone, a couple of pine twigs, and a few stones, all stuck on to a piece of white cardboard.

Figure 195.1 shows how many different materials you can use, including thick stalks of grass and dried moss.

Jewellery from natural materials

* sunflower seeds
  small stones
  twigs
  pine cone scales
  poppy seed capsules
  feathers
  glue.

You can use a piece of bark or a thin sliver from a branch as the background to your jewellery.

Fig 195.1

Gather together the jewels you want to use and see if the layout looks attractive before gluing it all together.

Use a piece of thin wire to fix a pendant to the piece of jewellery.

Necklace of pine cone scales
✂ ✱ ⌂ 🔨 ✂

✣ *large pine cone with tough scales,*
  file or sandpaper
  thread or chain

Saw the pine cone in two and use pliers to pull off the scales one by one. Cut off the pointed rear part of the scales and cut or sandpaper that side until it is pleasantly rounded. Sandpaper the rear until it is smooth. Drill two small holes in each scale. Lay the scales in the proper order and push the thread through them. Tie one or two knots in the thread. Perhaps you may be able to buy a clasp in a shop.

Decoration:
The necklace shown below has only been given a small yellow tip. You can decorate the scales much more if you wish.

Mobile using natural materials
🐞 🐌 ✂ ✱ ⌂ 🔨 ✂

✣ *twigs*
  pine cones
  moss, etc.,
  thin wire

Many different materials were used for the mobile shown below. When making a mobile, you have to ensure that each twig is balanced.

A mobile can be very simple, with only a couple of pine cones, for example, but you can also create one with many sections and subsections.

First gather all the materials together and spread them out on a table in the shape that you want to end up with. You will then be able to recognize what goes well together and what does not.

Begin with the lowest twig. When you have hung everything on it, find out its centre of gravity and tie the wire that will hold it. You should only tie the knot tight when you are completely sure that the twig is balanced.

Then move on to the next twig, and so on.

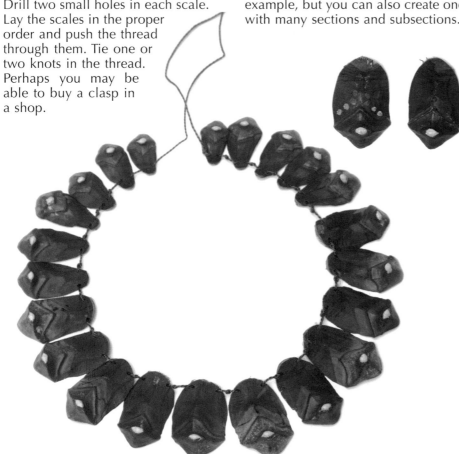

Creative with stones

Painting large pebbles

⚒ ❀ ✳ ⌂ ♀ ☝ ✂

✥ stones
paint
varnish

We often simply walk right over stones on the path, but if you take a good look, you will see that they have many different colours. You can sometimes see something exceptional in a stone, such as a face, for example. However, you can also make the stone to speak for itself, by turning it into a small creature, just like the group of gnomes we saw nestled in a corner of a house we visited. If you are really clever, you can use the lines that are already in the stone and paint a face around them.

Look for some large pebbles — or get the children to do that themselves while out on a walk — and have the children paint these with watercolours. As soon as the stones are dry, they should be coated or sprayed with quick-drying varnish (see figures on the right).

Stone mosaic

❀ ✂ ✳ ⌂ ☝ ✂

✥ small stones
acrylic paint and sand
plank

You may be lucky and come across a lot of stones that you can use to make a mosaic. We found the stones shown in the adjacent figures in a quarry in Italy, the land of the mosaics.

First draw your design (not too small) on a piece of paper and check to see if you have sufficient stones. Then draw your design on the plank. Make a thick mixture of acrylic paint and sand that you can use as cement. Work on your mosaic piece by piece, not too much at once. The acrylic *cement* will need 5–6 hours to dry.

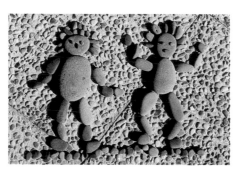

Working with shells

Shells are often beautiful and it is interesting to try to make things with them. You may not have realized that those marvellous small objects could be so hard and it is actually very difficult to make a small hole in a shell. You need a diamond drill to do so. They are not very expensive, but you probably won't have the opportunity to use one during the vacation. Nevertheless, you will probably be able to find many shells with a small hole in them already.

The shells shown in the pictures in this book have all been found on different beaches.

Using shells to decorate a box
⚙ ❀ ✂ ✳ ⌂ ♀ 𝌀 ✄

✢ shells
　all-purpose glue or acrylic paint
　　with sand
　small box

You can decorate a small box in the same way as you make a shell picture, see page 199.

Shell dolls
❀ ✂ ✳ ⌂ ♀ 𝌀 ✄

✢ shells
　any other pretty objects from the
　　beach
　all-purpose glue

It is not easy to stick shells together. Spread a little glue on each surface and wait until the glue is almost dry. Then press the surfaces together.

This is a job that is best spread out over a couple of days. First collect all the shells you want to use and then begin sticking them together.

Shell wind-chime
❀ ✂ ✳ ⌂ ♀ 𝌀 ✄

✢ shells
　twig
　cord
　small beads if desired

You can create a *wind-chime* by threading together some shells with a hole in them on several pieces of cord or thread. When you hang it from a branch, the wind will blow through it. When the wind blows hard enough, the shells will rustle together.

1 Look for shells with a hole in them and lay them in the order in which you want to thread them.

2 As you can see in the picture opposite, the shells ought to hang at a slight distance from one another. First tie a knot in the thread or cord and then insert the thread. Then tie a new knot for the next shell, etc.

You may wish to alter the distance between the shells later. It is not easy to do this until the knot in the thread has been tied. If you

have some beads, you can insert these between the shells when you are making the chime. They make it easy to alter the distances between the shells.

3 Tie the threads to the twig and hang the chime outside at a place where it will catch the wind.

Shell pictures
⚜ ☘ ✂ ✳ ⌂ ♀ 🔨 ✂
❖ *shells*
   all-purpose glue or acrylic paint with sand
   piece of firm cardboard
   hardboard or plywood

First lay the shells as you think they should be placed, just to see if the composition is agreeable. You can then stick them down using the glue. Put the picture in a safe place until the glue is properly dry.

You can also make your own glue using a tube of acrylic paint and some sand. This mixture is extremely easy to work with. As long as the paint is wet, it can be washed off easily, which makes it very suitable for young children. Spread a layer of the mixture on the background (cardboard, etc.) and push the shells into it. Allow the picture to dry out properly.

17. When It Rains ...

Home-made party games

Party games are ideal for rainy days. They are also good for aiding concentration and help calm children down. Do not take too many of these with you on vacation. You should certainly not take any games that you can easily make yourself with simple materials. Involve the children in making these games and integrate elements of your surroundings into the game.

Game of goose

🎲 🦢 3⁺ ⌂ 🔨 ✂ ▦

✥ *piece of firm cardboard*
various shells or stones
two dice

The game of goose is a very old Dutch game and has a fixed layout with 63 squares. There are 13 squares with a goose: 4, 9, 14, 18, 23, 27, 32, 36, 41, 45, 50, 54, and 59. In addition, there are a number of squares with other special functions.

Rules of play:
Everyone gets a 'man' and six tokens.

✿ Everyone throws the dice and the highest throw starts. He can move his man the same number of squares as shown on the dice.

✿ If on the first throw a player gets 4 and 5, he can move to square 53; if he throws 3 and 6, he goes to 26.

✿ Anyone landing on a goose can move on further by the same number of squares as shown on the dice.

✿ At the bridge (6) a toll has to be paid (one token). If the player pays double, he can move on to 12.

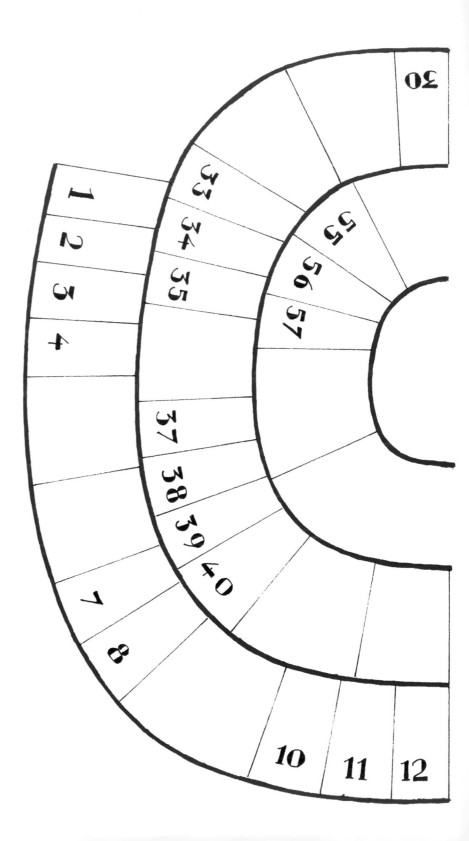

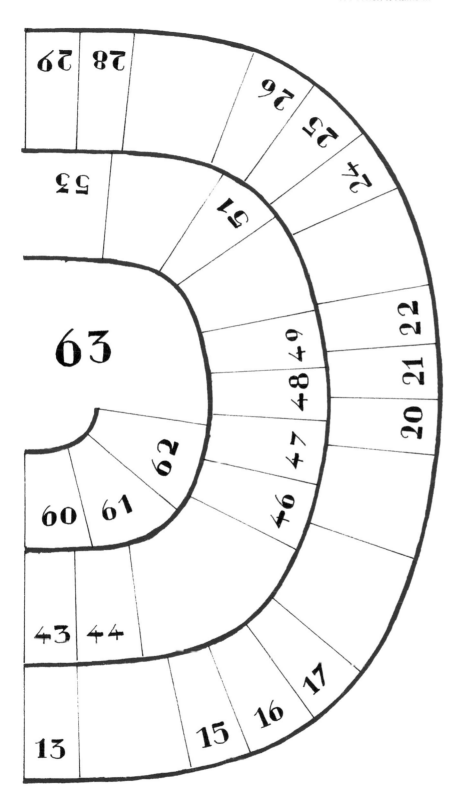

- In the inn (19), you miss two turns and have to pay two tokens for food and drink.
- Down the well (31) and in prison (52), you have to wait until you are freed by someone else who lands on your square. In prison, you also have to pay one token.
- If you land in the maze (42), you pay one token and go back three squares.
- Square 58 represents death. You have to pay two tokens and start all over again.
- First to square 63 is the winner. If you throw too many to land exactly on 63, you have to count to 63 and then count the rest backwards.

You can make your own game of goose and integrate the surroundings into your own game. Think up new obstacles. The well could be a ravine, the campsite could be closed, you could miss a turn because the bus didn't come, etc. You can copy the board shown here as the basis for your own board.

Puzzles

‡ *picture postcards or pictures from a magazine*

Take a large picture from a magazine or brochure and paste it to a piece of cardboard. Cut it into many small pieces. If you like, you can introduce a competitive element by taking two identical postcards or pictures from a magazine, pasting them to a piece of cardboard, and cutting them into an equal number of pieces. The children have to put them together as quickly as possible.

Happy families
☝ ✤ ✂ 3-6 ⌂ ✗

✤ *firm paper or thin cardboard*
  coloured pencils
  glue

A game of happy families should consist of at least 8 x 4 sets. You can extend the number of sets, depending on the number of family members. You can make a family from all kinds of ideas, including your surroundings. You can pick up some brochures at the tourist office and cut out the pictures. Make series of fours using: animals, trains, buses, flowers, mountains, buildings, etc.

Cut 32 cards of around 7 × 10 cm (3 × 4 in). Make sure that there are no special marks of recognition on the back. Write the four topics on *each card* of that set and underline the topic on *this* card.

Rules of play:
Shuffle the pack and give each player six cards. The rest lies face down on the table. The players have to try to get as many sets of four matching cards as possible. The player with the most sets is the winner. To get a set, the player looks at his cards and determines which set is nearest

completion. Then he asks one of the player: 'May I have from (name of player) the owl from the animals set, for example?' If the player asked has that card, he must give it to the person asking. The asker then goes on to ask again. If the asker does not get the card he was seeking, he takes a card from the stack. It is now the turn of the person who was last asked.

Pick-up sticks
☝ ✤ ✂ 2-6 ⌂ ⚑ ✗

✤ *Pick-up sticks or cocktail sticks*
This game is played with a number of thin sticks that are pointed at either end. You can buy pick-up sticks, but you can also play the game with cocktail sticks.

Rules of play:
One of the children takes the whole bunch of sticks in his hand, holds it just above the table and releases it. They fall on the table and lie in a heap all topsy-turvy. The first player now tries to pick up as many sticks as possible, on by one, without causing any of the other sticks to move. If that happens, it is the next player's turn. The person with the most sticks at the end is the winner.

Variation 1:
When the players have acquired a little skill in this game, each player can pick up the whole bunch, let it fall on the table and see how many he can pick up in one turn. When he is out, the other player gets the opportunity to pick up the whole bunch.

Variation 2:
You can also do this game with cheese sticks. They are smaller, which sometimes makes it more difficult to pick them up.

Bingo
⬡ ☝ 2⁺ ⌂ ⚑ ✗

✤ *thick cardboard*
  coloured chalk
You need two things for this game:
♣ A number of bingo sheets, with eight, ten, or twelve pictures.
♣ The same number of bingo cards with the same pictures as shown on the sheets. You can perhaps draw simple pictures yourself; you can also cut them out of brochures.

Rules of play:
Lay a stack of bingo cards face down on the table. Give each child a bingo sheet.

One by one, the children take a token from the stack and lay it on their sheet if it matches a picture there. If not, the card is put back on the table in a new stack. The first player to complete his sheet is the winner.

Tip:
Colours may be enough for very young children. In that case, it is advisable to make cards with only four colours.

Memory

⬡ ⬢ 2⁺ ⬠ 🎀 ✂

✣ *cardboard*
  coloured pencils
  brochures or picture postcards

For this game, you need various pairs of cards with the same picture. The picture can be colours or simple shapes, such as a triangle, a circle, a square, etc. You can also use picture postcards or pictures from brochures or magazines.

Rules of play:

The cards lie face down on the table and one by one the children turn over two cards so that everyone can see them. If the pictures are different, the player turns them face down again. If they are the same, the player keeps them and gets another turn.

The art of the game is to remember which cards lie where and to turn over the pairs that one can remember. The player with the most cards is the winner.

Dominoes

⬢ ⬡ 2⁺ ⬠ 🎀 ✂

✣ *firm cardboard*
  coloured chalk
  pictures, etc.

Each complete set has 28 dominoes, each of which consists of two squares measuring approximately 4 cm ($1\frac{1}{2}$ in). They normally display numbers (1 to 6) but may also have shapes, colours, animals, or something special to do with the vacation (see the picture below).

Rules of play:

Depending on the number of players, each player gets four or five dominoes. The others lie face down on the table. The first player lays a domino and the next player has to try to lay a domino that fits on to this one; it has the same number of dots or the same colour, etc. If he cannot do so, he must pick up one of the dominoes on the table. The player who plays out all his stones first is the winner.

Making other games

If you take a firm cardboard box from the supermarket, you can cut small or larger cards to make all kinds of number or letter games. It is a good idea to take the rules of play of your favourite games with you when you leave home.

Being creative when it rains

Cutting patterns
🐚🌱✂✳⌂🐘✂
✣ *coloured paper*

1 Fold a square piece of paper double in both directions. You have made a small square.
2 Fold this square along the diagonal. The long sides of the triangle are closed and the short side is open. If you have very thin paper, you may be able to fold it diagonally once more.
3 Cut all kinds of shapes into the closed side of the paper. Fold the paper open and see the beautiful shapes you have made.

Boxes for small treasures
🌱✂✳⌂🐘✂
✣ *coloured paper*

1 Fold a square sheet of paper twice in both directions to make 16 squares.
2 On two opposite sides, make an incision from the outside edge along one of the outer squares.
3 Spread a little glue on the loose flaps and stick them to the sides.
4 To make the lid, repeat step 1 with another sheet of paper and fold the outer strips in two.

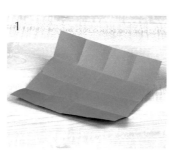

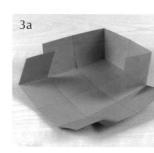

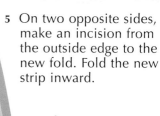

You can decorate the lid with one of the paper patterns you have made (see previous section).

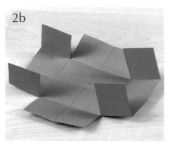

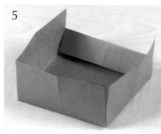

5 On two opposite sides, make an incision from the outside edge to the new fold. Fold the new strip inward.

Twisted paperchains
🎲🖐️✂️❋⬡🔔✄

❖ *strips of coloured paper*

1 Stick the end of the green strip at right angles to the red strip.
2 / 3 Fold the red strip over the green strip and then the green over the red.
4 Continue until you have reached the desired length.
5 If you are making animal figures, you can vary the colour, the width, and the length of the paperchain for each body part. Tape or

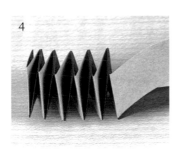

glue all the components together. Twister paperchains can become puppets if you suspend them on a thread.

Painting T-shirts
⬡🎲🖐️❋⬡🔔✄

❖ *simple T-shirts*
   indelible felt-tips

Simple white T-shirts are not expensive and are available almost everywhere.

1 Take a piece of firm cardboard the same size as the front of the T-shirt. Put it inside the T-shirt and stretch the front of the T-shirt tightly across it. Fasten the back of the T-shirt with a safety pin to keep the material taut.
2 Each child can use a felt-tip pen to decorate his own T-shirt.
3 When the children have finished, iron the T-shirt to fix the colours.

Paper painting
⬡🎲🖐️✂️❋⬡🔔✄

❖ *various pieces of*
   coloured paper
   glue

You can make your painting with the simplest things. Tearing the paper rather than cutting it places the emphasis on general impression rather than on form.

Newspaper hat
🎲🖐️❋♀✄

❖ *newspaper*

You can make a simple paper hat by following steps 1 to 4 in paper boats on page 136.

Friendship bracelets

✂ ✳ ⌂ 🏷 ✂

✥ *coloured cotton thread*
   safety pin
→ tied with the right hand
← tied with the left hand
•• double knot

All the armbands are made with the same basic knots. The differences are due to tying the knots with the right or left hands. The choice of colours also makes a difference of course.

The patterns

You can make a friendship bracelet according to your own ideas or you can work according to a pattern.

Basic knot, tied with the right hand →

1 Choose the colours and cut some pieces of thread about 100–120 cm (40–50 in) long. See the patterns (p. 207). Tie a knot at about 15 cm (6 in) from the end. Fasten the knot to your knee with a safety pin or bind the loose ends to a table leg. Hang the threads neatly next to one another in the desired order.

2 Take the red thread in your right hand. Take the blue thread in your left hand and pull it tight.

3 *Single knot.* Tie a knot around the blue thread and pull it nice and tight (steps 3a to 3e).

4 Double knot ••. Repeat this knot with the same threads.

5 Let go of the blue thread and take hold of the yellow thread. Tie a •• with the red thread around the yellow thread.

6 Repeat this until there are red knots around all the threads and the red thread is on the right.

7 Begin again at the left-hand side with a new thread (blue in our example). Tie this around all the other threads (See bracelets 1 and 2).

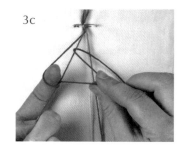

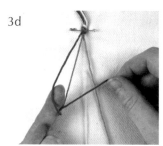

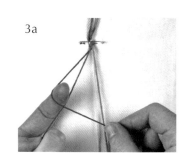

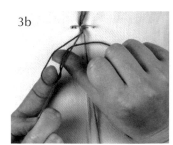

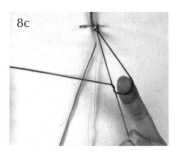

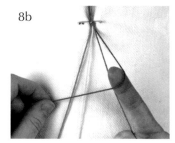

3c
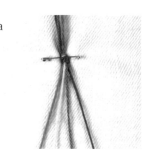

3d

1

3a

3b

3e

5

6

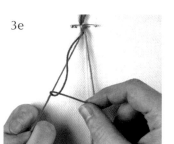

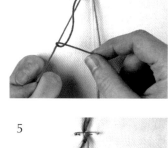

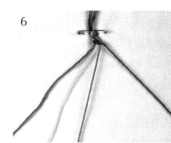

Basic knot, tied with the left hand ←

8 Take the red thread in your left hand. Take the blue thread with you right hand (see above and steps 8a to 8c).

9 See picture of bracelet with → and ←.

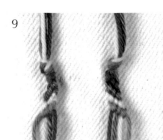

8a

8b

8c

9

Bracelet 3 and 4 with single knots

Bracelet 3

1 Choose a colour (140 cm, 55 in) and 2 supporting threads (50 cm, 19 in). See step 1 of Basic Knot, p. 206.
2 Use the long thread to tie single knots around the supporting threads.

Bracelet 4

1 Choose 2 colours for tying (120 cm, 47 in) and 2 supporting threads (50 cm, 19 in). See step 1 of Basic Knot, p. 206
2 Use the left-hand thread to tie a → single knot around the supporting threads.
3 Use the right-hand thread to tie a ← single knot.
4 Repeat steps 2 and 3.

Finishing off

Loosen the bracelet from your knee or table leg, untie the knot and braid the loose threads.

Reverse knot

A reverse knot is used to change a *right tie* → into a *left tie* ← and vice versa. In the pattern, a reverse knot is represented by a ■ in place of a single knot • (see bracelet 5).

1 If you are busy with a →, begin with a single knot →
2 Take the tying thread in your other hand.
3 Tie a single knot ←

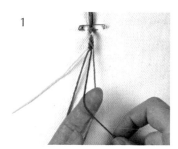

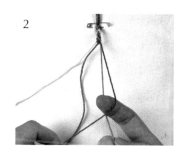

Bracelet 5

1 blue   165 cm (64 in)
4 yellow   90 cm (35 in)

6   7

Bracelet 6

1 red   160 cm (62 in)
1 green   80 cm (31 in)
2 yellow   100 cm (39 in)
2 blue   140 cm (55 in)
2 supporting threads
(black)   55 cm (21 in)

Bracelet 7

2 red   110 cm (43 in)
2 white   135 cm (53 in)
4 blue   120 cm (47 in)

Tying pattern

1 You require eight threads (120 cm, 47 in), two in each colour. See 'The patterns,' step 1, p. 206

2 Tie a •• with the yellow threads.

3 Tie three •• → with the red thread on the left-hand side.

4 Tie four •• ← with the red thread on the eighth-hand side.

5 Repeat steps 3 and 4 until you have used the red thread three times.

6 Tie a •• →, then a reverse knot, and a •• ← with the blue thread on the left-hand side. Repeat this with the blue thread on the right-hand side.

7 Tie three •• ← with the red thread on the left-hand side. Repeat this with the red thread on the right-hand side.

8 Tie a •• with the yellow threads. Repeat step 7 with the yellow thread.

9 Repeat step 8 with green and blue.

10 Repeat step 8 with red, by make the outside knot a reverse knot this time.

11 Tie a •• with the yellow threads. Use the yellow threads to tie a reverse knot around the green threads. Tie a •• with the yellow thread.

12 Turn the pattern around and tie everything back to front so that you get a mirror image.

1
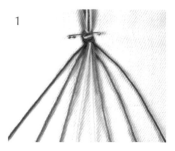

2
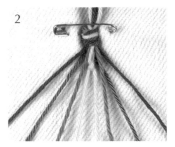

3
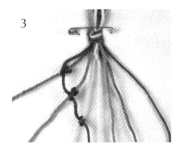

4a
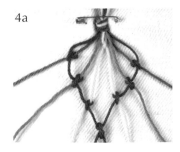

4b
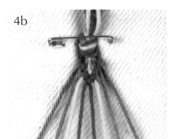

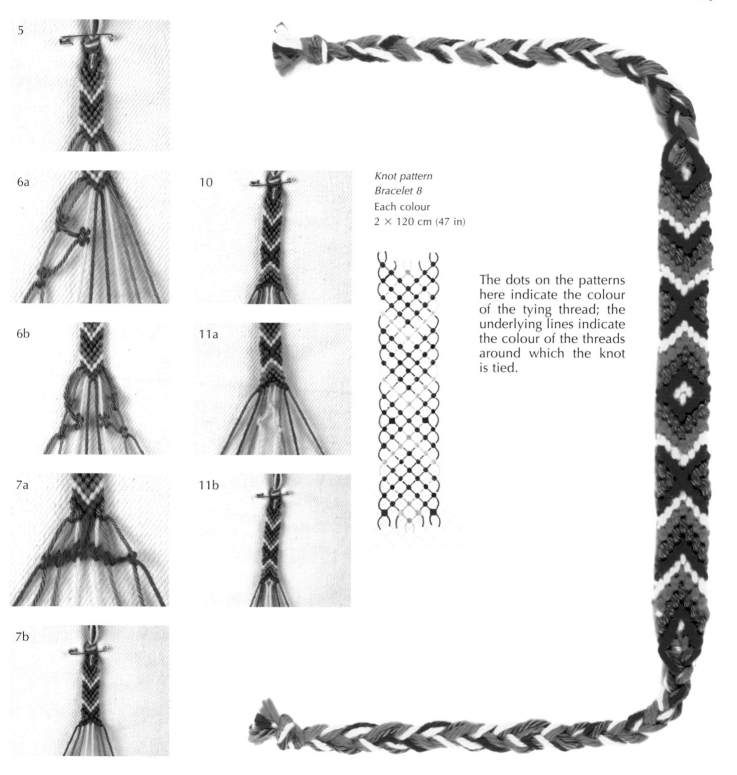

5

6a

6b

7a

7b

10

11a

11b

*Knot pattern
Bracelet 8
Each colour
2 × 120 cm (47 in)*

The dots on the patterns
here indicate the colour
of the tying thread; the
underlying lines indicate
the colour of the threads
around which the knot
is tied.

Songs

Frère Jacques (round)

Frère Jacques, frère Jacques, dormez vous, dormez vous?
Sonnez les matines, sonnez les matines: ding dang dong! Din dang dong!

There's a hole in my bucket

1. There's a hole in my bucket, dear Liza, dear Liza.
   There's a hole in my bucket, dear Liza, a hole.
2. Then mend it, dear Georgie, dear Georgie, mend it.
3. With what shall I mend it, dear Liza, with what?
4. With a straw, dear Georgie, dear Georgie, a straw.
5. The straw is too long, dear Liza, too long.
6. Then cut it, dear Georgie, dear Georgie, cut it.
7. With what shall I cut it, dear Liza, with what?
8. With a knife, dear Georgie, dear Georgie, a knife.
9. The knife is too blunt, dear Liza, too blunt.
10. Then sharpen it, dear Georgie, dear Georgie, sharpen it.
11. With what shall I sharpen it, dear Liza, with what?
12. With a stone, dear Georgie, dear Georgie, a stone.
13. The stone is too dry, dear Liza, too dry.
14. Then wet it, dear Georgie, dear Georgie, wet it.
15. With what shall I wet it, dear Liza, with what?
16. With water, dear Georgie, dear Georgie, with water.
17. In what shall I get it, dear Liza, in what?
18. In a bucket, dear Georgie, dear Georgie, a bucket.
19. There's a hole in my bucket, dear Liza, a hole.

Row, row, row your boat

Row, row, row your boat, gently down the stream.
Merrily, merrily, merrily, merrily, life is but a dream.

What shall we do with the drunken sailor?

1. What shall we do with the drunken sailor, what shall we do with the drunken sailor. What shall we do with the drunken sailor, early in the morning? Hooray and up she rises, hooray and up she rises, hooray and up she rises, early in the morning.

2. Put him in the long-boat 'till he's sober.
3. Pull out the plug and wet him all over.
4. Put him in scuppers with a hose-pipe on him.
5. Heave him by the leg in a running bolin'.
6. That's what we do with the drunken sailor.

Three white mice (round)

Three white mice, three white mice,
See how they run, see how they run
They run away from the farmer's wife
Who cuts of their tails with a carving knife.
Three white mice ...

There were ten in the bed

1. There were ten in the bed and the little one said:

   Roll over! Roll over! So they all rolled over and one fell out.

2. There were nine in the bed and the little one said: ...
3. There were eight in the bed and the little one said: ...
   ...
11. There were none in the bed, so no one said: ...

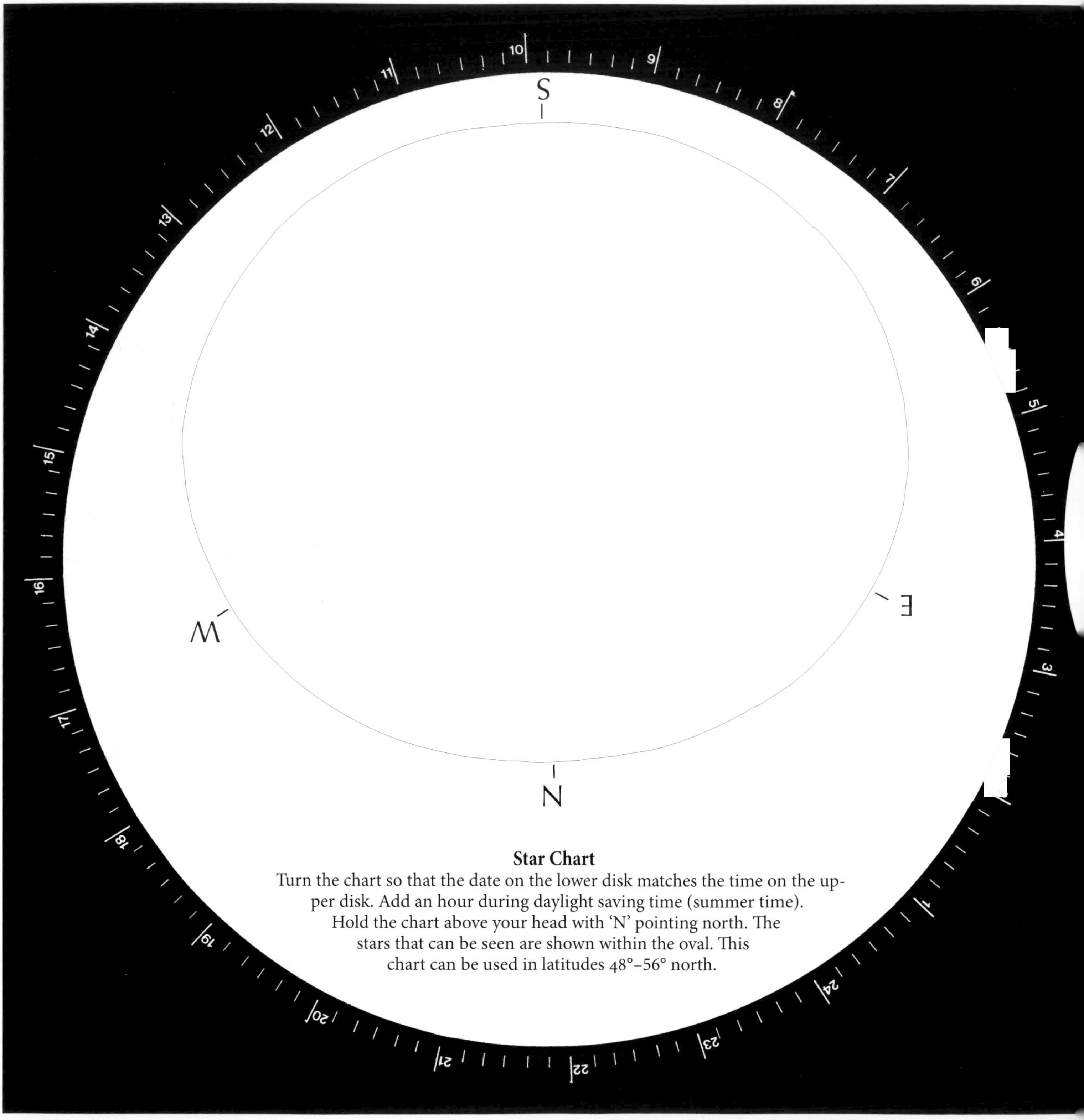

S

10
11
9
8
12
7
13
6
14
5
15
E
16
4
17
3
W
18
3
19
4
20
24
21
23
22
N

Star Chart
Turn the chart so that the date on the lower disk matches the time on the upper disk. Add an hour during daylight saving time (summer time). Hold the chart above your head with 'N' pointing north. The stars that can be seen are shown within the oval. This chart can be used in latitudes 48°–56° north.

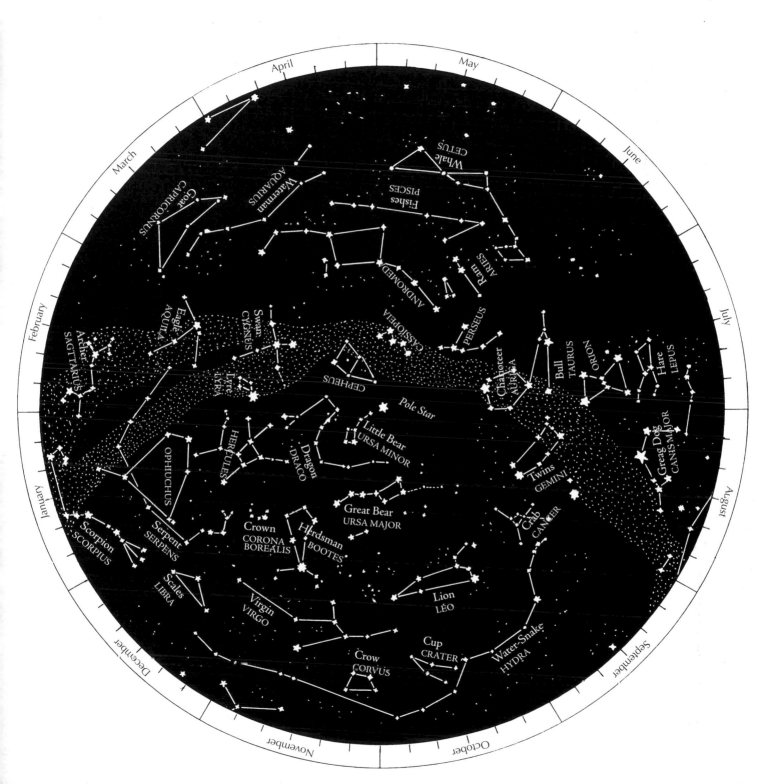

Alphabetical Index of Games and Other Activities

Explanation of the symbols

Age
⬡ end of third, fourth year
⬡ five to six/ beginning of the
 seventh year
⬡ seven to nine years
✂ ten years and older

Number of participants
✳ unlimited
N number of participants is N
N⁺ minimum number of participants
 is N; there is no maximum
N± minimum number of participants
 is N; there is no maximum,
 preferably an even number of
 participants
N± minimum number of participants
 is N; the is no maximum, preferably an uneven number of
 participants

Indoor or outdoor
⌂ indoor activity
♀ outdoor activity

Type of activity
⚑ table game
✂ creative activity
♪ music game
◐ ball game
✎ game with a blindfold
🚗 suitable for in the car
⊞ game with dice

Materials
► *rope*

Index According to Type of Activity and Age

The symbols after the name indicate age, number of players and type. See left for the symbol key.

Guessing games

Games with pencil and paper

Active indoor and outdoor games

Being creative with natural materials

Home-made party games

Folding techniques

Simple crafts